750

Wittgenstein and Meaning in Life

Wittgenstein and Meaning in Life

In Search of the Human Voice

Reza Hosseini
Rhodes University, South Africa

palgrave
macmillan

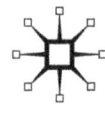

© Reza Hosseini 2015

All rights reserved. No reproduction, copy or transmission of this publication may be made without written permission.

No portion of this publication may be reproduced, copied or transmitted save with written permission or in accordance with the provisions of the Copyright, Designs and Patents Act 1988, or under the terms of any licence permitting limited copying issued by the Copyright Licensing Agency, Saffron House, 6–10 Kirby Street, London EC1N 8TS.

Any person who does any unauthorized act in relation to this publication may be liable to criminal prosecution and civil claims for damages.

The author has asserted his right to be identified as the author of this work in accordance with the Copyright, Designs and Patents Act 1988.

First published 2015 by
PALGRAVE MACMILLAN

Palgrave Macmillan in the UK is an imprint of Macmillan Publishers Limited, registered in England, company number 785998, of Houndmills, Basingstoke, Hampshire RG21 6XS.

Palgrave Macmillan in the US is a division of St Martin's Press LLC, 175 Fifth Avenue, New York, NY 10010.

Palgrave Macmillan is the global academic imprint of the above companies and has companies and representatives throughout the world.

Palgrave® and Macmillan® are registered trademarks in the United States, the United Kingdom, Europe and other countries.

ISBN: 978–1–137–44090–7

This book is printed on paper suitable for recycling and made from fully managed and sustained forest sources. Logging, pulping and manufacturing processes are expected to conform to the environmental regulations of the country of origin.

A catalogue record for this book is available from the British Library.

A catalog record for this book is available from the Library of Congress.

To my father

*Don't look for anything behind the phenomena;
they themselves are the theory.*

Johann Wolfgang von Goethe

Contents

Acknowledgements viii

Introduction 1
1 Book of Facts, Book of Values 13
2 The Limits of Justification 24
3 Aspect-Seeing and Meaning in Life 47
4 In Defence of the Ordinary 67
5 On Detachment or Why the Shopkeeper Does Not Investigate His Apples 84
6 The Human Voice: The Confessional Nature of Enquiring into Life's Meaning 117
Coda 147

Notes 152
Bibliography 163
Index 175

Acknowledgements

An idea expands like a seed in the soil. So many things have to happen for it to grow. There are people involved here; places are involved here too, like the streets of Tehran.

I am grateful to many people whose comments, suggestions or company over the years have influenced the development of my thoughts in this work: Johan Snyman, Thaddeus Metz, John Cottingham, Alex Broadbent, Ward E. Jones, Samantha Vice, Hans Sluga, David Kishik, Raphael Winkler, Oisín Eoin Keohane, Tyler Burge, Neil Van Leeuwen, Kianoush Eslami, Ehsan Bateni, Jan Koster, Leon Marincowitz and Arianne Conty.

I received valuable comments on the entire manuscript from James C. Klagge and David E. Cooper, which were crucial in the development of some of the ideas in this book. I'm indebted to their generosity. It goes without saying that none is to blame for the results.

I am grateful to the Philosophy Department at the University of Johannesburg for providing financial support to present a chapter of this work at the 35th International Ludwig Wittgenstein Symposium in 2012. I am thankful to the Allan Gray Centre for Leadership Ethics (AGCLE) at Rhodes University for giving me the support to work on the manuscript. I am especially thankful to Julie Borland, Lindsay Kelland and Pedro Tabensky for their friendship and collegiality.

An earlier version of Chapter 6 was presented at a research workshop organised by the University of Adelaide in 2014. The feedback I received from the participants of this workshop was reassuring, and the hospitality of Andrew Gleeson made my trip a memorable one. I'm grateful to Andrew, and I thank Christopher Cordner and Craig Taylor.

An earlier version of Chapter 3 was presented at the 37th International Ludwig Wittgenstein Symposium in Austria, and I'm grateful to the participants, especially Alois Pichler, for their useful comments and suggestions.

I should also thank Brendan George, senior commissioning editor at Palgrave Macmillan, for his confidence in the project, Ryan Dunlop, the copy editor of the book and the entire team at Newgen Knowledge Works for their prompt typesetting and proofreading, and the anonymous readers for their constructive comments and suggestions.

In 2008, I left my home country, Iran, in search of something I couldn't tell what it was by then, something I was conscious of but could not apprehend, and I landed in South Africa out of all the places. But now I can tell what it was and for which I am deeply grateful to my wife, Lebo Makubetse, who made me feel at home by virtue of which I came to realise why I had begun my journey in the first place. *Kea go bona, wa mpona!*

'On the 28th of August, 1749, at mid-day, as the clock struck twelve, I came into the world'.
>Goethe, *Poetry and Truth: From My Own Life*

'When I was fifteen years old or sixteen I carried around in the streets of Brooklyn a paperback copy of Plato's *Republic*, front cover facing outward. I had read only some of it and understood less. . . How much I wanted an older person to notice me carrying it and be impressed, to pat me on the shoulder and say . . . I didn't know what exactly. I sometimes wonder, not without uneasiness, what that young man of fifteen or sixteen would think of what he has grown up to do'.
>Robert Nozick, *The Examined Life*

'Midway upon the journey of our life
I found myself within a forest dark,
For the straightforward pathway had been lost'.
>Dante Alighieri, *Divine Comedy*

'Tell them I've had a wonderful life'.
>Ludwig Wittgenstein

Introduction

The research question

Though for a large portion of the 20th century the question of life's meaning wasn't a favourite question among analytic philosophers, recent developments, especially in the last 40 years, show that the meaning of life is no longer 'the black sheep of the normative family' (Metz 2002: 811). As Thaddeus Metz and others have noted, most normative philosophers had been more comfortable discussing notions such as 'happiness', 'well-being', 'morality' and 'value', and the notion of 'meaningfulness' has not been considered as a distinct category that could account for a good life.[1] However, it seems safe to say that the question of life's meaning 'has come firmly back onto the philosophical agenda' (Cottingham 2012: 115). Gone are the days when a distinguished analytic philosopher announced in his presidential address to the American Philosophical Association that 'once in a time of weakness and lapse of judgement' he wrote a paper on the meaning of life (Adams 2002: 71). The very existence of a growing body of literature on the meaning of life shows that 'the problem does not go away' (Cottingham 2003: 2).

The aim of most analytic philosophers who write on life's meaning is to develop and evaluate theories and principles that indicate what can confer meaning on one's life. That is to say, the fundamental question of the literature is to enquire about the necessary and sufficient conditions of a meaningful life. Note that the question here is not 'What makes my life a happy life?' or 'What is a moral life?' Rather, the idea here is that meaningfulness is at least as important, if not more, as morality or happiness in providing a justifiable account of a good life. For one thing, we consider the lives of Séraphine,[2] Van Gogh and Schubert to be good lives not because their lives were happy or moral but because they were meaningful. In this view, there is a limit to what the subjective sense of happiness and the universal claims of morality can offer in deepening our understanding of the human life. Obviously one might argue that a meaningful life ultimately cannot be devoid of morality or that one's life is meaningful as long as there is a sense of happiness, resulted from the satisfaction of one's strong desires, but these are matters of further enquiry once the idea of meaningfulness as a separate category has been established.

The aim of this book is to address some of the main questions and assumptions of the rapidly growing literature on life's meaning from a Wittgensteinian perspective. By Wittgensteinian perspective I am not only referring to what we can gather from the bulk of Wittgenstein's documented reflections on the 'sense of life', but also to exploring the literature from a viewpoint inspired by Wittgenstein's way of doing philosophy and, more importantly, to appraise whether his insights and claims on this topic are defensible at all. I don't want to explain, in yet another book on the subject, Wittgenstein's views about value and ethics; instead, I want to talk about Wittgenstein as the iconic representative of a movement in philosophy which aims at not 'building elaborate theories' but at 'considering the simple and obvious facts', as pithily stated by Iris Murdoch (1970: 1). I shall argue that some facets of Wittgenstein's philosophy and his 'way of looking at things' portray different landscapes and perspectives to appraise the question of life's meaning, and my task in this book is to set forth and highlight those landscapes with a stroke of my own brush. Some of the ideas that are pertinent to the literature and yet have not been addressed in a systematic fashion are, to name a few, the relation between meaning in life and what Wittgenstein calls 'world-picture', the non-cognitive and existential character of any attempt to talk about the meaning of life in his early works, the precedence of life over the intentional pursuit of meaning and the collapse of the dichotomy between 'superlative' and 'ordinary meaning'.

So, the key question of the book is this: Considering the literature on the meaning of life among English-speaking philosophers, what would a Wittgensteinian view add to it?[3] It is a strange irony that Wittgenstein, who spent most of his philosophical career on the question of meaning and on 'private' reflections on the problem of life, is mostly absent in the literature and that commentators 'write, for the most part, as though Wittgenstein had never existed' (Phillips 2004: xviii).

Let me commence by giving you a broad picture of the principal strands in the literature on life's meaning. There are three main camps in the meaning of life debate (Klemke (ed.) 1981; Klemke & Cahn (eds) 2008; Seachris (ed.) 2012; Metz 2013):

Supernaturalism: According to the dominant strand of this approach, the meaning of life is founded in relation to a god or God, a transcendental being who created the world. In this view, without the existence of God, life would be meaningless (Hartshorne 1984; Morris 1992; Craig 1994; Adams 1999; Cottingham 2003, to name a few). In the literature a distinction has been made between 'God-centred' theories and 'soul-centred' theories of supernaturalism. While the former suggest that the meaning of life would depend on believing in God who is omnipotent, who is omniscient and who is the ground of the physical universe (Hartshorne 1984; Davis 1987; Craig 1994; Adams 1999; Metz 2000), the latter concentrate on immortality as the only thing that ultimately matters and thus for which having a soul is necessary. (Morris 1992; Fischer 1994; Harris 2002; Metz 2003)
Naturalism: Denying the claim that the meaning of life is dependent upon the existence of a transcendent being, naturalists hold that since there is no good reason to believe in the existence of a transcendent god, there is no good reason to believe that the meaning of life is contingent upon the existence of a god. One can also believe in God but deny that his existence is sufficient for meaning in life. In other words, human beings, independently of any supernatural being, are capable of having meaningful lives, whether we believe life's meaning is subjective – that is, depending on an individual's set of desires and choices – or objective – that is, mind-independent.[4] Subjectivists, in general, claim that any conception of a meaningful life is dependent on one's 'propositional attitudes', which are defined as 'mental states, such as wants, emotions, goals' that are about states of affairs (Metz 2013: 164). One's life is meaningful, then, if one obtains the object of one's propositional attitudes. For example, Harry Frankfurt (1988) highlights the significance of the elements of love and care in conferring meaningfulness on one's life. Likewise, Richard Taylor (2000), by reconstructing the myth of Sisyphus, argues that one's life is meaningful as long as one obtains whatever one strongly desires. On the other hand, objectivists search for the common element(s) that are meaning-conferring and yet mind-independent. Alan Gewirth (1998), for example, holds that the meaning of one's life depends on transcending oneself by exercising reason in a way that goes beyond self-interest. Likewise, Robert Nozick (1981) argues that one's life is meaningful to the extent that it transcends and connects with an

object of worth, and Susan Wolf (2010) argues that a meaningful life is a life in which one's 'subjective attraction' to one's projects and activities is of 'objective worth'. Wolf's account is a synthesis of objectivism and subjectivism. In general, the notion of transcendence or going beyond one's self-interest is of key significance among objectivists.[5]

Moral objectivism and moral subjectivism differ from objectivism and subjectivism with regard to meaning, but they are closely related. Think of the way a moral objectivist and a moral subjectivist defend their claims. A moral objectivist suggests that there are ethical propositions that are true in virtue of their relation to some features of the world, irrespective of one's judgement or attitude. On the other hand, a moral subjectivist denies that moral propositions refer to such objective facts and claims that these kinds of propositions are about, or expressive of, people's attitudes. Objectivists with regard to the meaning of life believe that there are objective values that can confer meaning on our lives, values like orienting one's life towards the good, the true and the beautiful. So, whereas moral objectivists are concerned with only moral values, objectivists with regard to meaning are concerned with, and refer to, meaning-conferring values broadly construed. Likewise, subjectivists with regard to meaning deny that the source of meaning in life is objective, whereas moral subjectivists deny that moral values are of objective nature. So when a person says that there are objective moral values in the world, she is a moral objectivist, but if the same person suggests that there are meaning-conferring objective values, then, she is objectivist with regard to meaning. And if a moral subjectivist claims that meaning of one's life is a function of one's attitudes or choices, she is a subjectivist with regard to life's meaning as well. Note that all scholars in the literature take a stance towards meaning that is perfectly compatible with their moral stance. There is no one in the literature who thinks moral values are objective and at the same time claims that meaning of life is a totally subjective affair. This goes to show how one's moral stance deeply affects one's approach towards life's meaning.

Nihilism: Traditionally, the main argument of nihilists is that life is meaningless or absurd because the world fails to meet our demands for meaning. Viewing life *sub specie aeternitatis*, that is, from the standpoint of eternity, nihilists claim that life is valueless, insignificant or always harmful.[6] As Metz has noted, it is interesting that 'most contemporary arguments for nihilism...contend that the relevant naturalist requirements for a meaningful life are nowhere present' (2007: 20). A more recent argument for nihilism is provided by philosophers, such as Thomas Nagel, who claim that life is absurd because there is an incongruity between the meaning we ascribe to our lives and their significance from an objective point of view.[7]

Clarification of the project

In this book, I shall argue that there are a variety of parallels that could be drawn and points of contention that could be highlighted between a Wittgensteinian approach and the current literature on life's meaning. Wittgenstein left some 'scattered remarks' (Kober 2006: 110) about value and ethics in which he made a clear connection between ethics and our enquiry into 'the meaning of life' (Wittgenstein 1965: 4). But, more importantly, some elements in his philosophy have far-reaching implications for our way of approaching the question of life's meaning. I want to explore the literature from this standpoint. Further, I want to examine whether his insights and claims on this topic are justifiable. For example, I explore the implications of the *Tractatus'* fact/value dichotomy and what we can take away from it. I also ask how we can apply Wittgenstein's 'anthropological method' of doing philosophy in his later works to address the questions of life's meaning.

My aims in this book are not primarily exegetical. Nor is it my intention to provide a detailed analysis of the literature on life's meaning. Instead, the aim here is to advance a fresh outlook by taking Wittgenstein's thoughts as my point of departure. So the scope of my research is rather narrow. My aim is to engage with the literature on life's meaning, and thus I will refer to the secondary literature on Wittgenstein only to the extent that it is of assistance to the present concerns, which is an enquiry into life's meaning. This research has obviously benefitted from the rich debates among Wittgenstein's interpreters, but the primary concern here is not to affiliate my research with one of the established readings of Wittgenstein but to follow the movements of thoughts about life in his personal reflections and to explore the implications of some of his philosophical writings for the issues of life's meaning.

So far, few works have been written on Wittgenstein's account of life's meaning.[8] What distinguishes my research from the previous works, however, is that I shall provide an extensive exploration of some of Wittgenstein's ideas and apply those ideas as conceptual tools to engage with the literature on life's meaning. I agree with Peter Tyler that 'the aim of Wittgenstein's approach is to cultivate...a "change of aspect" in our way of seeing the world' (2011: 40–41). That is, I shall argue that the aim of a Wittgensteinian approach towards the question of life's meaning is 'to bring about the understanding which consists precisely in the fact that we see the connections' (Wittgenstein 1958: § 133). My aim is to show the 'connecting links' between life and meaning in everyday life.

Another key difference between this work and previous works on Wittgenstein's account of life's meaning is that there is one major theme running through all the chapters of this work and that is the limits of a theoretical approach towards the meaning of life. What binds the different chapters of this study together, beyond being about Wittgensteinian ideas, is their anti-theoretical nature. This is not to belittle a theoretical approach towards the topic, but to show its limits. Let me explain what I mean by theory to clarify, then, what I mean by the limits of theory.

I take a theory of life's meaning to be an answer that philosophers provide in searching for the essential element(s) of a meaningful life. Suppose an extraordinary person could present a list of all the things that would confer meaning on a life. Driven by a 'craving for generality' (Wittgenstein 1969: 17), one might ask, 'Is there something that all the elements on the list have in common?' As Metz suggests, an answer to this question is what we can call a 'theory' or 'principle' of meaning in life (2013: 7). It would be intriguing to search for and find a promising theory of life's meaning, 'akin to discovering that the rain, the ocean and the liquid that runs from the tap and one's eyes are all $H_2\Theta$' (ibid.). In this view, there is a claim for the universality of a theory of life's meaning. A successful theory, then, would be a principle that can plausibly explain why wide ranges of lives are meaningful (or meaningless). For example, a theory that claims fulfilling God's purpose makes one's life meaningful is a standard theory of life's meaning in that it is not concerned with any particular individual's life; it refers to a condition or some conditions in virtue of which all people's lives can be meaningful. I will use the word 'anti-theoretical', and by it I mean that in my research I am not hankering after an affirmative or negative theory about the constitutive elements of the meaning of life, which can be applied to all or most human beings. My research is anti-theoretical in three senses:

1. theory alone is not enough to lead to a perspicuous understanding of the ways people experience life's meaning;
2. theory alone is not enough to change one's attitudes or one's way of seeing the world, which is something that philosophers focusing on life's meaning should be concerned with;

3. general theories of life's meaning fail to convey the 'senses' of their claims.

Having said that, I should also make it clear that the implication of an anti-theoretical approach is not the idea that with regard to life's meaning 'anything goes'. The upshot of an anti-theoretical approach is not necessarily a self-congratulatory Monty Pythonesque attitude, which takes the meaning of life to be 'nothing very special', encouraging us to 'try to be nice to people and avoid eating fat'. Instead, what I would like to advance in this study is the idea that by 'faithful observation' of modes of our 'complicated form of life' we would reach, as Goethe once observed, 'a point where the grounds of our judgment' about life 'might be stated at the same time as the judgment itself' ([1833] 1913: Part III, Book XI).

Put differently, *my approach is anthropological rather than metaphysical*. I am concerned not with the philosophical conditions of a meaningful life but with the ways in which those conditions are met and experienced in everyday life. My research is an attempt to move away from theory and back 'to the things themselves' as captured in Edmund Husserl's injunction. The aim is to reach a perspicuous understanding of life's meaning through what Rush Rhees once called the 'anthropological method' (1970: 101). This method is in a sense similar to what John Cottingham calls the 'holistic' method. By discussing various theoretical methods of approaching questions such as the nature of morality and value and highlighting their limitations, Cottingham reminds us:

> Here it is worth stepping outside the seminar room for a moment, and remembering that in our ordinary human life and experience, the characteristic way in which we normally achieve understanding within the domain of meaning, as opposed to the domain of physical phenomena and their explanation, is not analytically but holistically: not by taking things apart but by reaching across and outwards. (2009b: 11)[9]

Likewise, I might say, my aim is to step outside the 'seminar room' and be mindful of the ordinary life and the ways in which we think of the meaning of our lives. One of the key features of the argument I am advancing here is the idea that there are certain things in life that we learn 'through long experience and not from a course in school' (Wittgenstein 1998a: § 925), and such is the case with life's meaning. The idea, ambitious as it might sound, is to take you out of the 'seminar room' to talk to you about an ancient question and answers given to it: 'How shall one live?'

Overview of chapters

In Chapter 1, 'Book of Facts, Book of Values', I provide a brief introduction to the Tractarian account of life's meaning. The reason I discuss the Tractarian view is to provide a background against which I examine the key arguments for supernaturalism and naturalism in Chapter 2. The *Tractatus*'s main claim is that all the problems of philosophy arise because we misunderstand the 'logic of our language'. To avoid this, Wittgenstein claims, we have to draw a sharp line between what can be meaningfully said and what cannot be said but can only be 'shown'. The *Tractatus* concentrates on the conditions of 'sayability' of propositions. In fact, the showing/saying dichotomy is at the core of the *Tractatus*. Judgements about value, Wittgenstein has it, cannot be expressed in meaningful propositions. We would arrive at the realisation that value is inexpressible if we understand the 'structure' of the world. So, I briefly address the arguments of the *Tractatus* for the inexpressibility of value. Although the main arguments of the *Tractatus* are not directly related to the discussions of life's meaning, they have far-reaching implications for the Tractarian conception of life's meaning, and that is the reason I will discuss them in this book.

After presenting the Tractarian account of value in Chapter 1, I analyse a set of key views of naturalists and supernaturalists in Chapter 2: 'The Limits of Justification'. The *Tractatus* revolves around the notion of limits: limits of language, of ethics and of justification. I focus on the justificatory nature of most supernatural and natural theories of life's meaning, for example, by discussing Peter Singer's account of 'ethical life' as an objective source of life's meaning. I argue that even when one accepts the validity of these justificatory arguments, they are unlikely to be successful in bringing about a change in one's attitude and one's way of seeing the world. This, in turn, leads to the fundamental idea that was implicit in Wittgenstein's early philosophy but cultivated in his later writings, namely 'the primacy of praxis'. And in the final section, I argue that the Tractarian view, besides all the plausible objections that it raises against most theories of life's meaning, is oblivious to the communal nature of human life, and thus it remains an unliveable view. The Tractarian view was yielding, in its own way, to the same tendencies and orientations that it tried to warn philosophers against; it was yielding to the same 'longing for the transcendent', for the final solution and for the ultimate answers. In fact, Wittgenstein was the one who first noticed the prevalence of this tendency in his Tractarian philosophy, and thus a turn in his philosophy was bound to happen. I discuss some of the objections to the Tractarian view, and I argue that most objections are variations of one single problem: the Tractarian account of life's meaning, and indeed of meaning in general, was oblivious to the *ordinary* forms of experiencing the world. However, as early as the 1930s Wittgenstein began to *see* the 'grave mistakes' (1958: x) in his Tractarian philosophy, the most important of which was the realisation that our language has some functions that are not descriptive of facts at all. He recognised that the endless varieties of human experience can be conveyed through language, and they don't need to be factual in the Tractarian sense to make sense. The 'grammar' or the function of the words in our everyday life determines their meanings and not their logical forms. And thus it seemed that the door was open for a dramatic turn in his view of philosophy that is pithily described as a turn 'from detachment to immersion' (Thomas 1999: 195).

In Chapter 3, 'Aspect-Seeing and Meaning in Life', I address Wittgenstein's discussions of aspect-seeing and aspect-blindness in his later works and discuss their implications for issues of meaning in life. I argue that very often seeing an aspect of life amounts to having an attitude towards that aspect, and in dealing with different views about life's meaning it is important to be aware of this connection. For Wittgenstein, the significance of the notions of 'aspect-seeing' and 'aspect-blindness' lies in the connection between the concept of seeing-as and 'experiencing the meaning of a word' (1958: 214). Likewise, I argue that there is a connection between the concept of seeing-as and experiencing the meaning of life. In other words, I argue that the way we experience the phenomenon of life's meaning is analogous to the way we see an aspect. Seeing the world as a 'friendly home', seeing the vicissitudes of one's life as the will of God and seeing the human life consumed by our 'cosmic loneliness', are some examples of seeing-as. Most supernaturalist accounts of life's meaning fail to pay due attention to the significance of one's attitude and one's 'way of seeing' (ibid.: § 461) in arriving at a religious understanding of life's meaning. That is, they fail to bring about the dawning of religious aspects on the nonbeliever. A supernaturalist who argues that life would be meaningless without believing in God and making a connection with Him would be successful in changing the nonbeliever's way of seeing the world only if, and to the extent that, her arguments make the nonbeliever *see* that this 'dust of the earth', as a supernaturalist might believe, is indeed made in the 'image of God'.[10]

A theoretical discussion of the conditions of meaningfulness would have a limited impact if it doesn't lead to a change of aspect. I might agree with a believer that God is the ultimate source of meaning and yet remain unable to see the world religiously. Conversely, you might lose your belief in God but continue seeing the world from a 'religious point of view': searching for reconciliation with the world or experiencing life to be something akin to a transcendent gift – an inner mode of being, expressed in things like being preoccupied with the concept of guilt or wondering at the existence of the world, attitudes such as humility and thanksgiving that are usually associated with having a religious outlook and manifested in one's 'texture' of being (cf. Murdoch 1997: 80–81). What is lacking in the literature is precisely attention to these details, which are usually of significance in our appraisal of a person's life's meaning. By paying attention to the regulatory effects of religious beliefs on the life of a believer, we arrive at an understanding of her life and the meaning ascribed to it that is different from the understanding that a detached theoretical approach would provide.

Due to the significance of the ordinary in Wittgenstein's later works, I dedicate the rest of the book to exploring the implications of the ordinary for our understanding of life's meaning from three different perspectives: the ordinariness of meaning, the certainty of life and the confessional aspect of enquiring into the meaning of life – all of which, I shall argue, are related to everyday life. Thus, in Chapter 4, 'In Defence of the Ordinary', I challenge theories of 'great meaning' and draw attention to their one-sidedness. My tools to do so are the views of Wittgenstein and Odo Marquard. The latter's account of the meaning of life in his essay 'On the Dietetics of Expectation of Meaning: Philosophical Observations' (1991), is similar to that of Wittgenstein's account in that both emphasise the significance of the ordinary. I discuss Marquard's criticisms of 'sensational' approaches towards the problem of life's meaning, and afterwards I raise objections to what I call 'exclusivism' in the literature. The exclusionary accounts of life's meaning distinguish between the great and the ordinary and provide us with what they consider to be the constituents of 'great meaning' in life. Some of the exclusionary accounts of meaning that I shall address include Richard Taylor's theory of 'artistic creations' (1999), Neil Levy's 'work theory' (2005), and Metz's 'fundamentality theory' (2013).

In Chapter 5, 'On Detachment or Why the Shopkeeper Does Not Investigate His Apples', the aim is to view the notion of 'detachment' from a perspective different from that of most sceptics about meaning. I shall focus on Thomas Nagel's account of 'the absurd' as I think his thought on this topic is exemplary of sceptical approaches towards the meaning of life. My response to Nagel will take its cue from Wittgenstein's last text, *On Certainty*, as it is concerned with the problem of scepticism, the solutions to it, and the role of certainty in our lives. I also discuss Taylor's subjectivist theory of life's meaning and highlight the pessimistic background against which he arrives at his theory, a point mostly ignored by the commentators in the literature. Furthermore, I shall dedicate a section to discuss the implications of *On Certainty* for the ways most naturalists and supernaturalists in the literature approach the question of life's meaning. I will also make a distinction between what I call the 'deflationary' and 'inflationary' responses to the absurd, and I argue that though Nagel's objections to the 'inflationary' responses (e.g. Schopenhauer's 'negation of the will', Nietzsche's *'amor fati'*, Camus' 'heroism' and Benatar's 'anti-natalism') are well taken, his own deflationary solution, that is, 'irony', is problematic. Furthermore, by making a distinction between philosophical and existential scepticism, I discuss three different views about philosophical scepticism, which are Stanley Cavell's distinction between 'knowledge' and 'acknowledgement', Franz Rosenzweig's distinction between the 'sick' and the 'healthy' and Wittgenstein's allusion to 'indifference' and its relevance to philosophical scepticism.

Finally, in Chapter 6, 'The Human Voice: The Confessional Nature of Enquiring into Life's Meaning', I attempt to bring all the elements of my views in previous chapters together. So, I shall draw attention to what I call the 'confessional' aspect of human enquiry into the meaning of life. Arguing for the confessionality of our enquiry into life's meaning is paralleled with my views in previous chapters in that it is not concerned with the essence of life's meaning, it focuses on the ordinariness of this phenomenon and it argues that it consists of one's way of seeing the world. I suggest that in our everyday life the grammar of the question of life's meaning is most often *confessional*. I take confession to be an act of declaration or introspection that is meant to express one's judgement about (one's) life as a whole. It is an *activity* in which one shares or narrates one's understanding of life. I discuss and defend my suggestion in more detail by referring to various philosophers, including Wittgenstein, Cavell and Nussbaum. Afterwards, I provide two examples of a confessional approach by examining James Joyce's *Dubliners* and Wittgenstein's 'private conversations' with himself in his diaries. Furthermore, I suggest that a confessional approach can provide a convincing account of the apparent inconsistency in Wittgenstein's views of the 'problem of life' in his diaries.

To sum up, the aim of this book is to initiate a conversation by introducing certain ideas and themes to the literature. I would also like to make it clear that what you will find in these pages is not based on a comprehensive survey of the literature. It is possible that some of the views expressed here will have criss-crosses with other works in the rapidly growing literature in which case the non-comprehensive nature of my work should be considered. In thinking about life, it happens time and again that one contemplates things that have been contemplated by other people before.

1
Book of Facts, Book of Values

'It is difficult not to exaggerate in philosophy'.

Wittgenstein, *The Big Typescript*

Introduction

In the literature a distinction has been made between 'individualist' and 'holist' or 'personal' and 'cosmic' questions about life's meaning (Wong 2008: 123; Metz 2013: 3). Holist or cosmic questions about life's meaning enquire about life as a whole; in this line of enquiry you would like to define yourself and your role or your purpose in the world. For a large portion of the history of philosophy, cosmic or holistic questions were the gateway through which we would arrive at an answer to the individualist or personal questions. That is, the assumption was that an individual's life's meaning is defined primarily by its role in the larger schemes of things.

But currently, as Metz has noted, most works in the literature have individualist concerns and questions. In other words, the question is 'What makes my life meaningful?' and not, for example, 'What is the point of existence' or 'Where do we go from here?' However, it is worth pausing for a moment to ask whether cosmic and personal questions about life's meaning can be as easily separated as indicated in the literature. It seems to me that this division overlooks the interlocking connection between the two, because, in a sense, cosmic questions can be 'personal' questions as well since a specific person might find it to be of significance in her appraisal of life. Pascal, for example, didn't have the notion that life's meaning can be separated as having two senses, and the source of his individual agony was realising that a universal meaning might be absent. In our quest for the meaning of life, one's remembrance of stealing fruit from the neighbour's tree or one's 'Rosebud', as in the film *Citizen Cane*, can be as significant as the purpose of the emergence of life on a tiny portion of Milky Way Galaxy. Saint Augustine's recollection of his innocent mischiefs in his youth is a good example:

> Yet I lusted to thieve, and did it, compelled by no hunger, no poverty ... A pear tree there was near our vineyard, laden with fruit ... To shake and rub this, some lewd young fellows of us went, late one night ... and took huge loads. Behold my heart, O God, behold my heart. ... It was foul and I loved it. ... Fair were the pears we stole, because they were Thy creation, Thou fairest of all, creator of all. ([398] 1966: Book II)

Add to this Augustine's intense affairs with his concubines (Book VI), the significance of his mother in his life, his restless heart and his 'destructive pleasures'.[1] Every single human being, one might say, begins the question of the meaning of life with the vicissitudes of her life at the background, like the way Augustine did. We want to know what, if anything, confers value on the things we consider to be of value. In other words, it seems that a different version of the question of life's meaning is the relation between facts and values, and our judgement about this relation has an impact on our understanding of the meaning of life. For example, a subjectivist who claims that the meaning of life is only a matter of obtaining what one wishes is already denying that there are things in life that are objectively valuable and meaning-conferring. On the other hand, a supernaturalist would say what confers value on facts is defined in terms of their relations to a Supreme Being who is the source of all values.

In this chapter, I examine a radical answer in the history of modern philosophy to the question of the relation between fact and value, and then I discuss the implications of this answer on one's understanding of the meaning of life. I am referring to the *Tractatus Logico-Philosophicus*. The *Tractatus* can be seen as a treatise on the meaning of life in that it takes propositions of value to be the manifestation of our tendency to say something about the 'sense of life' (1966: § 6.5). I should mention that a critical understanding of the *Tractatus*'s account of life's meaning needs an analysis of its arguments the large portion of which might appear to be of remote relevance to the issues of life's meaning. That is, first I have to discuss the premises that led to the book's conclusions about value. My aim in this chapter is to provide a Tractarian picture of meaning in life. It is against the background of this picture that in the next chapter I examine some theories of life's meaning. And although, in Chapter 2, I ultimately reject the Tractarian view itself, the aim is to judge what we can take away from it.

Making a case for fact/Value dichotomy

During the course of World War I, Wittgenstein, a young soldier by then, used to write down his thoughts in his notebooks. His notes were mainly on logic and its relation to our language, but one could also find notes of a personal nature that would reflect his existential concerns, from fear of death to the implications of 'living in agreement with the world'. It was based on these notes that Wittgenstein published his first book, the only one he published in his lifetime.[2] The book's main aim is to show that the problems of philosophy arise because we misunderstand the 'logic of our language'. In order for us to avoid this misunderstanding, Wittgenstein suggests, we have to draw a sharp line between what could be meaningfully said within the boundaries of language and what cannot be said but can only be 'shown'.

But how are we to determine what is sayable and what is not? By logical analysis of the structure of our language, Wittgenstein thought. He starts his book by claiming that the world consists of the 'totality of facts'. For example, it is a fact that it is raining now, that the cat is by the window now and the earth revolves around the sun. Facts are 'existent states of affairs' (§ 2), and states of affairs are made of combinations of objects. Objects, in turn, combine with one another based on their internal and logical properties. The logical form of an object is all the possibilities that it has in virtue of its internal properties. These properties make states of affairs either actual or possible. In other words, the states of affairs that do exist could have been otherwise. For example, in our world the earth is approximately 8.20 light-minutes away from the sun, but it is possible to imagine a world in which the distance is shorter or longer. According to the *Tractatus*'s ontology, the totality of states of affairs makes up the whole of reality. The world is precisely the combination of all the states of affairs that do exist.

Wittgenstein tried to explain this by introducing his famous picture theory of language. Imagine in a court the judge is presented with a miniature model of a car accident which describes how it has happened. Now each of these elements in the model (cars, trees, houses, etc.) have a function; they are picturing a states of affairs. Wittgenstein took this model as an analogy to the way language functions and suggested that the whole language is in a sense a picture model of reality. That is, a proposition shows how things stand in the world. A proposition offers a picture of reality. If the states of affairs, pictured by the proposition, actually exist, then we say the proposition is true. Once again, reality is the totality of all the states of affairs that do exist. And, as Alfred Nordmann puts it, 'a complete list of all those possible states of affairs that actually obtain would provide a complete description of the world' (2005: 39). That is, a complete description of the world provides the 'totality of facts' but not more. Think of that miniature model of a car accident as a picture of language again. What Wittgenstein wants to say is that you can think of all sorts of things that can be put in a miniature model, things like objects and states of affairs, but there is not any place for value in such a picture of reality and of the world. When you talk about 'natural sciences', the cat on the couch, a general snow in Ireland, and so on, there is a way to find out whether these sentences correspond with the reality out there. In this view there is a limit to what language can convey, and the limits of language is seen as 'the limits of my world' (1966: § 5.6).

In a sense, what Wittgenstein does in the *Tractatus* is similar to a thought experiment introduced by William James in *The Varieties of Religious Experience*. The difference is that James and Wittgenstein arrive at two quite different conclusions by the same thought experiment. James wants to demonstrate the impossibility of abstracting oneself from the attitudes and emotions that colour our experience of the world and asks to

> Conceive yourself, if possible, suddenly stripped of all the emotion with which your world now inspires you, and try to imagine it *as it exists*, purely by itself, without your favourable, hopeful or apprehensive comment. It will be almost impossible for you to realise such a condition of negativity and deadness. No one portion of the universe would then have importance beyond another; and the whole collection of its things and series of events would be without significance, character, expression, or perspective. ([1902]1987: 141)

Whereas James denies the psychological possibility of a value-stripped world, the *Tractatus* claims that not only is it possible to 'conceive' a value-stripped world but also that, ontologically, this is how the world is. The world that the *Tractatus* tries to describe is 'stripped of all the emotion' and 'purely by itself' – a world where only the 'law of causality' decides what we can describe. As Wittgenstein says, 'what can be described can also happen: and what the law of causality is meant to exclude cannot even be described' (§ 6.362). Wittgenstein claims,

In the world everything is at it is, and everything happens as it does happen: in it no value exists – and if it did exist, it would have no value. If there is any value that does have value, it must lie outside the whole sphere of what happens and is the case. For all that happens and is the case is accidental. What makes it non-accidental cannot lie within the world, since if it did it would itself be accidental. It must lie outside the world. (§ 6.41)

The claim that 'in the world everything is as it is' is crucial in understanding the Tractarian account of value and the meaning of life. The *Tractatus* is about an individual who faces the world and tries to see it as *it is*. In such view, the fact of human life is something that 'belongs with the rest of the world'. When we read in the *Tractatus* that 'Death is not an event in life' (§ 6.4311), we can see its relation to a view that considers human beings to be part of the world like a 'beast' or 'stone' or tree. However, as we will see in the next section, the raison d'être of ethics is precisely our deepest tendency to deny that human beings belong with the rest of the world; it is to deny that the only things we have are facts and not values.

The Tractarian account of the 'sense of life'

The last four pages of the *Tractatus* address the implications of the Tractarian worldview for Wittgenstein's understanding of the sense of life. These pages contain a number of concise claims about the unsayabilty of ethics, the nature of the will, death, the insufficiency of our temporal immortality to solve the problem of life, the mystical, and silence. And there is a reason for the brevity of these statements. For the author of the *Tractatus*, the 'correct method' of doing philosophy was 'to say nothing except what can be said, i.e., propositions of natural science ... and then, whenever someone else wanted to say something metaphysical, to demonstrate to him that he had failed to give a meaning to certain signs in his propositions' (§ 6.53). Ironically, however, as Russell noted, Wittgenstein managed to say 'a good deal' about the unsayable.[3]

One might say the gist of Wittgenstein's propositions concerning ethics is that in the world the only thing we have is 'facts, facts, facts, but no Ethics' (Wittgenstein 1965: 7). There is a limit, in this view, to what can be said, and all the propositions that can be said are of 'equal value' (1966: § 6.4). The common characteristic of all the facts in the world is only one thing: They are all 'accidental' (§ 6.41), and what is accidental cannot convey value. Wittgenstein's argument can be restructured as follows:

- Facts of the world are accidental.
- All propositions concerning facts are contingent.
- Ethics is concerned with value.
- If there were propositions of value in the world, they would be contingent.
- This would make propositions of value accidental.
- Value cannot be accidental since if it were accidental, it wouldn't be value; it would, then, be a fact. Therefore,
  - in the world, it is impossible to have propositions of ethics;
  - value must lie outside the world.

If the answer to the question of value cannot be put into words, as Wittgenstein claims, then one might begin to ask whether the *question* itself can be meaningfully expressed. Thus, Wittgenstein claims that the unsayability of an answer would render the question itself unsayable as well (§ 6.5). Put differently, when a question can be expressed meaningfully, it is 'possible to answer it', and the only questions that can be asked are the questions of 'natural sciences'. However, even if we answer all the questions of science, we won't be able to answer the problem of life:

> We feel that even when *all possible* scientific questions have been answered, the problem of life remains completely untouched. Of course there are then no questions left, and this itself is the answer. (§ 6.52)

One feels that the chain of thoughts in the *Tractatus*, expressed in a numeric order, has a domino effect. That is, what has been started with the first proposition of the book, which claims the world to be 'all that is the case' (§ 1), reaches a mystifying end in one of the key points of the book:

> *The riddle* does not exist. (§ 6.5)

The point is that the only way to solve the problem of life is to make it disappear – to see that the riddle of life, for which an answer was supposed to be found, does not exist.[4] The problem will vanish when one realises that it cannot be framed into a question, and thus no meaningful answer can be found for it (§ 6.521). In a sense, the only solution to the problem of life is taken to be changing one's way of seeing the world. The craving to find an ultimate answer to the problem of life will fade away once we come to realise that there is no such thing as 'the riddle of life'. In the penultimate section of the *Tractatus*, Wittgenstein famously writes:

> My propositions serve as elucidations in the following way: anyone who understands me eventually recognises them as nonsensical, when he has used them – as steps – to climb up beyond them. (He must, so to speak, throw away the ladder after he has climbed up it.)…He must transcend these propositions, and then he will see the world aright. (§ 6.54)

Philosophy here is seen as an 'activity' and not 'a body of doctrine' (§ 4.112). This activity is a transcendental activity in the sense that by virtue of undertaking it one ultimately reaches a point where one sees the world aright. And when one sees the world aright one sees the limits of the world and the stance one should ideally take with regard to them. The last proposition of the book alludes to this point when in one of the most controversial claims of the book we read: 'What we cannot speak about we must pass over in silence' (§ 7).[5]

Wittgenstein's style of writing and his reluctance to explain his arguments in the *Tractatus* has led to different interpretations of his ethical views. When Russell begged him to clarify and explain the declarative remarks of the *Tractatus*, Wittgenstein retorted that explaining them was like 'dirtying a flower with muddy hands' (Monk 1990: 54). However, eight years after the publication of the *Tractatus*, in 'A Lecture on Ethics', Wittgenstein was willing to 'step forth as an individual and speak in the first person' about ethics as a tendency to enquire about the meaning of life. As I will argue in Chapter 2, the identity of ethics with our tendency to say something about the meaning of life is one of the key ideas that Wittgenstein held throughout his life.

Ethics as enquiry into the meaning of life

'A Lecture on Ethics' might be seen as a footnote to the *Tractatus* and is written in the same spirit, though in the former Wittgenstein is more charitable in clarifying his views about value. That includes the nature of value, the mystical, morality and the meaning of life. The core idea of the lecture is that though we might feel the presence of values in our lives, we should be aware of the limits of our language in conveying these feelings. Metaphorically speaking, we would be able to talk meaningfully about value if we could 'destroy' the structure of our language and of the world.

> If a man could write a book on Ethics, which really was a book on Ethics, this book would, with an explosion, destroy all the other books in the world. (1965: 7)

That is to say, writing the book of ethics entails destroying the book of facts. Wittgenstein's claim is that if I can write ethics, it means that I can 'say' it, and if I can say it, it means that ethics has a 'sense'. If it has a sense, it means that it is factual. Whatever is factual is accidental. However, ethics is not accidental, and thus it cannot be written. Note that words like 'saying', 'sense', 'factual' and 'accidental' follow Wittgenstein's terminology in the *Tractatus* and have specific meanings. Of course, I can say, for example, that harming innocent people for selfish reasons is morally wrong. But this is not Wittgenstein's point. His point is that the sense of a moral value cannot be expressed by justificatory explanations. If someone asks why harming innocent people is morally wrong, I might respond because human life has absolute value and harming the innocent disregards that value. If he asks, then, why human life has absolute value, I might say because humans are autonomous or because it is in the interest of society, etc. However, none of these explanations can convey fully the absolute value that you might ascribe to human life.

Why are we, then, still 'tempted' to use expressions such as 'absolute value', and what do we try to express by them? The lecture is disconcerting. On the one hand, Wittgenstein says there are experiences of absolute value, and on the other hand, he immediately warns us that any attempts to express these experiences are nonsensical. I think there are two reasons for Wittgenstein's 'disquietude' throughout the lecture. The first one is Wittgenstein's self-conscious attempt to avoid sounding like a logical positivist. While for the logical positivists all that matters is the verifiable meaningful propositions, and they are content with them, for Wittgenstein, the most cardinal problems of life are precisely the ones that cannot be talked about (Engelmann 1967: 97–111). The second reason has to do with Wittgenstein's disapproval of what he calls 'claptrap about ethics' (Monk 1990: 282). He was always disapproving of the tendency to view ethics as a science alongside other branches of knowledge. In this view, reducing ethics to a science that deals with human actions fails to do justice to the way we experience ethical problems. He had the same thing in mind when he once said to Rhees, 'it was strange that you could find books on ethics in which there was no mention of a genuine ethical or moral problem' (Rhees 1970: 98–99). Ethics, in such view, is primarily an attitude towards the world as a whole and, hence, it is about a way of being, about one's vision of life. Wittgenstein's ethics, in Hans Sluga's words, is a 'visionary' ethics as opposed to 'prescriptive or normative' ethics (2011: 147).

Wittgenstein finishes his lecture with an avowal of reverence towards ethics:

> Ethics so far as it springs from the desire to say something about the ultimate meaning of life, the absolute good, the absolute valuable, can be no science. What it says does not add to our knowledge in any sense. But it is a document of a tendency in the human mind which I personally cannot help respecting deeply and I would not for my life ridicule it. (1965: 11–12)

In other words, for Wittgenstein, ethics as far as it aims at giving an answer to our existential questions about life, as far as it stems from our innermost experiences that shape our understanding of the world, cannot be 'science'. Note that he is not denying that these experiences exist. Instead, the concern here is that they are senseless because they don't deal with describable states of affairs. I think Nordmann's distinction between nonsensicality and senselessness can be of use here. As he writes, 'a great many expressions are nonsensical and yet not senseless' (2005: 160–161). A proposition is nonsensical if it cannot be made to 'look like good scientific sentences and if it cannot be analyzed or clarified' (ibid.: 164).

Implicit in such understanding of ethics is the idea that there is a limit to what we can successfully communicate.[6] For example, in a state of *jouissance*, I might whisper 'Everything that lives is holy', or a believer might say this world is a 'friendly home', or a destitute soul might argue that 'Better never to have been' or that 'There is but one truly serious philosophical problem and that is suicide' (Camus 1955: 72). But here the arguments and the whispers stand at the same level in that all try to express something about life emphatically but the 'sense' of these utterances is nowhere to be found. As another example, think of the way we communicate our feelings when we are in love. How do we make sure that the message is delivered? Examining the ways we approach and experience these kinds of questions, Nordmann writes, 'When I say that I love you...I am reaching across an unbridgeable abyss. You have no means to compare the content of this statement to the real state of affairs in my head and heart, nor can I be sure that what you understood me to say is just what I meant by it. In fact, I cannot control the meaning of this phrase even for myself' (2005: 205).[7] Likewise, one might think of other experiences that one finds hard to express. The expressions and the phrases we use to describe 'the domain of the existential', Pierre Hadot writes, are 'conventional and banal' like the words you use to 'console someone over the loss of a loved one' (1995: 285). Wittgenstein refers to some of these experiences in the *Tractatus* and the lecture, and he highlights the 'hopelessness' of any attempt to treat them like describable states of affairs that can be easily communicated. As I will show in the next chapter, Wittgenstein's main objection to the current strands in the literature on the meaning of life would be precisely the fact that the communicability of the meaning of life is taken for granted.

What Wittgenstein calls the 'strictly correct method' of doing philosophy is to pay attention to what one says (1966: § 6.53). In the *Tractatus* there is a demand upon the reader, as D. Z. Phillips notes, 'to examine his life with words' (1999: 43). This demand might be viewed as what Wittgenstein once called 'the ethical point' of his book.[8] Whereas most commentators in the literature on the meaning of life freely use normative concepts and terms and take their communicability for granted, Wittgenstein would suggest that we pause and ask what meanings they have given to certain signs in their propositions. Philosophers in the literature appeal to words like 'love', 'transcendence', 'purpose of God', 'salvation', 'objective value', and so on without considering the possibility that those words might not convey the same message that they intend to deliver. In *Notebooks, 1914–1916* where Wittgenstein contemplates happiness, he reminds himself of the 'complete unclarity' of his statements (1979a: 79). We tend to assume that there is a mutual understanding between philosophers who write on the meaning of life and the readers, that someone sends a message and the other receives it. We all tend to forget that most of what we say with regard to ethical, religious and aesthetic matters is hard to convey, that we might have a feeling of 'mutual understanding' when we talk about some matters in life, but that doesn't mean that what we say is clear. As Nordmann says,

> It is easy to lose sight of the categorical distinction between ... agreement on the truth and falsity of a descriptive sentence and a feeling of mutual understanding. And far from being a harmless philosophical misunderstanding, the confusion of these things can actually be dangerous. If we start believing that our co-ordinated use of words

(She says: 'I love you,' he says: 'I love you, too'.) somehow contains real understanding, shared values or common truths, we may take the fact of communal co-ordination as evidence for a grounding in meaning, values, cultural norms. (2005: 216)

As I will argue in the next chapter, most theories in the literature on life's meaning overlook this categorical difference. I will argue that the *Tractatus*, as it stands, can draw the attention of philosophers to the limits of their theories to convey their senses and bringing about a change in one's life. I will also raise some objections against the Tractarian account of life's meaning, the most important of which is Wittgenstein's 'aspect-blindness' to the modes of our 'complicated form of life' (Wittgenstein 1958: 174). So, critically analysing major theories in the literature from a Tractarian perspective does not mean that I agree with the Tractarian conception of life's meaning. And rejecting the Tractarian conception of life's meaning does not necessarily mean that the Tractarian objections to the common strands in the literature should be overruled. I discussed the Tractarian account of life's meaning in this chapter to portray the background against which Wittgenstein arrived at his later approach to philosophy. As we will see in the next chapter, the movements of thought in Wittgenstein's philosophy can be traced back to the movements of his life.[9]

2
The Limits of Justification

Introduction

The *Tractatus* is about the limits of theory; it is about paying attention to what we say and write about problems of philosophy and 'the ultimate meaning of life'. It also recognises that there is a 'tendency' in us to talk about these matters. This tendency, by the criteria of the book, is epistemically futile, but it existentially shows something about the human condition. It is not a trivial tendency. It has an effect on one's life; it makes you 'step forth as an individual and speak in the first person' about value and the meaning of life (Wittgenstein 1979b: 117). From this vantage point, and in this chapter, I want to address two major approaches towards the meaning of life in the literature – that is, supernaturalism and naturalism. This will provide an insight into what I think has often been neglected in the literature, which is the limits of theorisation. However, my aim is not only a comparative study, but also to provide new ways of looking at familiar themes, particularly with regard to religion and meaning as well as attitude and meaning.

In the second part of this chapter, I raise some objections to the Tractarian approach towards the meaning of life, the main of which is the *Tractatus*'s 'autistic' conception of life, to borrow a term from Ernest Gellner (2005). I argue that the Tractarian view of life suffers from an 'aspect-blindness' with regard to a fundamental aspect of our life, which is our communal life. In other words, Wittgenstein, in his Tractarian philosophy yielded, from a different route though, to the same metaphysical tendency that he tried to warn philosophers against. However, the fact that Wittgenstein himself was bewitched by similar urges to provide a universal solution to the 'problem of life' does not necessarily imply that his criticisms of the tendency to theorise the meaning of life are not well founded.

Supernaturalism

Let me briefly clarify a point here. I think the assumption that there is a clear-cut distinction between all three approaches towards the meaning of life, that their titles clearly represent various theories within each approach, can be very misleading. For instance, supernaturalism is often defined as the theory that holds the meaning of life is found in relation to God and that without the existence of God and making a relation with him life would be meaningless. However, this broad definition does not say much about the vast differences between friends of supernaturalism. Believing in God as the ultimate source of meaning is not merely a simple affirmative answer to the question regarding whether God exists. As Cottingham says, an answer to the 'Yes/No question' of this type 'often tells us surprisingly little about how far a religious worldview informs someone's outlook' (2005: 80), and, as I will show, there are differences between friends of supernaturalism in their ways of advancing their conceptions of life's meaning. So, I view terms like 'supernaturalism' or 'naturalism' only as umbrella concepts for a wide variety of perspectives with family resemblances between them.

What is the key idea of supernaturalism? I think the answer is that supernaturalists, at least in the Abrahamic tradition, believe in a Supreme Being who confers value on the facts of the world. According to this view, in the presence of God Almighty the fact/value dichotomy collapses. Everything has an ultimate purpose and value. 'Every soul shall taste of death ... and unto us shall ye return' (The Qur'an III, 185; XXI, 35; XXIX, 57). In the Qur'an the earth is seen as a sacred place; one walks on earth beholding God's presence.[1] Interestingly, in the Arabic language there is no word for 'fact'.[2] To put it in the Tractarian terms, in supernaturalism the whole world of facts 'waxes and wanes' completely, so that it becomes a completely different world.[3] In Wittgenstein's words, 'to believe in a God means to see that the facts of the world are not the end of the matter' (1979a: 74). According to supernaturalists, if everything could be ultimately reduced to facts, then human endeavours in life would be pointless. Without God even our benevolence and good will, which are the sources of meaning for some naturalists, would be of little significance. Cottingham writes,

> If there is nothing to support the hope that the good will ultimately triumph, if essentially we are on our own, with no particular reason to think that our pursuit of the good is any more than a temporary fragile disposition possessed by a percentage (perhaps a minority) of a

certain class of anthropoids – then ... the very idea that some lives can be more meaningful than others begins to seem a fantasy. (2003: 72)

Cottingham's point is that the pursuit of the good is necessary, as objectivists suggest, but it wouldn't be sufficient to confer conclusive meaning on one's life, and only the existence of God could give an ultimate purpose to our good will. In other words, only a supernatural transcendence can confer an ultimate meaning on life.

On the other hand, some objectivists defend the view that the mere existence of God and relating to him in the right way does not rule out other possible ways of acquiring meaningfulness, such as engaging in objectively valuable activities. Moreover, one can believe in God and yet be convinced that only one's deeds in life, apart from one's belief in God, determine whether one's life is meaningful. Cottingham doesn't deny that one's actions play a significant role in determining whether one's life is meaningful, but what he denies is the assumption that all that there is to a meaningful life is adherence to a set of values which are supposedly mind-independent. It would be a 'fantasy' to assume that our good actions are both necessary and sufficient conditions of a meaningful life: what is more fundamental is to examine and ascertain whether the framework within which our actions are undertaken is in any way connected to a transcendent Being.

In response to this challenge a naturalist might come up with a thought experiment to show the reason supernaturalists appeal to the idea of God. She might say, suppose God created the world and, out of his infinite wisdom, decided to create human beings, but let us imagine that he denies their eternal survival after their death. That is, in this scenario people's death would be the end of the matter (no resurrection, no residence in God's memory, no reincarnation, none of those theological solutions). If God is omniscient and if 'God's ways are beyond human understanding' (as most supernaturalists believe) then at least we should be willing to acknowledge that there would be a reason for our ultimate annihilation. It seems that in principle a supernaturalist would be in agreement with this scenario. However, the naturalist goes on, believers would give you many reasons to undermine this absurd scenario. It would be against God's wisdom, they might say, to create human beings and then let them be wiped out from the face of earth *purposelessly*.[4] A rock, a fish, a lion, a rose, a dinosaur would vanish with no trace, but a human being shall remain because she is made in the image of God, and the image of God shall not perish. As Robert Nozick says,

A significant life, in a sense, is permanent; it makes a permanent difference to the world – it leaves traces. To be wiped out completely, traces and all, goes a long way toward destroying the meaning of one's life...Mortality is a temporal limit and traces are a way of going or seeping beyond that limit. To be puzzled about why death seems to undercut meaning is to fail to see the temporal limit itself as a limit. (1981: 582, 595)

From this vantage point, our naturalist says, supernaturalism or theism boils down to one fundamental belief: that mortality *destroys* the meaning of life.[5] We attribute to God all properties that we can't possibly have (omnipotence, omniscience, omnipresence, etc.) as long as he confers immortality on us – a fair trade. In general, most supernaturalists take immortality to be a necessary condition for a meaningful life.[6] But when a naturalist asks why immortality is so important for obtaining meaningfulness, the answer is because only immortality of our souls can *solve* the problem of life. For most supernaturalists, believing in God and believing in the immortality of the soul are two sides of the same coin. However, for the author of the *Tractatus*, what supernaturalists fail to take into account is that immortality might procrastinate our encounter with the riddle of life, but it does not solve it:

Not only is there no guarantee of the temporal immortality of the human soul, that is to say of its eternal survival after death; but, in any case, this assumption completely fails to accomplish the purpose for which it has always been intended. Or is some riddle resolved by my surviving forever? Is not this eternal life itself as much of a riddle as our present life? (1966: § 6.4312)

By alluding to the above position, Metz suggests that no supernaturalist 'maintains that mere extension [of human life] is sufficient for life's meaning' (2002: 790). Instead, 'an infinite amount of time is a necessary condition' of other elements that confer meaning on life (ibid.). For example, immortality is necessary for obtaining 'perfect justice'. The idea here is that for life to be meaningful, justice must ultimately prevail in the hereafter, if not in this world, for which our temporal survival after death would be necessary.

But, how can justice solve the problem of life? I want to use my imagination and imagine a world wherein ultimate justice is fulfilled and still see myself asking 'And now what?' What else would keep us going after justice is being served? Mightn't we say 'perfect justice' is the nickname for immortality? For even if you are doomed to eternal damnation, you know deep down, at the same time, that you are not expired, that you are alive to witness something, that you are in God's memory even though you are far from him. I will be sent to hell, but I will be in his memory, too; and that's a relief.

Here a supernaturalist might come up with a new idea: Life is meaningful in virtue of something more fundamental than 'perfect justice', something like God's love or God's recollection of us in his memory (Hartshorne 1984). But in what sense shall we remain in God's memory? Is it going to be like the way I recall someone who is long gone, or is it an altogether different phenomenon? In other words, would I need to survive temporally to reside in God's memory, or can I simply rest content with the assurance that I will be somewhere in God's recollection? Is he going to remember me like the way I would prefer to be remembered, with all the defining details that are central in shaping one's identity? Is he going to remember my childhood, the street fights, the second grade teacher who was, to our surprise, beautiful yet kind and my pigeons on the roof who would fly around the neighbourhood and descend as the sun went down? Will he remember that on 27 July 1890 someone did what he did 'for the good of all'?

Let us pause for a second here and ask ourselves what these sad and obscure speculations and questions try to convey. For the author of the *Tractatus*, these kinds of metaphysical solutions, whether it be 'love', 'recollection', 'perfect justice' or 'immortality', all try to run against 'the walls of our cage'. The cage is language and what is uttered outside the cage fails to convey what it means to convey, but it points at something. It points at our strong 'tendency' to say something about the ultimate meaning of life. The correlation between one's life and one's religious tendency is of a key significance in understanding Wittgenstein's account of religion in both his early and his later philosophy. He wrote 16 years after the publication of the *Tractatus* in February 1937:

> A religious question is either a question of life or it is (empty) chatter, this language-game – one could say – gets played only with questions of life. Much like the word 'ouch' does not have any meaning – except as a scream of pain. (2003: 211)

That is, a religious question, like a 'scream of pain', says something about the believer's life. Wittgenstein's statement is not merely trying to propose a non-cognitive account of religion, the view that religious utterances do not express factual propositions and thus cannot be true or false. Rather, I submit, it tries to highlight a 'way of seeing'; it says the life of the questioner gives 'sense' to his urge and tendency to ask these questions. As far as the literature on life's meaning is concerned, one might wonder how questions such as whether we are immortal in virtue of being recollected in God's memory or merging with God's identity could be related to one's life. On the other hand, Wittgenstein suggests that we should view religion not as a theory but as an 'event', not as a 'doctrine' but as a 'tendency':

> Christianity is not a doctrine, not, I mean, a theory about what has happened and will happen to the human soul, but a description of something that *actually takes place* in human life. (1980: 28, emphasis added)

The connection between life experiences and religious utterances is a recurrent theme in Wittgenstein's writings throughout his philosophical career. A religious conviction shows itself in its regulatory effects on the believer's life (I shall discuss this in more detail in Chapter 3).

To sum up, unlike most supernaturalists who concentrate on the existence of God and a soul to indicate what would make a life meaningful, Wittgenstein concentrates on the effects of such beliefs in the life of the believers. For friends of supernaturalism, the idea that there are non-theological objective values that confer meaning on life is seen as insignificant compared to the 'comprehensive meaning' that God would confer (Hepburn 1966; Craig 1994). Undermining naturalists' values in order to glorify religious beliefs has become a trend among most supernaturalists:[7]

> God loves and cares for us.... We live not by impersonal rules but in relation with a Cosmic Lover... Secularism lacks this sense of cosmic love, and it is, therefore, no accident that it fails to produce moral saints like Jesus, Maimonides... Gandhi... From a secular point of view altruism is not only stupid, it is antilife, for it gives up the only thing we have, our little ego in an impersonal, indifferent world. (Pojman 2002: 28)

Supernaturalists seize hold of an 'interpretation' of life, and religious beliefs for them is like 'a passionate commitment to a system of reference' (Wittgenstein 1980: 64). This is why religious instructions take the form of a 'description', a 'portrayal' of that system of reference. In this regard, undermining other systems of reference is seen as an effective way to highlight the advantages of one's system of reference. As Wittgenstein says, 'it would be as though someone were first to let me see the hopelessness of my situation and then show me the means of rescue until, of my own accord...I ran to it and grasped it' (ibid.). Pojman claims above that secularism does not offer 'special love' and that it denies any possibility of altruism and benevolence. In other words, you will be *hopeless* if you follow the naturalists' path. But, it seems that their success in letting me see the 'hopelessness' of my life does not prove the logical coherence of their system of reference. Their success in disclosing the depth of my hopelessness can show only the fragility of the human condition, our 'longing for the transcendent', but not more (ibid.: 15). Along with Wittgenstein, a supernaturalist might say the fragility of life might educate us to a belief in God.[8] But, a naturalist might reply, the same life might educate you to a disbelief in him.

As I hope I have made it clear by now, Wittgenstein's stance towards a supernaturalist account of meaning in life is twofold. On the one hand, we see a Wittgenstein who wants to put an end to all the 'claptrap about ethics' (Monk 1990: 282) and who discards all supernaturalist attempts to *say* something about the ultimate meaning of life, and on the other hand, we see a Wittgenstein who 'deeply' respects the human tendency to quest for the ultimate meaning of life. However, respecting a tendency is one thing, and being approving of the claims made due to the existence of that tendency is quite another. Wittgenstein's main criticism of the supernaturalist accounts of life's meaning would target their tendency to turn their experiences of what can give life value into theories and doctrines. This partly explains Wittgenstein's dismissive attitude with regard to the questions of value, as we see in his conversations with logical positivists, recorded by Waismann:

> Is value a particular state of mind? Or a form attaching to some data or other of consciousness? I would reply that whatever I was told I would reject and that not because the explanation was false but because it was an *explanation*. (1979b: 116)

And further on,

> What is valuable in a Beethoven sonata? The sequence of notes? No, it is only one sequence among many, after all. (ibid.)

By the same token, supernaturalist theories of the meaning of life are undermined precisely because they are only explanations. In a sense, what Wittgenstein targets in his Tractarian view of life, and obviously in his later works, is the gap between an intellectual understanding of any given account of life's meaning and the existential commitment to the implications of that view on one's life. The common element in most supernaturalist accounts of life's meaning, no matter if instead of God's purpose (Davis 1987; Moreland 1987; Craig 1994) we deal with God's love (Hartshorne 1984), 'infinity' (Nozick 1989) or 'simplicity' (Metz 2000), is that they fail to pay due attention to the lives of believers in God. What is lacking in the literature is the awareness that 'the adoption of a religious worldview does not hinge on the plausibility, let alone conclusiveness, of philosophical argument' (Cottingham 2009a: 266). As Cottingham puts it in a Wittgensteinian vein, it depends on 'coming to see the world in a different way' (ibid.). That is, the problem of life is solved not by learning certain facts about life but by 'seeing the existing facts in a particular light' (Child 2011: 66).

There is a growing body of texts in the literature, especially thanks to Cottingham's contribution, that takes the regulatory effects of religion on the believer's life seriously. Cottingham suggests that if religious discourse is to 'engage us on more than a narrowly intellectual plane', it may help if we shift the focus of discussion from the domain of religion to the closely related domain of 'spirituality'. There is widespread agreement, Cottingham has it, on the value of spiritual domain 'despite the polarisation of outlooks'. Spirituality, Cottingham writes,

> has long been understood to be a concept that is concerned in the first instance with activities rather than theories, with ways of living rather than doctrines subscribed to, with praxis rather than belief.... We have to acknowledge what might be called the *primacy of praxis*. (2005: 3–5)

By 'primacy of praxis', Cottingham means that our practical involvement with religion comes before, and is more important than, a theoretical discussion of its doctrines. In this regard, to understand religion, or rather supernaturalist views of the meaning of life, we should shift the focus to the praxis, to the effects, of belief in the believers' lives. We should shift our focus from the strategy of 'logical analysis' to the 'strategy of involvement' and the 'strategy of praxis' if we are to understand religious answers to the problem of life (Cottingham 2005: 12). Understanding the life of a believer, Cottingham suggests, needs a kind of 'openness' and 'responsiveness' with regard to the praxis of religious belief. A 'certain mode of receptivity' should be in place if we are to understand the religious outlook (ibid.: 83). This mode of receptivity is neither ashamed of the flaws in the traditional arguments for the existence of God nor concerned with finding a scientific evidence of his existence. Rather, it passionately believes that in this world of contingency and vulnerability one may discern 'unmistakable traces of that unexperiencable reality that transcends it' (ibid.: 136). These traces, of course, are not qualified as 'evidence' in its naturalist sense. But, according to Cottingham, it doesn't mean that they can be simply dismissed for being subjective. You need to develop the capacity to 'appreciate' traces of the transcendent reality, and that is a lifetime process. You do not acquire a religious way of looking at things in a vacuum. We do not arrive at a religious point of view in our respective lives as a result of investigation based on the 'classroom model'; rather, 'we gradually, laboriously, stimulated by examples, moved by parables, humbled by error, purged by suffering' begin to form a religious way of appraising life (ibid.: 144). You live and you learn many things in the process, one of them could be religiosity of the type Wittgenstein and Cottingham have in mind when they talk about religion.[9] For Cottingham, arriving at a religious view or seeing the traces of the transcendent in the world is not only a subjective affair, produced in the imagination factory of a restless mind. It is also the outcome of 'a living commitment'; it develops bit by bit, like the way you learn how to appreciate a piece of music. As he writes,

> A lifetime of musical discipline may enable the committed musician to discern profundities and beauties of musical form that are in large part quite literally inaccessible to the novice, but that does not mean that they are mere idiosyncrasies of subjective feeling. (ibid.: 138–139)

So, on the one hand, Cottingham emphasises that belief in God cannot be a 'straightforwardly empirical hypothesis', and on the other hand, he suggests that such belief is based on the observation of traces of the transcendent. 'The *trace* remains' (ibid.: 133). The believer's leap of faith is not a 'blind leap'; rather, it is guided by what Wittgenstein would call the 'imponderable evidence' (Wittgenstein 1958: 228).

If one objects that talking of the 'traces' of a transcendent reality is incompatible with the nature of that reality and that a transcendent reality with traces cannot be transcendent, Cottingham replies that he is not using the term 'trace' in its 'literal sense' (2005: 137). And 'once literality is abandoned, there seem to be several possible ways in which one might understand the idea of a divine trace in the created cosmos' (ibid.). In other words, the believer, with a 'certain mode of receptivity', is equipped with a certain mode of appraising life which is informed by traces of a divine reality.

In general, what is implicit in such a view of the nature of belief is the limits of theory, as explicitly discussed in the *Tractatus*. However, whereas Wittgenstein is against any talk of 'traces', Cottingham considers them to be a philosophically coherent source of our knowledge of the transcendent. I think Cottingham plays very powerfully with the remaining cards that are left for theists in the literature, but I also think there is a limit to what these cards can offer to supernaturalists. For one thing, Cottingham's talk of traces is effective and accessible only to those who are already *at home* with the idea of a transcendent being who leaves elusive traces. A Dawkinsian type of mind-set doesn't have access to these traces, and this doesn't mean that he has an agenda to close his eyes to everything that might lead him to the traces of the transcendent. Cottingham talks of traces but, at the same time, he treats them like evidence.

One concern here is that such an approach might eventually lead to a kind of exclusivism, which doesn't seem to be helpful. If, as Cottingham suggests, appreciating traces of the divine would be available 'only to those in an appropriate state of trust and receptivity' (2007: 36), then the question arises what qualifies as 'appropriate' here and who is going to decide what sorts of actions and attitudes need to be had to arrive at this state of receptivity. On various occasions, Cottingham talks of a set of values and attitudes that are embedded in theistic traditions – values such as 'humility, hope, awe, thanksgiving' (ibid.: 29). Religious traditions offer a 'complex interpretative framework' in which some of the key values of human life 'find a secure place' (ibid.: 28), a framework that, according to Cottingham, the naturalist or humanist outlook would fail to offer. But this raises the question whether these values are contingent upon believing in God or whether believing in God is a result of having them? In other words, did I become a humble, hopeful and thankful person because at a certain point in my life I came to believe in God, or am I a believer now because I have been humble and hopeful? I think it makes sense to say that belief in God brings about and highlights certain ways of being and perceiving life, usually manifested in attitudes that Cottingham associates with religion. But if belief in God is hinged upon having certain traits and attitudes, then the implication is that those who are not in the possession of these traits and attitudes will probably be excluded, or deprived, from the truth of theism. But, as I argue below, there is a flip side to that coin which can be used by naturalists.

I wonder if Cottingham is willing to accept that naturalists can also appeal to the trace argument and claim that even if they don't have conclusive evidence that there is no God, there are enough non-literal traces that point at his nonexistence. They might point at what happened in Gulags and Dachaus. Mightn't we say as in religious belief 'a certain mode of receptivity' should be in place to see the traces of God's absence in the world? Mightn't a naturalist say that a certain mode of objectivity has to be in place to see that beyond our deep expectations, there is nothing to support the idea that we are not on our own? It takes more humility or 'courage', a naturalist might say, to accept and, even more, to appreciate the human finitude (Wielenberg 2005: 117). The Scriptures are right, the naturalist says, 'every soul shall taste of death', but unto star dusts shall we return, not to God.

If both believers and nonbelievers can appeal to the traces of God's availability or absence, we might say believers and nonbelievers reach a conceptual impasse in their debate, one that can be overcome now and then not in the realm of theory but in the lives of believers and nonbelievers. That is, life might educate a nonbeliever to a belief in God and his traces. Conversely, a believer might begin to struggle to see the traces of divinity in the vicissitudes of her life. Wittgenstein goes so far as to suggest that 'if you want to stay within the religious sphere you must *struggle*' (1980: 86). As I will discuss in Chapter 3, in a sense, this struggle alludes to the believer's struggle to *see* the world religiously, that is, to keep seeing the world religiously once a religious aspect has dawned on her.

To sum up, Wittgenstein's concern with regard to supernaturalists' attempts to *explain* the ultimate sense of life springs from his fundamental conviction that theorising value is equal to *destroying* it. The second issue that I have tried to highlight is the intimate connection between one's life and one's belief system in Wittgenstein's views of value, something that is often neglected among supernaturalist theories of life's meaning.

Naturalism

Whereas supernaturalists believe that only God can confer comprehensive value or meaning on life, naturalists question God's monopoly in conferring value. In this section, I confine myself to analysing what I think is the defining idea of naturalism, the view that the meaning of life is not necessarily found in a relation with God. I think this key idea is vividly expressed in Peter Singer's book, *How Are We to Live? Ethics in an Age of Self-Interest*, and so I focus on this work.

Singer defends the idea that our lives can be meaningful by engaging in activities that are 'objectively worthwhile' (1995: 231). According to Singer, pain is intrinsically evil and reducing the total amount of avoidable pain in the universe is an objectively worthwhile activity. Reducing the total amount of pain, however, is not merely one objectively worthwhile activity among others. Singer goes so far as to suggest that the *best* way to make one's life worth living is to devote it to the reduction of 'avoidable pain in the universe'. He calls this 'an ethical life', and declares that 'living an ethical life enables us to identify ourselves with the grandest cause of all, and ... is the best way open to us of making our lives meaningful' (ibid.: 259). After a brief discussion of subjectivist approaches to the problem of life's meaning, Singer suggests that subjectivism leads to problematic results. If we reduce meaning to a phenomenon that's subject to our inner desires and wishes, we shall face the problem of boredom and loss of purpose in the societies where 'the narrow pursuit of material self-interest is the norm' (ibid.: 277). A connection is made here between subjectivism and its manifestation in consumerism. You can have your desires and wishes, but in consumerist societies these desires and wishes are already defined. Subjectivism says your choices would make your life meaningful as long as you are passionate about them, but consumerism says it is obvious what you should choose. As Renton, the junkie in Danny Boyle's black comedy, *Trainspotting*, narrates, 'Choose Life. Choose a job. Choose a career. Choose a family. Choose a ... big television, choose washing machines, cars, compact disc players and electrical tin openers. Choose good health, low cholesterol, and dental insurance. Choose fixed interest mortgage repayments. Choose a starter home. Choose your friends. Choose leisurewear and matching luggage. Choose a three-piece suit on hire purchase in a range of ... fabrics. Choose DIY and wondering who ... you are on a Sunday morning' (Boyle 1996). But, what Singer, Renton and most of us want to ask is, 'why would I want to do a thing like that?' (ibid.) As for Singer, there is more to life than yielding to the narrow materialist options offered by the society.

An ethical approach to life, as an ideal alternative to the narrow subjectivist approaches, gives us a better picture of life and its meaning. And since it is possible to live ethically regardless of the existence of God or lack thereof, the absence of God does not render human lives meaningless. Singer ends his book with a hopeful message:

> If 10 percent of the population were to take a consciously ethical outlook on life and act accordingly, the resulting change would be more significant than any change of government.... You will find plenty of worthwhile things to do.... You will know that you have not lived and died for nothing, because you will have become part of the great tradition of those who have responded to the amount of pain and suffering in the universe by trying to make the world a better place. (1995: 278–280)

So, there is an explanation of why we should follow what Singer calls the 'ethical life': We become part of something bigger than us, the humanistic tradition of all the people who have struggled to improve the human condition by alleviating some of its pain. You are what you are striving for in the world, Singer would say; better to choose something worthy of striving.

Now, let me briefly discuss Wittgenstein's views about the unexplainability of value in order for me to highlight vast differences between two ways of approaching value. Waismann relates a conversation between Wittgenstein and his friends in Moritz Schlick's house in 1930. They discussed Schlick's new book in which Schlick distinguishes between two theological interpretations of ethics. According to the first interpretation, which, for Schlick, is the 'shallower', an action is good if it is what God wills. The second interpretation, and the 'deeper' one, is that the good has intrinsic value, independent of God's will. Wittgenstein's dismissive response is as follows:

> I think that the first interpretation is the profounder one: what God commands, that is good. For it cuts off the way to any explanation 'why' it is good, while the second interpretation is the shallow, rationalist one, which proceeds 'as if' you could give reasons for what is good. The first conception says clearly that the essence of the good has nothing to do with facts and hence cannot be explained by any proposition. If there is any proposition expressing precisely what I think, it is the proposition 'what God commands, that is good'. (Wittgenstein 1979b: 115)

Let us unpack Wittgenstein's way of answering the Euthyphro dilemma.[10] His response to Schlick is, to say the least, counterintuitive, but it shows his firm conviction that there is a limit to what can be explained. Viewing God as the source of the good is 'profounder' because it *cuts off* all the explanations. It is profounder, that is, to stop explaining value as if it stands in need of an explanation. Wittgenstein writes,

> The *absolute good*, if it is a describable state of affairs, would be one which everybody, independent of his taste and inclinations, would *necessarily* bring about or feel guilty for not bringing about. (1965: 7)

I might try to define the absolute good as if it is a describable state of affairs, but then my description would fail to convey the 'coercive power' of the absolute good. On the other hand, I might say, for example, benevolence is good because it is God's will. The explanation is over; I find a terminus for my explanation. 'What is good', Wittgenstein writes, 'is also divine. Queer as it sounds, that sums up my ethics' (1980: 3). This queer stance towards ethics only makes sense against the background of naturalists' justificatory attempts to defend their account of the good life. For Singer, the final justification for living an ethical life is that we can avoid boredom only by self-transcendence, best exemplified in striving for alleviating suffering. But a supernaturalist might go further and question the value of our disposition towards the good. From a naturalist point of view, a supernaturalist might suggest, we are only 'members of a species, who, at a given epoch of evolution, [have] a particular collection of characteristics and potentialities' (Cottingham 2005: 53). We value benevolence and disvalue cruelty because in the long process of 'genetic lottery' of natural selection we happened to learn that altruism pays, that it was better to isolate some behaviours and attitudes and cultivate some others. As Michael Ruse claims,

> Our moral sense, our altruistic nature, is an adaptation – a feature helping us in the struggle for existence and reproduction – no less than hands and eyes, teeth and feet. It is a cost-effective way of getting us to cooperate, which avoids both the pitfalls of blind action and the expense of a superbrain of pure rationality. (1986: 99)[11]

The evolutionary ethicists claim that most human beings tend to commit themselves to a set of principles that cut across their own desires because it is a 'cost-effective' way of dealing with community. However, the objectivist says the reason people tend towards a specific set of actions is that they find them morally right. In other words, we tend to act morally not only because of our subjective dispositions but also because it is the right thing to do. She might point to the intuitive force of moral claims felt by most moral agents and arrive at the conclusion that these claims are objective or at least universal. But as Paul Johnston says, the fact that most people act as if their moral judgements are independent of them does nothing to change the logical status of these claims (2003: 5). In a sense, the objectivist holds a personal opinion and announces that her opinion is not, in fact, personal. In Johnston's words, 'having embraced a particular position, she congratulates herself on it being the correct position and wants us to take her self-endorsement as independent confirmation' (ibid.: 6).

The realisation that our search for a justifiable terminus for value would inevitably face contradictions and problems has led some philosophers to dismiss all explanatory attempts to justify value. Bernard Williams, for example, argues that the solution to the conflict between the ones who see ethics as a matter of 'disposition' and the ones who view it as a matter of 'truth', is to depart from the 'Christian method' of thinking about the conflict and return to the Greeks' method. By this, he means a return to a way of thinking that views ethics as a highly significant element in human flourishing, one that is not concerned with the idea of a morally correct view of the world. What is important, then, is the practical effects of ethics on human life in society and not the abstract concerns about the nature of ethical claims. We should leave, Williams suggests, the traditional obsession with objective ethics and move towards a modern conception of it, a movement that he considers to be a transition from 'ignorance' to truth. The realisation that there is no objective values, Williams believes, 'can be seen as a liberation, and a radical form of freedom may be found in the fact that we cannot be forced by the world to accept one set of values rather than another' (1985: 128).

It seems to me what Williams is saying is that we act ethically because, simply, it pays to be ethical; it leads to human flourishing. But isn't human flourishing another name for value? And if that is the case, it appears that what Williams actually conveys is that we identify with 'ethical considerations' (ibid.: 48) and values because they would lead us to a more fundamental value, perhaps the most important of them, that is, the human flourishing in life.

In light of my discussion of the justificatory nature of theories about the source of value, we can now take a fresh look at Singer's account of life's meaning. By emphasising the 'ethical life', Singer also tries to explain the meaningfulness of a life dedicated to the reduction of avoidable sufferings. Singer, with almost a messianic tone, announces that 'if, over the next decade, a critical mass of people with new priorities were to emerge, ... if their co-operation with each other brings reciprocal benefits, ... then the ethical attitude will spread, and the conflict between ethics and self-interest will have been shown to be overcome' (1995: 279). The reason we should take an ethical stance towards life is that it works, 'psychologically, socially, and ecologically' (ibid.). However, one might ask, what if it did not? Would an ethical life be less meaning-conferring then? It is beyond the scope of my topic to discuss whether success in one's projects is a key element in deciding whether one's life is meaningful, but one might intuitively suggest that not all the decisions we make in life are made with an eye to the prospect of their success. People commit themselves to moral life not because 'it works' but sometimes precisely in spite of the realisation that it might not work. That is, one might be concerned with the absolute value of, for example, modesty or compassion and not their consequences. More importantly, I'm not sure the conflict between an ethical life and the life of self-interest is as easy to overcome as Singer implies. Think of an entrepreneur who opens a production line in a developing country and recruits thousands of people with low salary. This would of course lead to the reduction of some sufferings in the world in that at the end of the day a group of people would be able to put bread on the table. It seems that, based on Singer's account, the entrepreneur would have a meaningful life because his enterprise leads to the reduction of some people's suffering, but I think this view is problematic, and I doubt Singer would call it an ethical life. What Singer fails to take into consideration in his account is the significance of one's attitude or 'one's way of seeing' in choosing an ethical life. He assumes that the moral weight of attending to people's sufferings is something like a truism. In Singer's words, 'in comparison with the needs of people starving in Somalia, the desire to sample the wines of the leading French vineyards pales into insignificance' (ibid.: 277). One cannot help sympathising wholeheartedly with what Singer says here. However, the fact remains that realising the insignificance of my way of life is important but not sufficient to make me change my attitude towards life. A person who drowns himself in debt to catch up with the unnecessary requirements of a comfortable stylish life might feel ashamed or sorry for what happens to less fortunate people, and at the same time, he might feel redeemed by donating $50 to Oxfam. In other words, 'indubitability' of the value of Singer's 'ethical life' 'wouldn't be enough to make me change my whole life' (Wittgenstein 1967: 57).

Finally, one might ask whether the reduction of avoidable suffering in the world is the only available option to people who are searching for meaning in their lives. An artist, a caring mother, a football player and a couple might view their lives as meaningful but not because they are doing anything especial to reduce the avoidable pain in the universe. As Erik J. Wielenberg notes, 'perhaps the ethical life needs to be characterised a bit more carefully' (2005: 30) because, based on Singer's account, 'the painless annihilation of all life would drastically reduce the amount of avoidable suffering in the world' (ibid.) and yet, obviously, Singer wouldn't consider it to be ethical.

Wittgenstein's rejection of justificatory attempts to explain the good or absolute value springs from his fundamental belief that 'if I could explain the essence of the ethical only by means of a theory, then what is ethical would be of no value whatsoever' (Wittgenstein 1979b: 117). A justificatory theory of value often fails to make me *see* the absolute value of a moral good. That is, it fails to give me the ethical attitude, which would have made all the burdens of justifying the moral good unnecessary. Likewise, someone who is blind to the sufferings of fellow human beings does not need philosophical promises of meaningfulness, advocated by Singer and other objectivists. What he needs is a change of attitude; an aspect of human life has to dawn on him (as I will discuss in the next chapter). According to this view, the dawning of an aspect *shows* what the objectivist fails to convey in his explanations.

The Tractarian view of value wants to do away with all explanations and justifications of value, and Wittgenstein wouldn't mind putting all normative philosophers out of their jobs. The irony, though, is that Wittgenstein puts himself in a normative position when he admonishes philosophers to avoid speculating about value. But I think there are things we can take away from this radical and 'queer' views about value, the first of which is the idea that an ethical life begins from within, not from without, as in Singer's account. The question is, how can I even begin an ethical life without leaving my vanity aside, without a change in my whole way of appraising life? It seems that the one who spends his life, out of vanity, pursuing his self-interest can also become the one who attends to the suffering of others out of vanity. Adam Smith's 'invisible hand' might have done a good job of reducing some avoidable suffering in the world, but I am not sure that we can conclude that the people who run this hand are living more meaningful lives in light of what their self-interest has ultimately brought about. People who have the luxury of searching for meaning only to avoid boredom might feel good upon being told that they can have very meaningful lives if they pay more attention to the pain of others (animals included), but this does not necessarily make their moral life more integrated. In less fortunate corners of the world people sometimes struggle for the things that are taken for granted in more fortunate ones. Depending on where you stand, you might find it tragic, absurd or unjust, but to act upon this realisation and live an ethical life is usually made possible by what we might call a gestalt shift in one's way of being, and that is not an easy task. Failing to live ethically is not only a failure of intellect; it is also a failure of the will.

So much for Singer's account of life's meaning. In the next section, I raise objections to the Tractarian account of meaning in life, and where needed I provide clarifications especially with regard to the 'queerness' of living in the Tractarian world. I argue that even though Wittgenstein's rejection of a justificatory approach towards value is plausible, especially considering his view of the nature of philosophy, his own picture of life in his Tractarian philosophy was limited with an aspect-blindness with regard to the ways we relate to life's meaning.

Unliveability of the Tractarian philosophy of life

I wonder what would have been the status of the *Tractatus* now if Wittgenstein hadn't included remarks about the 'sense of life' and value at the end of his book. What if Wittgenstein was literally silent about these matters in the book, without talking about not talking about them? Ray Monk sees a connection between the movements of life and the movements of thoughts in Wittgenstein's life, and he suggests that 'if Wittgenstein had spent the entire war behind the lines, the *Tractatus* would have remained what it almost certainly was in its first inception of 1915: a treatise on the nature of logic' (1990: 137). It was at the front that his thoughts on ethics began to find their way in his notes on logic. What is striking in these notes, as Monk notes, is that they are presented as if the former follow from the later. In the summer of 1916, in the head of a soldier in the Austrian Eleventh Army somewhere at the front, ethics and logic began to fuse because if logic shows the boundaries of the world and of language, ethics shows what lies beyond them.

However, the 'world' that Wittgenstein was referring to in his notes was not the world that he was experiencing; it was not the world of bombs and shells and hunger; it was not the world of the dead and the wounded. In the *Tractatus*, you don't hear the sound of loading guns; you hear the sound of *The World as Will and Representation*. Wittgenstein only refers to the 'misery of the world', and in his notes he is searching for a way to 'renounce' it. The ethics of the *Tractatus* is the ethics of renunciation by withdrawing to a silent sanctuary for the ideal self, a self that can fly over the 'totality of facts' and view the world *sub specie aeternitatis* and in his isolated reflections comes to an agreement with the world and accepts it as is. In the last four pages of the book, one can discern a philosophy of life, a way of looking at the world and living in it.

There is something formidable and bleak about this view of life presented in a few short statements. But, as David Wiggins suggests:

> a moment's thought about what it would take to practice the philosophy of life that is set out [in these passages] is enough to show how near to impossible it must be to live by this philosophy – either by its letter or by its spirit. (2004: 375)

I think the difficulty of a Tractarian way of living stems from the fact that it offers a static account of life, one that tries to transcend the world and view it *sub specie aeternitatis*. The unhappy result of such detachment from the world and its contingencies was the view that from a detached perspective there is no difference between the life of a human being and the life of an object, like a stone or a tree. It is in such a world that 'death is not an event in life'[12] (Wittgenstein 1966: § 6.4311). The Tractarian subject is surrounded by facts, and it has to come to terms with the unsayability of whatever that has something to do with value.

Implicit in such a static picture of the world is the absence, or insignificance, of the other. According to Louis Sass, the Tractarian philosophy advocates 'a certain kind of schizoid ideal, a life based on separation from the body, others, and the external physical universe, and on retreat to an inner and purely cerebral realm, devoid of any passion, yearning, and pain' (2001: 112). So, it is not a coincidence that throughout the *Tractatus* or *Notebooks, 1914–1916* one can hardly see any reference to the communal aspect of life. There is no moral message, no obligations, no duties and no universal commands. In those few pages about ethics he is referring to only himself. 'What history has to do with me? Mine is the first and only world', Wittgenstein writes in his notebooks (1979a: 83). History is a nightmare from which he is trying to awake by detachment.

The ethics of the *Tractatus*, thus, becomes the ethics of detachment or, as Liam Hughes says, an 'inward-looking ethics' (2009: 64) which is only concerned with the relation of the self to the world, and as a result, the other is absent in such ethics. What Dieter Mersch calls the 'paradox' of the Tractarian ethics is precisely the absence of the other. Mersch suggests:

> Turning away from the world, refusal, which first permits the attitude of non-intervention, is lastly rooted in the *negation of the other*. Therefore, in his solution lies a reversal and betrayal of what is precisely a constituent part of the ethical problem. Ethics beyond the question of *alteriority* remains blind; it forfeits, to think radically, its status as ethics. (2009: 48–49)

In short, I think most objections to the Tractarian account of life's meaning are variations of one single objection: the Tractarian view is oblivious to the *ordinary* modes of experiencing the world.[13] It is from this perspective that Ernest Gellner harshly characterises the *Tractatus* as an 'autistic work' (2005: 63). As Gellner says, 'if you accept the cognitive authenticity of nothing other than your own directly accessible data, in the end you are confined to a prison whose limits are indeed those data. If they are constituted by *your* immediate consciousness, by *yourself* in effect, then your *self* eventually becomes your prison' (ibid.: 43).

This limited conception of the self not only brings about a self-absorbed conception of ethics but also imposes a solipsistic way of looking at things. Such an approach amounts to disconnecting oneself from the locality and the contingencies of one's life, which in turn leads to what John Churchill calls viewing the world 'from everywhere and nowhere'. The *Tractatus* represents an inclination, Churchill writes,

> to portray our apprehension of the world on the model of a subject who surveys it from no particular perspective – from everywhere and nowhere, a perspective which is not essentially related to a particular, embodied, culturally and historically conditioned human being. (2009: 129)

One might say, at least as far as the Tractarian conception of life's meaning is concerned, one of the 'grave mistakes' in the Tractarian philosophy was Wittgenstein's yielding to a strong urge to see the world from nowhere. But, this is not to say that Wittgenstein is alone in this tendency. As Pierre Hadot eloquently explains in his book, *Philosophy as a Way of Life*, for a large portion of history 'the cosmic flight and the view from above' has been identified with 'the philosophical way par excellence of looking at things' (1995: 242). For the Platonists and the Stoics, according to Hadot, the goal of this exercise was to make 'imagination' speed through 'the infinite vastness of the universe', 'was to attain a greatness of soul,...to teach people to despise human affairs and to achieve inner peace' (ibid.: 242–243). We see a clear echo of this attitude in Wittgenstein when he writes, 'The only life that is happy is the life that renounce the amenities of the world' (1979a: 81). For Wittgenstein, renouncing the amenities of the world was made possible by detaching oneself from the hurly-burly of life, from culture and from history.

'There are diverse paths to loneliness', Gellner observes (2005: 43). The path taken by Wittgenstein was a result of the 'individualistic-universalistic, atomic vision of knowledge, thought, language and the world' (ibid.: 46). But it seems that the philosopher who thought he had found the final solution to the problems of philosophy spent enough time among ordinary people to rethink the lacunae in such a way of looking at things.[14] As early as 1930 he started to doubt whether it is possible to have a single general account of factual propositions, and he could see by then that there are different systems of propositions.[15] He also realised that our language has some functions that are not descriptive of facts at all. He recognised that the endless varieties of human experiences can be conveyed through language, and it does not need to be factual to make sense. The 'grammar' or the function of the words in our everyday life determines their meanings and not necessarily the predetermined, rigid logical forms.

Thus, Wittgenstein's philosophy evolved from the Tractarian search for the boundaries of what can be said to an acknowledgement of particulars. According to the *Tractatus*, as Russell Goodman suggests, 'there are just three things one can do with language: say, show, and utter nonsense' (2004: 173). By the time he was writing *Philosophical Investigations*, however, he had a completely different answer to the question: 'How many kinds of sentence are there?' The answer was as follows: 'countless kinds: countless different kinds of use of what we call "symbols", "words", "sentences"' (1958: § 23). He realised that his mistake in the *Tractatus*, as he once told Waismann, was to proceed 'dogmatically' (Monk 1990: 321), the conviction that there was a clear-cut way of capturing the ultimate structure of reality. Whereas the *Tractatus* was a book with a resolute beginning and a resolute ending, he begins one of his lectures in 1933 by acknowledging that 'There is a truth in Schopenhauer's view that...a book on philosophy, with a beginning and end, is a sort of contradiction' because in philosophy it is difficult to arrive at a 'synoptic view', which would have made possible a book on philosophy with a beginning and an end (Wittgenstein 1979c: 43).

These realisations led Wittgenstein to a turn in his thought from a metaphysical to an 'anthropological method' (Rhees 1970: 101). This method involves close attention to the use of words and practices in community. The new method made Wittgenstein abandon most of his Tractarian ideas, including the concept of the self and the world. He moved away from the conception of the self as a detached spectator who sees the world *sub specie aeternitatis* to one who is an actor in humans' 'forms of life'. In E. V. Thomas' words, Wittgenstein's later philosophy is a shift 'from detachment to immersion' (1999: 195). Consequently, Wittgenstein's account of the relationship of the self to the world was transformed and, in John C. Kelly's words, 'the door seemed to be open to a new account of ethics' (1995: 581) and, one might add, to a new account of the meaning of life. This new account of meaning was no longer concerned with the 'final solution' to the problem of life. Instead, it was more concerned with those little things that constitute our 'complicated form of life'. In other words, one might say, a transition or a gestalt switch happened. Iris Murdoch's allusion to 'a two-way movement' can aptly describe this transition. She writes, at the beginning of *The Sovereignty of Good*:

> There is a two-way movement in philosophy, a movement towards the building of elaborate theories, and a move back again towards the consideration of simple and obvious facts. McTaggart says that time is unreal, Moore replies that he has just had his breakfast. (1970: 1)

One might say, from an ambitious movement towards the construction of a universal theory in his Tractarian philosophy, Wittgenstein shifted towards the appreciation of 'simple and obvious facts' of life in his later works. Recall that in 'A Lecture on Ethics' Wittgenstein complains that no matter what happens in this world, the only thing we have is 'facts, facts, facts, but no ethics' (1965: 7). Some years later, thanks to his new turn, he could have also written somewhere in his diaries that whatever happens in this world, the only thing we have is life, life, life, but no theory of life's meaning.

In the preface to the *Philosophical Investigations*, Wittgenstein mentions that he had the intention to publish 'those old thoughts' in the *Tractatus* together with the 'new ones' in the *Investigations* and that 'the latter could be seen in the right light only by contrast with and against the background of my old way of thinking' (1958: ix). Likewise, the main reason I dedicated the first two chapters to Wittgenstein's 'old way of thinking' was to show the new ideas in the right light. The difference between the old and the new ways of thinking lies in the significance of shifting away from the abstract and the ideal and moving towards the concrete and the ordinary in the later works. So, my discussions in the next chapters, from the significance of our 'way of seeing' to the appreciation of that 'extraordinary thing called ordinary life',[16] from the absence of scepticism and our groundless 'trust' and 'certainty' in our everyday life to the confessionality of our quest for life's meaning, should be seen against the background of a way of thinking that searches for the ideal language and the ideal solution to the problem of life.

What can we take away from the Tractarian conception of life's meaning? There are some elements in Wittgenstein's Tractarian philosophy that have far-reaching implications for our enquiry and thus are worth considering. The first one is the idea that treating moral values as something explainable is not the right way of establishing a connection with them. The second element that we can take away is Wittgenstein's emphasis on the limits of what any *theory* of life's meaning can convey.

In his later philosophy, concepts and words have a 'home in our life', and they have meaning only in 'the flux of life', 'the bustle of life', or 'the stream of life' (Wittgenstein 1990: § 173). And the meaning of life is not an exception. The meaning of life is found, as it were, on the streets of life. According to this approach, the suggestion would be not to 'think' about the abstract conditions of a meaningful life but to 'look' and see the concrete circumstances in which those conditions are met and experienced (cf. Wittgenstein 1958: § 66).

What do we see when we look at countless modes of our complicated ways of living? I will attend to this question in the next chapter.

3
Aspect-Seeing and Meaning in Life

> 'Read the language of these wandering eye-beams.'
> — Emerson, 'Friendship'

Introduction

In previous chapters, I discussed Wittgenstein's Tractarian views about the inexpressibility of propositions of value, and I tried to highlight the implications of this radical, though prima facie defensible, view for issues of life's meaning. While in Chapter 1, I focused more on giving a broad picture of the Tractarian account of meaning in life, in Chapter 2 I tried to analyse some key views of naturalists and supernaturalists from a Tractarian perspective. Whereas most supernaturalists take the expressibility of their theories for granted, Wittgenstein draws attention to the limits of theory and justification. Furthermore, by discussing Singer's account of 'ethical life', I raised objections to the justificatory nature of his account of 'ethical life'. I argued that even when these justificatory arguments are accepted as valid, they are unlikely to be successful in bringing about a change in my attitude and my 'way of seeing the world', an issue that should concern philosophers. This is why I have dedicated this chapter to a discussion of 'aspect-seeing' and 'attitude' and exploring their various implications.

Though Wittgenstein was not the one who coined the phrase 'seeing-as', he showed the significance of this notion in the structure of concept formation and meaning, broadly construed. In this chapter, I will explore how notions of 'aspect-seeing' and 'aspect-blindness' can inform issues of life's meaning. The notion of aspect-seeing, as William Day and Victor J. Krebs (2010) show in detail, is of significance for

Wittgenstein, and the secondary literature on aspect-seeing is expanding rapidly. However, I refer to the literature on aspect-seeing only to the extent that it is relevant to the discussion of meaning in life. In the next two sections, I analyse Wittgenstein's views about aspect-seeing and its related discussions, such as attitude/opinion distinction, as discussed in *Philosophical Investigations*, and then, in the third and fourth sections, I apply those views to issues related to life's meaning.

Aspect-seeing and aspect-blindness

In part II of *Philosophical Investigations* (section 11), Wittgenstein explicitly discusses aspect-seeing and its related topics. However, the subject appears in several other texts.[1] A growing body of secondary literature on aspect-perception and aspect-seeing suggests that most scholars on the field have begun to take the importance of aspect-seeing in Wittgenstein's philosophy seriously.[2] In the *Investigations*, Wittgenstein begins the discussion as follows:

> I contemplate a face, and then suddenly notice its likeness to another. I see that it has not changed, and I see it differently. I call this experience 'noticing an aspect'. (1958: 193)

Here we are dealing with the two 'uses' of the word 'see'. The first use deals with our normal visual experience; we see an object, a drawing, and so on, and we use the expression 'I see this'. In the second use of the word 'see', we see a likeness; we notice a similarity or a likeness in the object of our visual experience to something else. In everyday life, we usually encounter this phenomenon when, for example, we see a facial similarity between a mother and her son, a similarity between two pieces of music (for example, the Adagio in G Minor by Albinoni might remind you of Air on the G string by Bach and vice versa), the likeness of a movie in terms of its theme to another, and so on. In all of these experiences seeing one object leads to discovering or seeing the other one. So, noticing an aspect, as Day and Krebs suggest, has a 'double aspect' (2010: 8). It is an experience in which we realise that something changes, and yet we know that nothing has changed. In other words, 'we know that the change is not (so to speak) in the world, but (so to speak) in us' (ibid.). This observation, as we will see, has far-reaching implications for our discussion. A classic example of seeing-as or noticing an aspect, one that is also used by Wittgenstein (1958: 194), is Jastrow's duck-rabbit as shown below:

The picture can be seen as a duck or a rabbit, depending on the centre of one's concentration when one looks at the picture. If you concentrate on the left side, you most probably first see a duck, but if you concentrate on the right side, you probably see a rabbit. Now imagine how someone who hasn't seen a rabbit in her life would see the duck-rabbit picture. In this situation she approaches the picture differently; an aspect is missing in her approach, though the picture is the same. In her visual experience she would see the same physical properties that we attribute to the shape of rabbit, but she wouldn't call it a rabbit-seeing visual experience.

Wittgenstein makes a distinction between 'continuous seeing' of an aspect and the 'dawning' of an aspect (ibid.). Suppose I see the duck-rabbit picture and see only a duck (continuous seeing), but when I manage to see the rabbit, an aspect of the picture 'dawns' on me. A new perception emerges. As Wittgenstein says, 'The expression of a change of aspect is the expression of a new perception and the same time of the perception's being unchanged' (ibid.: 196). Usually, the expression of a change of aspect is accompanied by an 'exclamation', which manifests the change of aspect. In the dawning of the rabbit picture I exclaim, 'I see a rabbit now!' The exclamation 'is forced from us' (ibid.: 197). We don't merely give a report when a new aspect flashes on us; the report is accompanied by an exclamation. One's 'tone of voice' or body movements usually express 'the dawning of an aspect' (ibid.: 206), like the way you close your eyes out of embarrassment when you realise you shouldn't have said what you have said to her. Or, 'the likeness makes a striking impression on me; then the impression fades' (ibid.: 211).

The other notion that has implications for the issues of life's meaning is the notion of 'aspect-blindness'. Wittgenstein asks

> Could there be human beings lacking in the capacity to see something as something– and what would that be like? What sort of consequences would it have? ... We will call it aspect-blindness. (ibid.: 213)

An aspect-blind person will have an altogether different relationship with the pictures to which he is blind. But aspect-blindness is not limited to pictures. Here is a point with far-reaching implications for the issues of life's meaning: One can be aspect-blind to various experiences in *life*. If I see someone and fail to see the smile on her face, then I am aspect-blind to her smile. Or, someone who is unable to appreciate and relate to a piece of music will be unable to recognise the subtleties and nuances that are usually hidden from a non-musical ear. In so many ways, Wittgenstein writes, aspect-blindness is 'akin to the lack of a musical ear' (ibid.: 214).

What makes the notion of 'aspect-blindness' important lies in the connection between the concept of seeing-as and 'experiencing the meaning of a word' (ibid.: 214). The question for Wittgenstein is: 'What would you be missing if you did not experience the meaning of a word?' (ibid.). Imagine yourself wanting to teach a child the meaning of the word 'friendly' or 'unfriendly'. I might assume the best way to do so is to use the ostensive method of teaching words, that is, by pointing at a face and telling her: 'This is a friendly face' or 'This is an unfriendly face'. We often tend to believe, as Verbin notes, that teaching a concept is as easy as teaching the name of an object, say, duck (Verbin 2000). Thus, I might show a human face to the child and call it 'friendly', but then the child might identify friendliness with smiling faces. However, we know that not all smiling faces are friendly; we learn that a smile sometimes reveals other attitudes or emotions besides friendliness, things like confidence, nervousness, condescension or cruelty. Children smile; politicians do too. I submit that the important point here, one that is pertinent to the question of life's meaning, is that there is a *history* or a life behind seeing an aspect, and when one is blind to an aspect, one is in fact blind to the life or the history related to that aspect. Pointing to an aspect is not enough; one needs to be equipped with the capacity to see that aspect, a capacity that is cultivated by experiences in life. The child will not learn the meaning of friendliness merely by an ostensive method of teaching words; *life's experiences will teach her what a friendly face is*. I mean a lot of training is required to learn these kinds of concepts. To learn what is a friendly face is to learn many other things as one lives. And if I were to learn these concepts, a certain level of agreement over definitions and judgements is required. Or, in Verbin's words, the learning of concepts presupposes 'a certain uniformity in experiencing and reacting to various facts of our world' (ibid.: 12). For example, the child should be able to distinguish between different forms of facial expressions and should be able to express different reactions to each of them. And in due time he might also acquire many other subtleties that help him arrive at a more informed judgement about what we call friendliness, subtleties such as a person's choices of words, his tone of voice, his attentiveness in greetings, his confrontational or invitational attitude in conversations, his mood consistency, his eye contact and the durations of various moments of eye contact, his general accessibility, and so on. But he might also realise that none of these can be taken as conclusive evidence for friendly demeanour (David Lynch's *Elephant Man* is scary and yet friendly; but he is a peculiar type of a friendly person. His retreat into darkness doesn't stop us from discerning friend-seeking behaviours and attitudes embodied in his recitation of Psalm 23 or crying out, when he is cornered by an angry mob, that 'I am not an elephant! I am not an animal! I am a human being! I am a man!').

On various occasions in his later works, Wittgenstein tried to advance and establish the basic idea that sharing a form of life is contingent upon agreement or uniformity on a wide range of issues – for instance, uniformity in our way of experiencing the world. He writes in *Investigations*:

> If language is to be a means of communication there must be agreement not only in definitions but also (queer as it may sound) in judgments. (§ 242)

In virtue of our agreement in judgement, for example, when I see someone in pain I do not *infer* that she is in pain; instead, I react to the pain. The human pain is transparent to us. However, not all behaviours and concepts are as transparent to us as pain behaviour. In Wittgenstein's words, 'One human being can be a complete enigma to another' (ibid.: 223). In these situations, I might feel 'I cannot find my feet' with them (ibid.). In certain respects they are not accessible to me.

Attitude/opinion distinction

Whereas our opinions are usually cognitive and have to do with our knowledge claims, which can be proven wrong or right, our attitudes are emotive and expressive (cf. Wittgenstein 1998b: 38). For example, you might have an opinion about the cause of someone's illness, but the way you would normally react to his pain is the result of having an attitude towards a human being in pain. While you are expressing an opinion by telling a patient about the cause of his illness, you express an attitude by holding his hands and keeping your voice down. A patient in bed forces new attitudes on you, like the way 'starry heaven', 'forest roads', or Paris might force different attitudes on you. You might know certain things about the origins of stars, about dead stars and ones that are yet to be born, but starry heaven might ignite in you a sense of wonder at the world; or, it might remind you of Kant's juxtaposition of the moral law within and the starry heaven above and make you contemplate the relation between the two. Likewise, we all know about Paris as the capital of a country, saturated with museums, tourists, love locks, and so on. But if you happen to know its history, the people who have been there and its endless conversations at the bars and cafés, and if, for example, you happen to know about its *400 Blows*, its *Samurai*, its *De battre mon coeur s'est arrêté*, its *Les Enfants du Paradis*, its *Rififi*, its *Breathless*, its *Bande à part*, its *Three Colours: Blue*, its *Jules et Jim*, its *Red Balloon*, its *Green Ray*, its *Moveable Feast*,[3] and the happiness that was promised to many in these works but delivered to a few, you might begin to form an attitude about the city.[4] It is only with the background of such knowledge and such subtleties that, then, you might see Paris not only as the capital of a country but also, among other things, as a place where a long time ago someone who was 'very poor and very happy' wrote with a very short pencil in his notebook that 'many are stronger at the broken places' (Hemingway 1964: 220). This is an attitude expressed in the form of an opinion.

At least on two occasions in *Investigations*, Wittgenstein alludes to the distinction between attitude and opinion. He invites us to imagine that all the people around us are automata. We might find this idea 'a little uncanny', but, he continues:

> Just try to keep hold of this idea in the midst of your ordinary intercourse with others, in the street, say! Say to yourself, for example: 'The children over there are mere automata; all their liveliness is mere automatism.' And you will either find these words becoming quite meaningless; or you will produce in yourself some kind of uncanny feeling, or something of the sort. (§ 420)

The reason we find this idea a little 'uncanny' is given in the second part of *Investigations*, as if Wittgenstein finds an answer to the question he has asked before. It is difficult to imagine a human being as an automaton because 'my attitude toward him is an attitude toward a soul. I am not of the *opinion* that he has a soul' (ibid.: 178).[5] In the course of our ordinary lives, we are already involved in a 'stream' of interactions with other human beings, and the meaning of our relations with fellow human beings seems 'transparent' to us (ibid.: 223). (I elaborate on the usual transparency of the human behaviour in more detail in Chapter 5.) The meanings of signs and codes of life are transparent to us precisely in the same way that the meanings of words are clear and transparent to us. I react to people's pain; I can respond to a smile with a smile. I do not see people in my community as robots, and I trust they don't either. Their 'liveliness' and their transparency make my attitude towards each of them an attitude towards a soul.[6] And I submit our attitude towards fellow human beings is a *'way of seeing'* and receiving them (1958: § 461). In short, usually our lives fit into 'life's mould' (Wittgenstein 1980: 27), and thus we do not view life as a problem. Life is transparent to us as long as we fit into 'life's mould'. However, every now and then, here and there, in the lives of some, the transparency of life fades away; it becomes an 'enigma' that needs to be solved. In the next section, I will analyse this enigma based on what I have discussed so far.

Aspect-seeing and meaning in life

In the *Blue Book*, Wittgenstein alludes to a person who constantly asks questions such as 'What is the meaning of a word?' or 'What is meaning?' He describes this situation as some sort of 'mental cramp' in which 'we feel that we can't point to anything in reply to [these questions] and yet ought to point to something' (1969: 1). On another occasion he talks about the same urge and mental cramp that makes us search for answers that will be 'given once and for all; and independently of any future experience' (1958: § 92). According to David Kishik, it is one's 'blindness to the way by which language meshes with life that is the cause of this mental cramp' (2008: 113). I agree with Kishik that we feel the same urge and mental cramp when we ask questions such as 'What is the meaning of life?' or 'What is the purpose of life?' But, unlike Kishik, I am not convinced that the question of life's meaning emerges as a result of our 'blindness' to the ways 'language meshes with life'. It seems to me that we ask the question because the sense of life is no longer transparent to us. That is to say, our blindness is not blindness towards the grammar of our language and its relation to life; rather, it is an aspect-blindness towards the transparency of life. In our everyday life we are not concerned with the grammar of our language (unless we are doing philosophy in the study); we are preoccupied instead with our daily tasks and routines that usually shape our social and individual life. These are what make life transparent to us. But as Thomas Nagel famously argues, when we begin to wonder about life's purpose we examine our lives as a whole. Tolstoy's narration of the way he arrived at the question of life's meaning is very illuminating. 'Five years ago', he writes,

> something very strange began to happen with me: I was overcome by minutes at first of perplexity and then of an arrest of life, as though I did not know how to live or what to do, and I lost myself and was dejected. But that passed, and I continued to live as before. Then those moments of perplexity were repeated oftener and oftener, and always in one and the same form. These arrests of life found their expression in ever the same questions: 'why? Well, and then?' (1905: 7)

I think it is not coincidental that most people who begin to enquire about the meaning of life find their quest 'uncanny'; the question of life's meaning sounds strange, as Tolstoy alludes above, in that while we are actually living, we quest for the meaning of life. That is, we feel mere living is not enough; there must be a purpose, a point behind living. It appears that we need to find an Archimedean point to see life as an observer for which a certain degree of detachment from life is required. In short, questions concerning the value and the meaning of life are often accompanied by being isolated from the surrounding circumstances of one's life. In other words, in these situations it is not easy to find one's feet within one's way of life. This is Wittgenstein's point when he writes,

> The way to solve the problem you see in life is to live in a way that will make what is problematic disappear. The fact that life is problematic shows that the shape of your life does not fit into life's mould. So you must change the way you live and, once your life does fit into life's mould, what is problematic will disappear. (1980: 27)

It is not clear here what changing one's way of life entails, since it does not merely mean changing one's lifestyle, diet, friends, partner, and so on, and it is quite possible to change every external factor in one's life and yet leave the problem untouched. Here, I think, the attitude/opinion distinction discussed above might clarify Wittgenstein's point. One might say, not what happens in our lives but rather our attitudes towards them, our 'way of seeing', determines whether we see life as problematic or not.

Furthermore, the implicit conformism of this view is also problematic. One might wonder whether the same 'life's mould' isn't part of the problem of life's meaning. And how can I fit into life's mould if I see it as the source of all problems? What does guarantee that the problem of life will be solved if I fit into life's mould? In a passage that alludes to the *Tractarian* view of life, and serves as a critique of it, Wittgenstein reconsiders his previous position:

> If someone believes he has found the solution to the 'problem of life' and is inclined to tell himself that now everything is simple, then to refute himself he would only have to remember that there was a time when this 'solution' had not been found; but at *that* time too one had to be able to live, and in reference to this time the new solution seems like a coincidence. (2005: 309e)

So, on the one hand, he suggests that the problem will disappear if one changes one's way of life, and on the other hand, he proposes that even without this solution one would be 'able to live' – as if he views the same problem from two different perspectives. I think what is meant by changing one's life, in the first statement, is the dawning of a new aspect on one's life. As Monk suggests, 'the consequence of a change of aspect might be a change of *life*' (1990: 516). A person who decides to change the way he lives does not necessarily do so after concluding that, for example, there are values such as 'benevolence' and 'compassion' that make one's life meaningful. His decision might as well be the consequence of the dawning of an aspect of life on him. Experiences of 'various sorts' in life might lead to a change in his perception of life. 'The expression of a change of aspect', in this case, 'is the expression of a new perception' (Wittgenstein 1958: 196).

The significance of aspect-dawning becomes clear when we consider the way people change or re-evaluate their religious beliefs. Nancy Bauer's account of the way her faith disentangled from her sense of 'moral rectitude' and sloughed off bit by bit 'like an old skin' is relevant here. 'I still cannot say', Bauer writes, 'exactly how or why this happened.... But I can say what did not happen: I did not lose my faith as a result of someone's advancing a philosophical demonstration of its inherent irrationality' (2005: 212). Here we should openly take into consideration the experiences of a person to whom the religious aspect of the world no longer dawns, the realisation that she is ultimately on her own or that what happens in the world 'is a matter of complete indifference for what is higher' (Wittgenstein 1966: § 6.432). In other words, not only does one lose one's belief in a set of ideas about the creator of the world and the purpose of life, but also one faces the realisation that a certain mode of being is no longer available.

Wittgenstein writes, 'if you want to stay within the religious sphere, you must *struggle*' (1980: 86). The struggle, I think, of wanting to stay in the religious sphere is the struggle to keep one's religious attitude towards the world. It is the struggle to experience the continuous dawning of religious aspects on one's life. One cannot see the vicissitudes of one's life as 'the will of God' unless such aspect is already dawned. By attributing an event to human nature, to biology, to poverty, to ignorance, and so on, I might think that I'm contradicting a person who relates that event to God's will. But by seeing God's will in that event, she expresses something more than a mere causal explanation:

> In the sense in which asking a question and insisting on an answer is expressive of a different attitude, a different mode of life, from not asking it, the *same* can be said of utterances like 'It is God's will' or 'We are not masters of our fate'. (ibid.: 61)

When a believer says that the vicissitudes of her life are God's will, she is not giving a causal explanation of what has happened in her life. She is 'expressing an attitude to all explanations' (ibid.: 85). The dawning of new aspects usually brings about new attitudes, new decisions. For example, a father, the absent figure of a broken family, might consider going back home thanks to the flashing of a new aspect on his life and not necessarily as a result of contemplating values of care and family. He might do so because the fact that his kids are the only living beings related to his life has dawned on him (an attitude has consequently flashed on him). Likewise, another person might fail to see sufferings of other human beings; he might fail to see 'humanity in a man':

> We tend to take the speech of a Chinese for inarticulate gurgling [while] someone who understands Chinese will recognise *language* in what he hears. Similarly I often cannot discern *humanity* in a man. (ibid.: 1)

Providing a solid proof that every person, in virtue of being a person, has inalienable rights, or arguing that despite our vast differences we are all made in the image of God, wouldn't be enough to make me see humanity in others. But when I finally see the humanness in a person, I might see curiosity of the eyes: I see 'the look in the eye'.[7] I look at him and he looks back at me. And then, in Emerson's words, I might be able to read 'the language' of his 'wandering eye-beams' ([1841] 1940: 222).

Religious ways of seeing the world

Lectures and Conversations on ... Religious Beliefs emphasises the centrality of aspect-seeing in the life of the believer. It is about the regulatory effects of religious pictures on the believer's life. For example, consider a religious picture that most believers appeal to: 'God's eye sees everything'. The way to understand the picture is to recognise the application of this picture in the believer's life. Wittgenstein says:

> 'God's eye sees everything' – I want to say of this that it uses a picture. I don't want to belittle the person who says it. ... We associate a particular use with a picture. ... What conclusions are you going to draw? ... Are eyebrows going to be talked of, in connection with the Eye of God? ... If I say he used a picture, I don't want to say anything he himself wouldn't say. I want to say he draws these conclusions. (1967: 71–72)

In other words, he is trying to describe only the effects of belief in God's eye in the life of the believer. We will go astray if we immediately start to ask questions that the picture appears to force upon us. If someone exclaims that God has spoken to him, asking him about God's accent is to miss the entire point. Putnam's reading of Wittgenstein's remark is worth quoting at length:

> If I speak of my friend as having an eye, then normally I am prepared to say that he has an eyebrow, but when I speak of the Eye of God being upon me, I am not prepared to speak of the eyebrow of God. But the impressive thing here is not what Wittgenstein says, but the limit he places on his observation. Pictures are important in life. The whole weight of a form of life may lie in the pictures that that form of life uses. (1994: lii)

And I want to add that not only a 'form of life' but also a way of seeing and a certain attitude lie in the pictures that believers employ. Consider the following examples: God as the Father, God as the Saviour, God as the Judge, God as Love, and so on. The picture itself, on its own, is silent; one's relation to it – that is, the 'application' – gives it its meaning. For instance, to a believer God as the Father means that we are all his children, that he cares about us, that he shelters us, that we are not lost, and so on. The picture of God as a father brings about or leads to other pictures and concepts. That is, it forces a way of seeing the world. Wittgenstein connects the world picture of religious people and its impact on their lives by the following example: 'Suppose somebody made this guidance for this life: believing in the Last Judgment. ... Asking him is not enough. He will probably say he has proof. But he has what you might call an unshakable belief. It will show, not by reasoning or by appeal to ordinary grounds for belief, but rather by regulating for in all his life' (1967: 53–54). The idea is that the language-game of empirical proof doesn't apply here. There is no evidence, and 'if there were evidence, this would in fact destroy the whole business' (ibid.: 56). As Cottingham observes, 'quasi-scientific or knock-down arguments' for God's existence 'are quite untypical of the route whereby people are normally drawn to give their allegiance to a religious worldview' (2005: 21–22). In other words, evidence, of the type a naturalist might request, is not enough to force a way of living on her. The believer appeals to a picture of the world, which has a regulatory effect on her life. Consider, for example, the picture of the world as a friendly home:

> There is life after death. Death is not the end of the matter. But we shall live on, recognising each other in a better world. We have eternity in our souls and are destined for a higher existence. So if Hebraic-Christian theism is true, the world is a friendly home in which we are all related as siblings in one family, destined to live forever in cosmic bliss in a reality in which good defeats evil. (Pojman 2002: 29)

Obviously, naturalists deny this picture and argue that an impartial observation of facts portrays an altogether different picture of the world from that of supernaturalists (Benatar 2006; Russell 1957). Some pessimists claim that, given the amount of suffering and injustice in the world, given the fragility of goodness and pervasiveness of evil, it is crazy to infer that the world is a friendly home (cf. Blackburn 1999: 170). The world, they say, is an asylum, not a friendly home.

One problematic feature of this way of criticising religious worldview is that it assumes the believer is like a colour-blind person who fails to see the true colour of the human condition.[8] But we shouldn't rule out the possibility that a person might arrive at a religious outlook not in spite of all the evidence of suffering in the world but precisely because of it, a point that naturalists usually fail to take into consideration. As Cottingham observes, the most passionately religious people 'were a people whose history was conspicuous by the most terrible suffering' (2005: 23). Moses crossed Sinai not in spite of the evidence of human suffering but precisely because of it. Religion, for a genuine believer, is, first and foremost, a 'passionate commitment to a system of reference' (Wittgenstein 1980: 64), which regulates her life, and the believer finds the meaning of life in the regulatory dimension of her commitment. This commitment is not an arbitrary commitment. It forces a certain type of seeing the world and acting upon it. It wouldn't, for instance, force a believer to commit herself to Sudoku or collecting autographs of celebrities, but it might lead her to *see* a strange beauty in realising that Mohammad and Jesus stared at the same moon that she does now.

So, in a sense, the believer wants us to see some aspects of the world in the way she does. Most supernaturalists refer to the scientific picture of the world and its destiny to bring home the key idea that without God we would be hopeless. As Craig writes,

> Scientists tell us that everything in the universe is growing farther and farther apart. As it does so, the universe grows colder and colder, and its energy is used up. Eventually all the stars will burn out, and all matter will collapse into dead stars and black holes. There will be no light at all. There will be no heat. There will be no life, only the corpses of dead stars and galaxies, ever expanding into the endless darkness and the cold recesses of space, a universe in ruins. (1994: 159)

That is a typical naturalist account of the ultimate destiny of the universe.[9] But, what is curious is the conclusions naturalists and supernaturalists draw from this. Whereas naturalists tend to believe the meaning of life is possible only through the recognition of our indifferent world[10] and through embracing either various objective values or subjective preferences of individuals, supernaturalists conclude that from a value-less world we can derive neither subjective nor objective values. In Pojman's reading of Russell's 'Free Man's Worship', 'on the firm foundation of unyielding despair we can only build that which is desperate' (2002: 28). In other words, according to supernaturalists, there is no happy end in the naturalists' picture of the world. We should look at 'the means of rescue' against the background in which our hopelessness is portrayed.

The supernaturalist's belief in God as the ultimate source of meaning of life did not begin with a philosophical conviction that could be discarded by a philosophical clarification later on.[11] However, the vicissitudes of life might flash new aspects on the believer's life. 'An aspect dawns and fades away' (Wittgenstein 1998a: § 438), and if we want to feel it and be aware of it, 'we must bring it forth again and again' (ibid.). In this view, losing one's faith might be the result of the fading of an aspect of the world. Conversely, one doesn't come to see the world religiously as a result of someone's advancing a philosophical or theological explanation of the existence of God (cf. Verbin 2000: 20). Suppose there are two books on the table, or a million books in the library, and someone picks one of them and says, 'This is God's word'. Here we might see what he means by the way he relates to the book in his life; by the way he holds the book, the way he leafs through the pages and the way he knows off by heart some verses of it and the way he quotes them, now and again in his human conversations. In other words, you can't believe a text is God's word and, at the same time, keep a neutral relationship with it. That is, one's attitude towards the text clarifies what one means by any explanation one offers to prove that a text is God's words.

Wittgenstein suggests that sometimes by asking for a causal explanation for an event we express an attitude. Let me clarify this with an anecdote by Nancy Bauer. She writes, in 2003, while she was reflecting on the question, 'Is there anything beyond human understanding?' a child in her son's elementary school went to bed with a mild stomach bug and never woke up. As the news spread all over the neighbourhood, the next day everyone had the same question: Why? Of course, there was a rational explanation for his death, but it didn't stop many people from continuing to ask 'why'. To the point that one night her eleven-year-old daughter came into her room, crying 'I just don't understand, Mommy. ... Why did Jordan die?' (2005: 212.), Bauer, unable to answer her question, remembers her own father's response to her when she was ten years old and suffering from juvenile depression:

> My father told me that God was crying for me ... and when he said this I burst into fresh tears, largely because I felt bad that my own sadness was making God, who had felt so far away during those days, feel so bad. I'm not sure whether it was my despair or my father's sense that he had failed to convey to me what he had meant to convey by saying that God was crying for me that caused his tears to well up and overflow. But I have always been grateful for that moment, in which I came to grasp the value – the gift – of ... something that no argument could have brought me to understand. This was not a gift that I was able to give to my daughter the night she came to me sobbing. (ibid.: 213)

In other words, Bauer was unable to explain the death of Jordan the way her father would have explained it because she couldn't see the world the way her father did. Her intellectual integrity would have been at stake had she told her daughter that 'God's ways are beyond human understanding'. For Bauer, the only available explanation for Jordan's death was a scientific one, but that could not stop her daughter and other people from asking 'why?' They continued to ask 'why?' because they were not searching for a 'causal explanation'. Rather, they were expressing an attitude towards all the explanations. A straight scientific explanation was that the child died of 'asymptomatic, undiagnosed juvenile diabetes', and that is the end of the matter, but a believer might not find it convincing. She might say 'God's ways are beyond human understanding' to give a transcendent sense to what is deemed unexplainable, but then a naturalist, like Kai Nielsen, might retort that it is confused to talk about God's plan not because God's ways are beyond human understanding but because all God-talk is either false or confused. 'If God is utterly beyond human understanding', Nielsen argues, 'then there is nothing to be said, nothing to be thought, nothing to be perplexed about, nothing to wonder at' (2005: 157). The vicissitudes in human life, Nielsen has it, 'happen for no rhyme or reason' (ibid.: 147). It seems that Wittgenstein is somewhat sympathetic to Nielsen's view.[12] However, unlike Nielsen, Wittgenstein suggests that the same vicissitudes in human life can educate one to a religious way of seeing the world. 'Life', he writes in his diaries,

> can educate one to a belief in God. And *experiences* too are what bring this about; but I don't mean visions and other forms of sense experience which show us the 'existence of this being', but, e.g., sufferings of various sorts. ... Life can force this concept on us. (1980: 86)

On another occasion, Wittgenstein talks about the necessity of having a 'certain kind of upbringing' to believe in God (ibid.: 50). In other words, by providing 'proofs' for the existence of God, one is unlikely to show the religious aspects of the world to a nonbeliever and even believers 'would never ... come to believe as a result of such [arguments]' (ibid.: 85).[13]

To sum up, I argued that supernaturalists appeal to a religious 'picture' of the world, which brings about a religious way of assessing life and its meaning. The disagreement between supernaturalism and naturalism is not merely over the theoretical conditions of life's meaningfulness. Rather, it is over different ways of assessing the vicissitudes of life. Even though some aspects of these different ways of appraising life might 'crisscross' and overlap, the fundamental aspects are not easy to reconcile.

Objections and clarifications

In this section, my aim is to address two related objections that might be raised against the ideas I discussed so far. The first objection is based on a misinterpretation of my suggestion, claiming that limiting the meaning of life to one's way of seeing amounts to reducing it to a 'subjective affair'. That is, if the meaning of life is nothing but a sort of aspect-seeing, then anyone can claim that the meaning of her life is rooted in the dawning of an aspect of life on her. A pessimist might claim that people who deny the absurdity of life are aspect-blind to the most fundamental aspect of human life, and an objectivist might retort that the former is aspect-blind to those objective values that most human beings share and respect, and so on.

This is an important objection, but it doesn't undermine my suggestion. The concern and the question here is that by connecting one's understanding of life's meaning to aspect-seeing whether I propose that there isn't any truth-value in seeing an aspect of life. But there is a yes and no to this question. Yes, in the contexts in which the aspect that is dawned or seen is configured in the overall structure of the object of experience. When a musician, upon listening to a piece of music, comes to see a resemblance between that work and another one, the grounds of her judgement and her aspect-seeing is in the object of the experience itself. This similarity or connection might be missing to someone who doesn't have a musical ear, but that missing recognition doesn't mean that the similarity is not there.

And the answer to above question is no in situations where the dawned aspect is either forced into the picture or is remotely related to the object, but the conclusions one arrives at do not follow from the picture itself. For example, if someone comes to believe that extra-terrestrials are sending him private codes through the blink of stars, then we are faced with the task of figuring out how they can manipulate stars to blink and how we can explain to him that he is wrong. Sylvia Nasar, the biographer of mathematician John Nash, who was diagnosed with schizophrenia in 1959, describes a conversation between Nash and his colleague while the former was at McLean Hospital. The colleague asks him how a mathematician, 'a man devoted to logic and truth', could believe that extra-terrestrials are sending him messages, to which Nash replies, 'Because the ideas I had about supernatural beings came to me the same way that my mathematical ideas did. So I took them seriously' (Nasar 1998: 11). A faithful observation of life's phenomena can be obstructed by many things, including psychological disorders, cognitive limitations and conflicted ideas. But what is important in our involved enquiry into life's meaning is to cultivate and strive for a mindset that searches for a kernel of truth, if there is any, in the dawned aspects of life on the people who are here but for a short period of time. If someone sees life as a never ending, absurd, Sisyphean stone-rolling, we might agree with him that some activities in life are absurd (prostitution to feed one's drug addiction, to borrow an example from Metz) but we could also point out to him that certain things and activities in life are valuable or meaningful regardless of our judgement about life as a whole. So what is important in the discussion of aspect-seeing and its relation to meaning is to pay attention to the implications and the *limits* of what one deems to be an aspect-dawning experience.

Moreover, explaining the experience of life's meaning within the framework of aspect-seeing does not amount to relativising it. By suggesting that one's understanding of life's meaning is akin to seeing an aspect, I want to draw attention to the ways we experience it. That is, I'm only making a *grammatical* remark about people's conceptions of life's meaning. My focus is not the conditions of a meaningful life, but, rather, the ways those conditions are seen and experienced in our lives. In other words, I suggest that the experience of life's meaning is a living experience in which one's whole way of seeing and assessing life is involved, whether we believe it is a subjective or objective affair. Recall that I suggested that there is a history or a life behind seeing an aspect. When we connect this idea to issues of life's meaning, we see that arriving at a picture of life and committing oneself to it are usually the result of an involved participation in a varieties of experience in the course of one's life. People arrive at different understandings of life's meaning not merely because they happened to read different philosophers and not because they happened to find an argument more appealing than others. In other words, to borrow a term from Murdoch, it takes a whole texture of a man's being to arrive at an understanding of life's meaning, and that is what I am trying to highlight. A person who believes every human being, in virtue of being human, deserves respect and dignity might provide very strong arguments in support of her claims. But her arguments would be of little help to a person who usually fails to 'discern humanity in a man' (Wittgenstein 1980: 1). What is lacking here is less a theory of human dignity and more the dawning of an aspect of life on him in which the human dignity is still inviolable or sacred. Seeing the world as a 'friendly home'; seeing the vicissitudes of one's life as 'the will of God'; seeing life as 'a tale told by an idiot, full of sound and fury, signifying nothing'; and seeing coming into existence as a 'harmful' event are not merely some theoretical views. They are ways of approaching life to either of which one arrives not merely as a result of someone establishing their philosophical coherence.

The other objection, which is related to the first one, is concerned about the unhappy consequences of a Wittgensteinian approach towards religious belief. If religious beliefs are a matter of 'seeing-as', if one's belief in God is a 'simile' (Wittgenstein 1980: 29) with no reference whatsoever to a Supreme Being, then we should conclude that religious beliefs are merely 'symbols' used to describe the believer's attitudes and emotions. In other words, we should conclude that for Wittgenstein religion is an autonomous phenomenon, which does not make any knowledge claims and only expresses the believer's emotions. Criticising the non-realistic, expressivist views of religious beliefs, Hick writes,

> The unacceptable feature of the position is that by treating religious language as autonomous...it deprives religious statements of 'ontological' or 'metaphysical' significance....Religious language has become a kind of 'protected discourse', and forfeits its immemorial claim to bear witness to the most momentous of all truths. (Hick 1964: 239–240)

It is beyond the scope of my discussion to judge whether Wittgenstein was a realist or an anti-realist with regard to religious beliefs, but a few words are in order here. A large portion of his reflections on religion, as we will see in Chapter 6, show a personal interest in addressing it from an anthropological perspective. At the same time, this anthropological method is fused with Wittgenstein's own struggle with availability or unavailability of a religious way of living. The kinds of questions Wittgenstein explores clearly show this dual aspect of his enquiry: What is it that defines being religious? What kinds of evidence do believers appeal to when they talk about the evidence of God's existence? How does religion affect one's way of appraising life? Is it possible to be religious without believing in a Creator? Supposing Christianity is only a 'system of reference', adhered by believers through thick and thin; if so, then what is the gist of this system of reference? The traditional theological questions such as the problem of evil or the arguments for God's existence or the relation between the divine and the profane are simply absent in his enquiries.

As a result, it isn't surprising to see that a majority of commentators first read Wittgenstein as an expressivist or emotivist with regard to religion and then discard his approach and what he has written entirely. But, as

Cottingham suggests, this dismissive way of approaching Wittgenstein's reflections fails to grasp 'important insights' that his writings about 'the nature of religious allegiance' provide (2009c: 205). Furthermore, it seems to me that there is something misleading in this way of rejecting or defending Wittgenstein's 'scattered remarks' on religion. Realists are right: most believers do believe in the Last Judgement; they do believe that actions have consequences in the next world, if not in this world. They do believe that a higher reality exists, but Wittgenstein is not primarily concerned whether these beliefs correspond to an objective reality. The tendency here is to think that the question of religion can or should be boiled down to a straightforward ontological question concerning the existence of God. Most realists insist that no matter how closely we analyse the internal structure of a religious language-game, the question remains whether our beliefs refer to an objective reality out there (Insole 2006: 1–2). But what Wittgenstein's notes try to emphasise is that belief or non-belief is not defined by *only* an affirmative or negative answer to the question of God's existence. And I am not sure that one can gather from Wittgenstein's notes alone that in his view religious belief is *nothing but* the expression of an attitude.[14] In fact, what is clear in most of his remarks on religion is that he tries to emphasise the primacy of praxis in religion and the interlocking connection between the question of religion and the question of life. One might question some of his remarks on religion, but that is a different issue from trying to find a realist or anti-realist label for them. In dealing with Wittgenstein's works on religion, in Cottingham's words again, it is 'important not to be put off by certain received interpretations' of his views (2009c: 205). It is important to approach Wittgenstein's remarks on religion critically and, at the same time, to be open to what his reflections try to highlight – the key idea being that the life of a believer informs much about the nature of her belief.

Another response to the above objection would be to refer to what we might call the spirit of a Wittgensteinian way of doing philosophy. A theory that discards other theories by introducing new theories and systems can be anything but Wittgensteinian. I never claimed that religious belief, or life's meaning for that matter, is nothing *but* the expression of one's way of seeing the world. Rather, my focus was to show the limits of theory in affecting one's attitude towards life and to argue that there is a life or history behind seeing an aspect, especially when it comes to issues of life's meaning.

The aim in this research is to understand the ways in which people relate to life's meaning in everyday life. To that extent, the concentration is more on what is 'clear and ordinary' (Wittgenstein 1975: § 347). In the next three chapters, I shall focus on the ordinary from three different perspectives: The ordinariness of meaning, the certitude of life and the confessional aspect of enquiring into the meaning of life – all of which related to everyday life. In the next chapter, I examine a pervasive tendency among some commentators to make, first, a distinction between the great and the ordinary and, second, to theorise what they deem to be the sources of 'great meaning' in life.

4
In Defence of the Ordinary

'For smallness is particularly contrary to the soul which always strives after the complete and perfect, both divine and human'.

— Plato, *The Republic*

'I ask not for the great, the remote, the romantic; what is doing in Italy or Arabia; what is Greek art, or Provencal minstrelsy; I embrace the common, I explore and sit at the feet of the familiar, the low. Give me insight into to-day, and you may have the antique and future worlds. What would we really know the meaning of? The meal in the firkin; the milk in the pan; the ballad in the street; the news of the boat; the glance of the eye; the form and the gait of the body'.

— Ralph Waldo Emerson, 'The American Scholar'

Introduction

The question of life's meaning has not been a favourite topic among normative theorists. As E. M. Adams notes, analytic philosophers have given enormous attention to the questions of morality or 'well-being' but 'scarcely' any to the question of life's meaning (2002: 71).[1] Metz suggests that there might be two reasons for the fact that the meaning of life has not received due attention. The first reason might be that normative theorists are not aware of 'any clear and precise analysis of the question of the meaning of life'. Philosophers, Metz writes, 'are more confident as to the senses of "well-being" and "right action" than as to those of "life's meaning"' (2002: 782). The second reason might be that common Kantian and utilitarian outlooks continue to dominate and define the way philosophers think of 'normative categories' (ibid.). It seems to me that there is yet another important reason for the fact that normative theorists are reluctant to address the question of life's meaning: The question sounds like a pseudo-religious question, one that you ask from sages and gurus but not from proper academic philosophers who have learnt that not every big question is worth racking one's brain over. Rumour has it that a taxi driver once had Bertrand Russell in the backseat of his cab, and since Russell was a famous philosopher the taxi driver asked him, 'What's it all about?' And, not surprisingly, Russell couldn't give an answer. For a large portion of the 20th century, philosophers have been reluctant to address these kinds of taxi driver-type 'pseudo-questions'. The strategy was to question the question itself instead of giving an answer to it and, by doing this, to make the problem hopefully disappear.

However, the growing body of texts on the meaning of life, especially within the last 40 years, shows the problem 'does not go away' (Cottingham 2003: 2). It appears that the question of life's meaning is even more pressing in the absence of religious traditions, which used to be the main supplier of answers to these kinds of questions. The question of life's meaning has become like a surrogate to one's religious feelings. I think Nietzsche was one of the pioneers of this new territory in Western normative philosophy. The question for him was that what would happen to our values in the absence of God. He writes:

> As we thus reject the Christian interpretation and condemn its meaning like counterfeit, Schopenhauer's question immediately comes to us in a terrifying way: Has existence any meaning at all? It will require a few centuries before this question can even be heard completely and in its full depth. ([1882] 1974: 308)

By announcing the death of God, Nietzsche claims that there are only two options left; nihilism or a humanistic attempt to establish new values by 'transvaluation of all values'. After him, many philosophers have tried, one way or another, to give an answer to Schopenhauer's and Nietzsche's key question by introducing new values like 'freedom and responsibility' (Sartre 1946), 'guardianship of Being' (Heidegger 1977: 36), or 'heroism' (Camus 1955).

A key feature of these kinds of solutions is what Odo Marquard would call their 'sensational' understanding of the ways we try to define ourselves or give a sense to our lives. In the next section, I discuss his views about the 'immoderateness' of our demand for meaning, and afterwards I discuss some theories of life's meaning which are mainly driven by the immoderateness that Marquard criticises. This immoderateness in the literature is manifested in the tendency to make, first, a theoretical distinction between the 'ordinary' and the 'great' or 'superlative' meaning and, second, to theorise ways of obtaining what is deemed to be the constituents of great meaning in life. I argue that theories of 'great meaning' are unjustifiably exclusionary and based on 'one-sided' examples. Some of the theories that I will be discussing are Taylor's theory of 'artistic creations' (1999), Levy's 'work theory' (2005), and Metz's 'fundamentality theory' (2013).

Marquard on inflated conceptions of meaning

Some of us are familiar with a situation where someone turns a casual conversation at a party into a confident soliloquy about the absurdity of life or the absence of meaning. For some people, talking about life with a pessimistic tone has come to be associated with profundity. Some of us might even sometimes wonder 'if not having a taste for a dark or tragic view isn't a mark of superficiality' (Nozick 1989: 24). But where does this feeling come from? What do we mean by the 'absence of meaning', and what kind of meaning are we referring to? Marquard takes up these questions in his work, 'On the Dietetics of Expectation of Meaning', and he offers a view that has a bearing on the dichotomy between the great and the ordinary meaning. For Marquard, the experience of meaninglessness of life in modern society is not necessarily 'due to lack of meaning; it can also result from excessive expectations of meaning' (1991: 36). In other words, it is not that there is no meaning in life but that our demands for meaning are immoderate. In our everyday life we undertake many meaningful activities, but we want something more significant than ordinary meaning. As the members of modern society, preoccupied with the mentality of demand, we are 'spoiled' by the repeated satisfaction of our demands, and we want to be spoiled with meaning as well.

One might object here that just because a person is thinking about the meaning of her life doesn't necessarily mean that, first, she does this with the mentality of demand and, second, she is a member of a modern society. But I agree with the main point of his claim – that in our quest for the meaning of life, some of us expect to find an answer that gives our life an absolute meaning, not a relative one. That is, we search for meaning in its 'cosmic sense', not in its 'individualist sense'.

Marquard's solution to the problem of 'the immoderateness of the demand for meaning' is, simply, a 'diet' with regard to our expectation of meaning (ibid.: 37). The aim of what he calls a 'dietetics' of the expectation of meaning is to sober up our intoxicated expectations and to moderate our demands for meaning. The first ingredient of this diet is to avoid what he calls 'aiming directly at meaning'.

By 'aiming directly at meaning', Marquard refers to an attitude that is best pictured in Hegel's story of the man who wanted fruit and who consequently spurned 'apples, pears, plums, cherries' because 'what he wanted was not apples but fruit; not pears, but fruit; not plums, but fruit; not cherries, but fruit' (ibid.: 39). Likewise, what a person who aims directly at the meaning of life wants is not reading, but meaning; not writing, but meaning; not work, but meaning;...not helping, but meaning;...not carrying out duties, but meaning' (ibid.). This person is not aware of the fact that *'no human being has a direct relation to meaning'* (ibid.: 40). What we call 'meaning' is always conferred indirectly by undertaking different projects and activities. Tolstoy's account of his misery during the time he was confronted with the problem of life is a good case of aiming directly at meaning:

> All that happened with me when I was on every side surrounded by what is considered to be complete happiness. I had a good, loving, and beautiful wife, good children, and a large estate.... I was respected by my neighbours and friends, more than ever before, was praised by strangers, and, without any self-deception, could consider my name famous.... And while in such condition I arrived at the conclusion that I could not live, and fearing death, I had to use cunning against myself, in order that I might not take my life. (1905: 8)

The question for Tolstoy began right at the time he apparently had all the reasons to consider his life happy. However, happiness was not enough, and since he was aiming directly at meaning, nothing could satisfy him. What Tolstoy wanted was not family but meaning, not wealth but meaning, not fame but meaning, not artistic creations but meaning, not good children but meaning. For Marquard, when we aim directly at the meaning of life, we fail to acquire it. Our tendency to aim directly at meaning makes the problem of the meaning of life 'sensational' and 'plunges human beings into unhappiness' (1991: 42). He suggests that the reason we have this tendency is 'the human need for excitement and sensation'. Even when we deny meaning, we might do so in a sensational manner in order to satisfy our need for excitement.

There is something simplistic, and to some extent condescending, about this view. If the driving force behind our search for meaning is merely a need for excitement and sensation, then it seems that we would be better off with gambling, bungee jumping, bull fighting and hitch hiking. But that doesn't mean that the bull fighter is less susceptible to enquiring about life's meaning than the solitary philosopher is in his study. For one thing, by all standards, Tolstoy led a much more exciting life than most people of his time and yet went through what he pithily called the 'arrest of life'.

But, in fairness to Marquard, I think there is a point in seeing a link between aiming directly at meaning and taking a sensational approach towards the meaning of life. His point is that there is an exaggerated, an all or nothing, expectation of meaning when one aims directly at meaning, and in doing so one is unlikely to rest content with the everyday concrete answers that are at our disposal.

It is in contrast with such tendencies that Marquard proposes the cultivation of un-sensational meaning through aiming indirectly at it. This strategy aims at reducing our expectation of meaning. In order to achieve this, we have to desist from some tendencies in our search for the meaning of life, like 'perfectionism' or 'making the affirmation of life depend on an absolute proof of meaning'. But, most importantly, we should desist from contempt for *small* answers to the question of life's meaning. By 'small answers', Marquard means all the immediate tasks that we usually deal with in everyday life. Think of occupations, family affairs, responsibilities and specific day-to-day activities and routines as examples of immediate tasks. Our daily tasks, the contextuality of our lives, give a sense of structure, order and purpose to a large portion of our lives. Kids need to be picked up from school, and someone has to fetch them; assignments have to be handed in, and someone has to finish them; deadlines are approaching, and something must be done; trains depart on time, and we have to arrive at the station on time; the cat is missing, and the sheep is lost, and we bring them back home, and so on. Put differently, for many of us the question is not 'to be or not to be' but rather more concrete questions such as to stay or to walk out, to say the word or to hide it, to accept the job offer or to stay with the family, to pick up the phone or to end the conversation, to decide whether the story should be resumed or terminated and other questions like that. In short, there is always something to 'attend to'. What Goethe once, in a letter to his friend, called 'the healthiness of the moment'[2] is in a sense made of being attentive to these daily tasks. The idea here is that most of us don't think of the unavailability of meaning when we are *actively* engaged with ordinary tasks and projects. In other words, there are always some 'delaying factors' in the course of our day-to-day lives to which we attend.

On account of these 'little delaying factors', we usually procrastinate encountering the question of life's meaning in a direct manner (Marquard 1991: 44). Our habits and daily tasks give a quiet, un-sensational meaning to our lives. The meaning of life, Marquard has it, depends more on immediate things than on ultimate ones. I surely cannot answer the question, 'Why is there anything at all, rather than nothing?', but it does not mean that I will lead a meaningless life due to my failure to find an answer to this question.

In the next section, I argue that the tendency among some scholars in the literature to idealise or aggrandise the meaning of life is driven by a similar kind of immoderateness and is mostly nourished by a 'one-sided diet', that is, by one-sided examples (Wittgenstein 1958: § 593). In other words, most philosophers who desire a theory of 'superlative meaning' neglect the *elusive* nature of what we might call 'great' in everyday life.

Great meaning versus the ordinary meaning

A theory of great meaning in life, as opposed to the 'ordinary meaning', is a theory that claims one's life can become significantly worthwhile and valuable in virtue of orienting one's life towards valuable goals, which usually require outstanding perseverance and vision. According to this view, the meaning that is acquired in virtue of writing, for example, *Anna Karenina* is substantially different from writing reviews in yellow pages or caring about one's garden. Note that perseverance alone in one's life projects and activities does not necessarily secure great meaning. Instead, it should be oriented towards activities that are objectively worthwhile. Moreover, what separates great meaning from the ordinary meaning is the transcendental characteristic of the former as compared to the latter. Think of artistic works, scientific discoveries and struggles for a just cause as examples of transcendental projects that go beyond self-interest.

Before discussing the great/ordinary dichotomy, I need to clarify something here. My objections to this dichotomy do not imply that I think there is no great meaning. The point is that any attempt to *theorise* it is bound to provide a selective and biased account of great meaning because it has to brush aside the *particularity* of human life for the sake of achieving a general account of great meaning.

In modern philosophy, I think, it was Nietzsche who first tried to highlight the distinction between the great and the ordinary, by his 'last men' and 'higher men' and by his 'free spirits' and 'herds'. 'The concept of greatness', Nietzsche claims, 'entails being noble, wanting to be by oneself, being able to be different, standing alone and having to live independently' (1966: 212). Or, 'A great man...is incommunicable: he finds it tasteless to be familiar' (1968: 962). The great men 'create themselves'. The death of God, therefore, is not necessarily bad news for men of high status and esteem. It also provides an opportunity for the rest of us to redefine ourselves. The father is gone, and the house is yours now, if only you have the courage to claim it back.

Though no one in the literature on life's meaning talks of the *Übermensch*, the Nietzschean project of exalting 'great meaning' and trivialising the ordinary is still alive among some commentators. For example, Richard Taylor, who is usually known for his subjectivist theory of meaning, in a gestalt shift from his previous position, writes:

> A meaningful life is a creative one, and what falls short of this lacks meaning, to whatever extent. What *redeems* humanity is not its kings, military generals and builders of personal wealth, however much these may be celebrated and envied. It is instead the painters, composers, poets, philosophers, writers – all who by their creative power alone, bring about things of great value, things which, but for them, would never have existed at all. (Taylor 1999: 14, emphasis added)

Note the Nietzschean tone of Taylor's allusion to the redemption of humanity by original artists and creative thinkers. In fact, on another occasion, Taylor claims that our capacity for creative activity is hardly exercised; it is only a possibility, and this possibility is realised only 'here and there, more or less, and [is] fully realised in exceptional persons' (2012: 303).

Taylor is of course alluding to a truth about the way we appreciate the great works of men and women. People who strive for 'the good, the true, and the beautiful' add value to the world; they leave traces; they make the world a better place to live; they go beyond; they transcend; and they push the limits of human imagination. Having said that, I believe there is something missing in such a picture of the ordinary and the extraordinary. What is missing is attention to the contextuality and particularity of the human life: the fact that most of us ascribe value (great or mundane) to people's lives upon appraisal of the contexts in which great or ordinary meaning is judged to be obtained.

First, there are many areas where it is hard to tell or where there isn't even a correct way of drawing a line between great and ordinary meaning. In these contexts, I think what defines the significance of one's life is not a set of predetermined criteria, as in Taylor's account, but the surrounding circumstances of the life in question. And it seems that there are ordinary people whose acts are significant in consideration of the context of their lives. That is, upon a detailed examination of their lives, some aspects might dawn on us that are missing in an exclusivist approach. These aspects make us see the connection between their lives and the meanings ascribed to them. Think of an ordinary person who realises that his 'destructive pleasures' are bound to destroy his family, and thus he decides to change his life. He might not have an extraordinary story, but he might share the same moral principle with, for example, an outstanding person who saves children from the Warsaw ghetto. After all, they might do what they do in virtue of an 'unshakeable belief' that 'Whoever saves one life, saves the world entire'.[3]

A further objection to the great/ordinary dichotomy has to do with the moral implications of such dichotomy. Here one cannot help noticing a sense of contempt for ordinary ways of acquiring meaningfulness.[4] Wittgenstein alludes to the moral implications of this segregation when he asks himself,

> Are *all* men great? No. – Well then, how can you have any hope of being a great man! Why should something be bestowed on you that's not bestowed on your neighbour? To what purpose?! If it isn't your *wish* to be rich that makes you think yourself rich, it must be something you observe or experience that reveals it to you! And what do you experience (other than vanity)! Simply that you have a certain *talent*. And my conceit of being an extraordinary person has been with me *much* longer than my awareness of my particular talent. (1980: 47)

Once the dichotomy is established, an exclusivist might be tempted to show the ways of achieving the great meaning. If, theoretically, we could establish what the great meaning is, then, why shouldn't we show the practical ways of achieving it? Neil Levy's account of 'superlative meaning' in life through what he calls 'open-ended activities' is such an attempt. I think Levy's account reveals, in an important sense, the unhappy consequences of theorising about the great/ordinary dichotomy and ways of achieving the great meaning.

Levy on 'Downshifting and Meaning in Life'

Levy's theory is an exemplary case of exclusivism in the literature. According to Levy, in the Western world affluence has led to a rise in people's sense of 'happiness'. However, they do not feel the presence of 'values' in their lives as much as they feel the presence of happiness (this is called a paradox). As a result, many people are reorienting their lives, 'away from the pursuit of wealth and toward the pursuit of meaning' (2005: 176) – and hence the emergence of the downshifting movement. For Levy, downshifters probably will be successful in finding meaning in their lives, but 'to the extent they seek superlative meaning, the highest, most satisfying...they are looking in the wrong place'. They have to search for 'supremely valuable' (ibid.: 186) and open-ended activities, such as artistic activity, the promotion of justice or the pursuit of truth. The pursuit of close-ended activities, Levy suggests, is 'circular' and ultimately leads to the problem of boredom. A good example of close-ended, circular activities is given by David Wiggins when he talks about a farmer 'who grows more corn to feed more hogs to buy more land to grow more corn'.[5] On the other hand, one cannot imagine an end for open-ended activities because as our activities evolve so do the ends at which we aim. Think of, for example, 'the pursuit of truth'. The idea of a 'finished and entirely true system of knowledge is literally inconceivable beforehand' (ibid.: 185). The open-endedness criterion guarantees that we will not have to face the problem of 'boredom'. These activities have common characteristics: They are 'hard', and they require intellectual and physical effort. And it often takes 'great courage' to undertake them. They require sustained 'effort, concentration, attention, striving and perhaps...failing' (ibid.). Levy's message to the *ordinary* downshifters is clear:

> Downshifters are only half right. Meaning in life can be pursued in just the way they have suggested. By cutting work hours, and thereby leaving more time for family, for friends, for the simple joys of a life which is less stressed and more in touch with beauty and the natural environment, we really can make our lives more fulfilling. But we cannot achieve superlative meaning in this way. Such meaning, the meaning which can be looked full in the face by the most reflective without fear or flinching, is only to be found in work. (ibid.: 187)

Levy treats great meaning like an expensive item that only an elite few can buy. Most downshifters don't have the capacity to undertake open-ended activities, and, so the argument goes, they rest content with the ordinary meaning. In fact, Levy goes so far as to claim that the fact that 'meaning-conferring' activities are difficult is 'a positive advantage' of his account (ibid.: 187).

The first objection that might be raised against such view has to do with the simple fact that in the presence of both ordinary and superlative meaning, one might reasonably value the former more than the latter. For example, consider a person who is leading a promising scientific project, and she is highly satisfied with it. Now, if the scientist decides to reduce her working hours to spend more time with her children, to the same extent, Levy claims, she would forfeit her chance of acquiring superlative meaning. But, she might consider her life most meaningful when she is with her family. Levy's response, I think, would be that the scientist rests content with the 'ordinary meaning' (2005: 188) and that she fails to see the significance of engaging in an open-ended activity. In other words, great meaning can be found in only valuable 'projects' and not in following what one judges to be of more importance in comparison to one's projects, which upon close examination might be more vital for the integrity of one's life than the mere pursuit of an open-ended activity is. It seems that you have to be in Levy's camp if you want to acquire superlative meaning.[6]

This last point leads us to the second objection to Levy's theory, which has to do with the moral implications of such account. By offering a theory of superlative meaning, we put ourselves in a situation to instruct people on how to live without considering the contexts in which people make decisions and act upon them. This reminds me of Wittgenstein's conversation with his friend about ethics:

> Ethics [is] telling someone what he should do. But how can anyone counsel another? Imagine someone advising another who was in love and about to marry, and pointing out to him all the things he cannot do if he marries. ... How can one know how these things are in another man's life? (Wittgenstein, as quoted in Bouwsma 1986: 45)

I suggest that the same questions apply to Levy' theory. His account neglects the *particularity* of one's life, which is usually the key factor in defining the nature of one's deeds. Imagine a scientist who has to choose between rejecting a prestigious job offer in another country in order to stay with his family and accepting the offer to actualise his intellectual capabilities. How can Levy's account help the scientist faced with such dilemma? Based on Levy's theory the answer is clear: If he is concerned with obtaining great meaning, he would need to leave his family, but such an attitude towards moral complexities is insensitively dismissive. What makes a moral decision such as this difficult, as Rhees suggests,

> Is not that I am bewildered by the rules or uncertain which rule applies here. It is that what I have to do goes against what I feel to be deeply important; I shall be doing what I feel I would give my life to avoid doing – harming those I least want to harm. The problem is difficult because whichever course I take I shall be doing something for which I can never forgive myself. (1970: 88)

Here 'we have all the materials of a tragedy' (ibid.: 99), and being concerned with 'superlative meaning' is usually the last thing one thinks of. In the face of moral predicaments such as this one, Levy's work theory shows its limits. In general, any theory that claims that it has an answer to the scientist's problem will probably fail to do justice to understanding the depth of his problem. Theories of great meaning are specifically most vulnerable when they address to the particularity of our lives.

A more lenient way of reading Levy's work theory is to say that according to him one's life is more meaningful if, all other things being equal, one pursues open-ended activities. That is, there is more value in creating artworks or making scientific discoveries than making some kids and spending time with them. That is fair enough, but we also know that in actual life all things are hardly being equal, and the decisions people make are usually influenced, and driven, by factors that attention to which would help us to arrive at more informed judgements about those decisions.

And finally, I think in Levy's account, engaging with a large portion of open-ended activities, except the pursuit of justice, has been considered as a function of 'wealth' (2005: 176). In other words, one's wealth largely determines whether one can pursue open-ended activities. As Levy claims,

> It seems to be the case that an enormous proportion of the world's population is cut off from the projects which might secure superlative meaning, including almost *everyone* in the third world. ... In a more just world in which resources, material and intellectual, were more fairly distributed, far more people could participate in [open-ended] projects. (ibid.: 189, emphasis added)

I find this type of determinism very limiting. For one thing, the reason we usually value the lives of many great achievers is their composure in the face of grave situations such as poverty, injustice and deprivation together with their ability to still engage with highly significant open-ended projects. When Wittgenstein asks, 'Why should something be bestowed on you that's not bestowed on your neighbour?' (1980: 47), I wouldn't be surprised if Levy responded, 'Because luckily I am a white male from the first world'.

Particularity and the curious case of Paul Gauguin

My objections to Levy's theory point at the significance of particularity in the issues of life's meaning. In this section, I discuss different views about Gauguin's decision to abandon his family for the pursuit of his artistic career and argue that attention to the singular conditions of his life provides a more perspicuous picture of what he did.

According to Williams, Gauguin was justified in abandoning his family since, retrospectively speaking, the final outcome of his decision was the creation of some masterpieces, and today we wouldn't say that he should have made a different decision (1976: 23–27). The idea here is that Gauguin's action is justifiable ex post facto by virtue of his artistic creations. But I wonder how far we can go with this line of argument because based on this argument many things would have been permissible if we consider what Gaugin achieved in Tahiti (cf. Johnston 2003: 18). Let me shift the focus from 'great art' to something else to show where this line of argument can take us. Imagine a father who abandons his child and leaves him destitute. In the absence of his father, the child has to go through hardships in life, which, retrospectively, has a character-building effect on him; it turns him into a self-actualised type of person. Now, should we follow from this that considering what the child has become, his father's action is less blameworthy? I don't think so. And there seems to be no difference between what Gauguin and the father have done except the fact that the former was an artist. Art has been exalted so disproportionately that it is now difficult to resist the charm of considering it to be a source of great meaning in life. In Johnston's words, art has become the 'last refuge of absolute value. Somewhat strangely, belief in art seems to survive belief in right and wrong, as if it were easier to accept that there can be no objective judgments about human actions than that there are no objective distinctions in art' (ibid.).

According to Cottingham, the achievements of great artists or intellectuals are naturally meaning-conferring. However, in the absence of a moral 'overarching structure' and a 'normative pattern to which the meaningful life must conform', a meaningful life would be reduced to an engaged life 'in which the agent is systematically committed to certain projects he makes his own, irrespective of their moral status' (2003: 26). Cottingham's worry makes more sense especially when we see that some friends of subjectivism are comfortable in biting the bullet of considering even immoral lives meaningful (cf. John Kekes 2000: 97).

It seems to me that Williams' view about the justifiability of Gauguin's action is not informed by the circumstances in which he decided to abandon his family. Instead of appealing to any given principle to judge Gauguin's action, one might *look and see* not only his 'solutions' to a specific problem but also his whole 'total vision of life'. In Murdoch's words,

> When we apprehend and assess other people we do not consider only their solutions to specifiable practical problems, we consider something more elusive which may be called their total vision of life, as shown in their mode of speech or silence, their choice of words, their assessments of others, their conception of their own lives, what they think attractive or praiseworthy, what they think funny: in short the configurations of their thought which show continually in their reactions and conversation. These things...one may call the texture of man's being or the nature of his personal vision. (1997: 80–81)

In other words, in appraising other people's lives we should ideally take a holistic approach towards the texture of their beings and pay attention to details. What is missing in Gauguin's case, one might say, is *particularism*. It seems to me that it would be difficult to arrive at an informed judgement about Gauguin's decision without knowing, among other things:

- whether his wife really loved him by the time he left;
- whether he provided his family with subsistence after his departure;
- whether there was a sense of family between them at all;
- whether Gauguin thought of his departure as a relief to the family;
- whether there was a possibility to take the family to Tahiti;
- whether he asked someone to look after his family while he was away.

We ask the above questions not to justify what he did and not based on an after the fact model, as in Williams' approach. Instead, the aim is to understand Gauguin's decision based on attention to the context the decision was made. In this approach, we are neither blinded by the belief that 'a meaningful life is a creative one' (Taylor 1999: 14) nor deceived by the promise of 'superlative meaning' through open-ended projects (Levy). We are neither seduced by the term 'great meaning' nor put off by the ordinary. To put it differently, an artist might abandon his family for pursuing art and yet we might be sympathetic to his action given the context in which he has done so. In Gauguin's case, knowing that his staying with the family would have brought more harm than good to the children certainly would affect the way we would judge his action. That is, his great art would be only one factor among many others in appraising his decision and not *the* main factor as the latter would be in Williams' view.

In light of the importance of the particular in informing our appraisal of people's lives, in the next section, I turn to a most recent attempt by Metz to capture in his 'fundamentality theory' the three elements of 'great meaning' in life – that is, 'the good, the true, and the beautiful'.

The good, the true and the beautiful

All objectivists in the literature appeal to at least one of the three sources of the good life in their accounts of what would make a life meaningful.[7] But most recently, in his book, *Meaning in Life*, Metz attempts to bring all the elements that would confer superlative meaning on one's life under a unified theory, which he calls the 'fundamentality theory'. Roughly, the idea is that the more one positively orients one's and others' rational natures towards fundamental conditions of human existence, the more meaningful one's life would be (2013: 219–239). The fundamental conditions in this contexts are the conditions that are responsible for much else about the human life. Metz then meticulously elaborates on how one's orientation towards these conditions figures into the good, the true and the beautiful. Think of the life of Mandela, for example. Based on this theory, his life was meaningful not entirely because he fought apartheid. Instead, his life was of significant value because he oriented his whole life towards the realisation of conditions that are fundamental for the realisation of other valuable conditions in human life. In this case, autonomy, freedom and equality were the fundamental conditions that Mandela strived for.

The fundamentality theory is able to explain why we think a wide ranges of lives are meaningful. Think of the lives of the people spent on the pursuit of moral achievement, intellectual discovery or artistic creativity. Metz's final version of the fundamentality theory is as follows:

> A human person's life is more meaningful, the more that she, without violating certain moral constraints against degrading sacrifice, employs her reason and in ways that either positively orient rationality toward fundamental conditions of human existence, or negatively orient it towards what threatens them; in addition the meaning in a human person's life is reduced, the more it is negatively oriented towards fundamental conditions of human existence. (2013: 233)

In examining Metz's theory I'm going to focus on the implications of his view for the realm of the beautiful or artistic creation. Think, for example, of an artist whose life is vacillating between negative and positive orientations towards fundamental conditions. Or, think of an artist, living in a moral sewer, who has excellent talent for creating good works of art. I wonder if we could talk, as in Metz's account, of the cancelling-out effect here – namely the idea that one's positive orientation towards certain fundamental conditions can be undermined or even nullified by one's negative orientations towards other fundamental conditions at the same time. Metz coins the term 'anti-matter' to describe this situation (ibid.: 234). He argues that certain actions and behaviours are not only devoid of value; they also devalue the overall meaning in a person's life. But I am not sure that when we judge an artist's life or her work we usually subtract the negative orientations in her life to reach a conclusion about positive ones. It seems that we take a holistic approach in appraising the significance of her life. In fact, struggling with anti-matter and its psychological and social implications is itself a very rich topic for exploration, and it wouldn't be difficult to see that people who are good at creating good works of art about this topic are sometimes the ones who themselves have struggled with anti-matter in their lives.

The other issue in Metz's theory which is not clear, at least in the domain of artworks, is the notion of fundamental conditions. In clarifying what he means by the fundamental condition in artworks, he refers to topics such as 'morality, war, death, love, family, and the like' (ibid.: 230). Of course, most works of art are about these topics; we don't doubt that. But, what Metz doesn't address is the fact that not all works on these topics can be called good works of art. In appraising an artwork we don't usually consider a work to be of significance only in virtue of being about fundamental conditions or 'deep themes'. We appeal to other criteria as well, depending on the type of works we are dealing with. Artists have made bizarre works and called them art, all of which allegedly tried to shed a fresh light on the human condition and yet, besides their publicity for being odd, have signified nothing but the poor and conflicted ideas of their creators. Further, we might even say one of the reasons for our fascination with good works of art is precisely the fact that good art is the realm of freedom. That is, artists allow themselves to experience new methods of expression with no guarantee that it will work, and yet we all know that in the hands of good artists they often do work but not merely because they are about fundamental conditions. Rather, we incline to differentiate these works from poorer ones by virtue of their novelty in looking at the old or fundamental themes. So, in the realm of art not what you talk about, as in Metz's account, but how you talk determines the value of your artwork. Every year so many cinematic works are being made with a very old theme: a man and a woman meet. However, only a very few remain with us precisely because of the reasons we cannot readily articulate. Cinema has always been about celebration of details that are lived or observed with perceptive minds who then reflect them on the screens. Metz's broad qualification is of no help here. We might readjust Metz's theory here and suggest that maybe a good work of art is one that talks about the fundamental conditions of human life in a revealing manner. But this in turn leads to the very complicated question about what it means in each case to create a revealing works of art – a question that yet requires a further clarification. Metz's account thus is much broader than it seems, which in turn makes the fundamentality theory a vague theory which might be on the 'right track', but it is too broad, too, at least with regard to what we aesthetically calls beautiful.

Conclusion

In this chapter, I discussed three theories of great meaning. The pervasive tendency among some scholars in the literature to idealise or to aggrandise the meaning of life is caused by what Marquard and Wittgenstein would designate as a 'one-sided diet', which mainly brushes aside the ordinary life by considering it inconsequential in the process of acquiring great meaning in life. Specifically, Levy's work theory was discussed, and I argued that his theory is based on unjustified assumptions about ways of achieving great meaning. And with regard to the fundamentality theory, I argued that Metz's theory is of little help at least when we judge whether an artwork is aesthetically good, bad or mediocre.

We should bear in mind that criticising the current exclusivist theories of great meaning does not imply that we stand in need of another theory. What must be questioned is the very assumption that we need a theory of great meaning, whatever that might be. The aim here is to observe the phenomena and see the connecting links between the varieties of individual cases. Exclusivists, on the other hand, want to redeem us by highlighting all that is interesting and admirable in us (e.g. artistic creation, moral heroism and scientific discovery) and, hence, an approach that only aims at examining the connection between life and meaning seems unsatisfactory to them. This approach might not lead to a 'great' or 'superlative' achievement in its enquiry into life's meaning, but it gets its strength and satisfaction from a humble observation of those human details in that 'extraordinary thing called ordinary life'.

The aim here is to clarify existent theories and to show their missing links, but not to build a new theory. That is to say, the aim is not to create new buildings to replace those that have been discarded. 'All that philosophy can do', Wittgenstein writes, 'is to destroy idols. And that means not creating a new one – say in the "absence of an idol"' (2005: 305).

And what does remain after destroying idols? Life itself, one might say, remains. We see that long before contemplating the meaning of life most of us have mastered ways of living. There is a certainty that usually runs through our ways of life. We usually don't check if the copies of newspaper are the same, if the sun rises from the same direction that it did yesterday, if we have two hands or three hands, if our child comes back home after school or decides to find another house, and so on. In short, we live and we see that some meaning is acquired through the act of living. And I will argue that these pre-contemplative natural modes of beings have implications for the way we enter into contemplative mode of appraising life as a whole. However, sceptics beg to differ. I will attend to their differences next.

5
On Detachment or Why the Shopkeeper Does Not Investigate His Apples

Sax player: What are you thinking about?
Ida: I'm not thinking.
Sax player: We are off to Gdańsk to do some gigs. Want to come?... Ever been to the seaside?
Ida: I haven't been anywhere.
Sax player: Come along then. You'll listen to us play, we'll walk on the beach.
Ida: And then?
Sax player: Then we'll buy a dog, get married, have children, get a house.
Ida: And then?
Sax player: The usual. Life.

— *Ida* (2013), Directed by Pawel Pawlikowski

Introduction

What do we do when we do philosophy or think about the meaning of life? Some philosophers say we detach ourselves from the contingencies of our lives and view the world from a broader perspective. In our everyday lives we are engaged with, and committed to, countless things, but we also have a 'special capacity to step back and survey' life from above (Nagel 1971: 146). Detachment from life is seen as the key factor in contemplating the meaning of life. Implicit in such a view is the idea that some level of distance, or separation, from life is required in order to contemplate it. The assumption here is that the very act of doing philosophy as a second-order enquiry requires stepping back and distancing oneself from that which is being enquired. As Alasdair Macintyre writes, 'philosophy inescapably involves some measure of self-alienation' (2006: 127). In particular, the notion of detachment is of high significance among sceptics and nihilists in the literature. They claim that the only way to arrive at the truthfulness of nihilism is through detaching ourselves from our individual concerns and viewing life as a whole.

In this chapter, my aim is to view the notion of detachment from a perspective different from that of most sceptics about meaning. I focus on mainly Thomas Nagel's account of the absurd as I think his thoughts on this topic are exemplary of sceptical approaches to the meaning of life. My response to Nagel will take its cue from Wittgenstein's last text, *On Certainty*, as it is mainly concerned with the problem of scepticism, the solutions to it and the significance of certainty in our life. I propose that *On Certainty* offers a different way of approaching the problem of scepticism and weighing it in the context of our day-to-day life, as compared to the current approaches in the literature. Some of the issues that have not received due attention in the literature are: (1) the centrality of one's 'world-picture' in one's conception of life's meaning, (2) the role of trust in the constitution of meaning and (3) conversion from one world-picture to another and the role of persuasion. In a sense, this chapter is on seeing the literature through the eyes of *On Certainty*. I believe this task is of importance, especially considering the fact that so far those few philosophers who have written on Wittgenstein's account of meaning in life have not addressed the implications of the text for the issues of life's meaning.[1]

I also briefly discuss Richard Taylor's subjectivist theory of life's meaning and highlight the pessimistic background against which Taylor arrives at his theory, an issue that is often neglected in the literature.

In the last section of this chapter, by making a distinction between philosophical and existential scepticism, I discuss three accounts of the difference between the two. So I will discuss Cavell's distinction between 'knowledge' and 'acknowledgement', Franz Rosenzweig's distinction between the 'sick' and the 'healthy' and Wittgenstein's allusion to 'indifference'. I argue that whereas philosophical scepticism might seem of interest to only philosophers, the 'arrest of life' is an existential experience, different from philosophical scepticism of the kind Wittgenstein describes in *On Certainty*.

Doubt in the stream of life

On Certainty is excerpted from Wittgenstein's notes in the final year and a half of his life. It consists of mainly Wittgenstein's comments on G. E. Moore's approach in 'A Defence of Common Sense' (1994a) and 'Proof of the External World' (1994b), originally published in 1925 and 1939, respectively. In the first article, Moore lists some propositions that he knows with 'certainty': 'A living body exists now, which is my body'; 'I have been continuously on earth since my birth'; or 'The earth existed many years before my birth'. In the second article, he provides a common sense argument against scepticism by raising his right hand and saying 'Here is one hand,' and then raising his left hand and saying 'And here is another,' concluding that there are at least two external objects in the world, and therefore he knows (by this argument) that an external world exists.

The main task in *On Certainty* is to explore the implications of Moore's apparently simple propositions. Wittgenstein asks under what circumstances we stand in need of a set of propositions like these to prove the existence of the external world. How is the language-game of doubt played? In what circumstances and how often do we doubt the things that we take for granted in our everyday lives?

Wittgenstein's main objection to Moore's anti-sceptical approach is that he has a confused conception of the language-game of 'knowing' (cf. Rhees 2003). To know something entails that one can offer justification, including evidence and reasons for that claim, but when Moore starts his propositions by saying that 'he knows', and uses it to prove the things that do not stand in need of justification (my hands, the earth, etc.), he begins to go astray. The common elements in Moore's propositions, Wittgenstein observes, is that we do not arrive at any of them 'as a result of investigation' (1975: §§ 137–138). That is to say, they cannot be doubted in *ordinary* circumstances. More importantly, the epistemic status of these types of propositions is more fundamental than usual knowledge claims. These propositions are the background against which we come to know the world, and they 'stand fast' for us (§ 151). They are not about epistemic certitude; rather, the whole epistemology is built upon these kinds of propositions. Fundamental propositions cannot be the subject of doubt; rather, they act like the 'hinges' on which the door of our epistemic enquiries turn (§ 341). That is why the fundamental propositions are also referred to as 'hinge propositions' (Moyal-Sharrock 2004: 33). Wittgenstein goes so far as to say, 'the game of doubting itself presupposes certainty' with regard to hinge propositions (1975: § 115). In other words, the language-game of doubt is played after learning the language-game of certainty and 'trust'. 'Doubt comes *after* belief' (§ 160). Imagine someone who doubts whether his hands are really his hands. The fact that he uses the word 'hand' without a second thought, that he should 'stand before the abyss' if he wanted so much as to try doubting every word he uses, shows that the 'absence of doubt belongs to the essence of the language-game' (§ 370). Everyone's 'world-picture' (§ 162) is founded upon this fundamental trust.[2] In Bob Plant's words, 'without trusting in *something* and *someone* (that I have a body; that the world is not a figment of my imagination; that, as a rule, people do not try to deceive me) one's orientation around the natural and social world would become hopeless' (2005: 50–51). Based on this fundamental trust, 'My *life* consists in my being content to accept many things' (Wittgenstein 1975: § 344). I accept that history books do not usually fabricate facts and figures in a systematic way, that a scientific theory is true even though I haven't investigated it personally, or that the date of my birth is the same as the one reflected in my identity card. Normally, I do not investigate any of these. I simply believe them. 'What we believe depends on what we learn' (§ 286), and we learn countless things as we grow. We learn that fire burns; that objects fall; that when it is cold, it is cold, and when it is warm, it is warm, and they are not the same. Examination and investigation is a capacity we acquire later in life. No child in this world arrives at the conclusion that the earth is round by investigation (§ 160). If he doubts literally everything the teacher says, he ends up not learning anything. He will acquire the language-game of investigation after learning how to leave a wide range of things unexamined.

From this perspective, the problem of scepticism is exactly its *failure* to understand that its very sceptical claims are based on trust and certainty with regard to something. For example, consider Cartesian doubt. Descartes sought to doubt the truth of all his beliefs in order to determine which beliefs he could be certain were true. But in this process there are things that remain intact. For example, as he doubts the existence of the external world or himself as a body, he takes for granted that his words refer to something, that the 'I' refers to something, that every time I use the word 'I', I don't need to check whether it refers to 'I' or someone else, and so on. Doubt comes after certainty.

The initial task of exploring the implications of Moore's propositions lead to other discussions with far-reaching implications for the issues of meaning in life:

1. *Groundlessness of belief.* Wittgenstein holds that one acquires a belief system based on trust: 'The schoolboy believes his teachers and his schoolbooks' (§ 263). The teacher says, for example, that Everest is in Asia, and she doesn't give a ground for it, because the pupil doesn't need a ground for his belief as yet. If he doubts the existence of Thomas Jefferson, he only fails to learn about America's history. One continues learning based on trust until one acquires the language-game of investigation and justification.
2. *Acknowledging the variety of world-pictures.* Usually, as one grows one might realise that not all world-pictures are the same. For example, one might learn at one's home that God created the world *ex nihilo*. At school, however, one might learn about Darwin and evolution. As he writes, 'I believe that every human being has two human parents; but Catholics believe Jesus only had a human mother' (1975: § 239). In these situations, one's 'frame of reference' or 'world-picture' is exposed to something fundamentally different. I can give many reasons to prove why my belief is right (human sexual life, human anatomy, biology, self-experience, etc.) but Catholics also say they have reasons. When we encounter people of other belief systems, we might feel bewildered not necessarily due to the queerness of what they believe but because we realise that the whole foundation of our belief system can be put into question. A nonbeliever might find it unreasonable to say, 'under certain circumstances wine transforms into blood'; he might say, if I accept this I might as well deny everything I have learnt so far.

However, we also know that what people consider 'reasonable or unreasonable' changes (§ 336). We know that sometimes people change their fundamental views about the world. In other words, conversion happens. One should read 'conversion' here as a change in one's world-picture, a change in one's 'whole way of seeing' the world (§ 291). We all 'stick' to the opinion that, for example, 'the earth is round' because it is part of our 'hinge propositions', but if we do change our views about this, our whole way of seeing nature changes. In other words, some beliefs will never change unless one's whole conception of the world collapses. Doubting the fundamental 'framework' of my knowledge 'would seem to drag everything with it and plunges it into chaos' (§ 613). Nothing major will happen, for example, if I doubt whether the results of a scientific experiment are well founded (there might be a mistake in calculation, or another variable involved, etc.), but I'm not sure what it would be like to doubt 2 × 2 = 4. If you doubt this, you should doubt the whole multiplication table as well. My language-game of investigation and doubt would reach its limit if I did so. However, in certain dimensions of life conversion from one language-game to another is possible. Experiences 'of various sorts' in life might lead me to a new language-game (Wittgenstein 1980: 86):

> Certain events would put me into a position in which I could not go on with the old language-game any further. In which I was torn away from the *sureness* of the game. Indeed, doesn't it seem obvious that the possibility of a language-game is conditioned by certain facts? (1975: § 617)

For example, if someone grew up with an unshakable belief that God shall shelter her if she cries his name in hours of desperation and if she does so for a long time without obtaining what she wishes, there is a *possibility* that either she ultimately abandons her belief in God or transcends her conception of God to one that is more like God and less like Spider-Man. In the latter case we then might say, 'sufferings of various sorts' has educated her to a different belief in God (Wittgenstein 1980: 86).

This kind of conversion happens of my own accord. On the other hand, we might encounter people of other world-pictures and try to encourage them to see the world the way we do. But, in doing so, we use our own language-game to defeat theirs. Suppose I am guided by 'the propositions of physics', and I meet people who 'consult an oracle'. Wittgenstein's view is worth quoting at length:

> Is it wrong for them to consult an oracle and be guided by it? – If we call this 'wrong' aren't we using our language-game as a base from which to *combat* theirs? ... And are we wrong or right to combat it? Of course there are all sorts of slogans which will be used to support our proceedings. ... Where two principles really do meet which cannot be reconciled with one another, then each man declares the other a fool and heretic. ... I said I would 'combat' the other man, – but wouldn't I give him *reasons*? Certainly; but how far do they go? At the end of reasons comes *persuasion*. (Think what happens when missionaries convert natives.) (1975: §§ 608–612)

In persuasion one shares or displays one's world-picture to the other with non-coercive measures. But in this process one's opinion is not enough to make the other change her way of looking.[3] Some principles cannot be reconciled with one another, because they embody opposing world-pictures. That is to say, these principles are arrived at by different criteria of right and wrong or reasonable or unreasonable (§ 559). In this situation, one might be forced to form a combative attitude towards the other and the prospect for communication looks bleak.

Such a view of the way different world-pictures encounter each other is quite cynical. Wittgenstein might be right that at the end of reason comes persuasion, but that doesn't necessarily mean that it is accompanied by a segregating – 'us and them' – attitude. People with opposing principles do encounter and they do try to *convince* each other to see the world the way they do, but this does not necessarily imply that they take an offensive approach. I might find someone's world-picture 'primitive' or 'unintelligible', but I'm not sure that I would declare him a 'fool and heretic'. It seems quite possible to face a different world-picture and yet find it intriguing. (Maybe that is why we find Werner Herzog's movies fascinating.[4])

According to James C. Klagge in his book *Wittgenstein in Exile*, Wittgenstein had a fixed understanding of the nature of interaction between opposing world-pictures which is not necessarily in conformity with the way we might experience these situations. In scenarios laid out by Wittgenstein 'where two principles really do meet which cannot be reconciled with one another' (1975: § 611), we need to undertake what he calls a 'diachronic anthropology' (2011: 64). That is, we should observe what will happen over time when apparently irreconcilable groups or principles meet and engage with one another – 'not simply in debate but in life' (ibid.). One advantage of Klagge's strategy is that it is open to the variety of possibilities that human communications might bring about – an openness which is not there in Wittgenstein's cynic view of the limits of human contacts. So, in this approach instead of declaring the other 'fool and heretic' from the outset, we bracket our obstructive judgements about the other and, maybe with an attitude of hoping for the best and planning for the worst, go along with the experience of encountering and meeting the other group or principle. And of course it is not insured that such an approach will turn out to be successful, but there might be successes as well if we manage to go beyond 'restrictive conditions' highlighted by Wittgenstein (ibid.).

In the next section, and in the light of what I have discussed so far, I address, once more, the disagreements between naturalists and supernaturalists and argue that the conflict might stem from a failure to see the fundamental impact one's world-picture has on one's conception of the meaning of life, and I show how most commentators rely on *reasoning* where it has the least effects – that is, when they are dealing with world-pictures. This, in turn, explains why 'indubitability' of a theory of life's meaning is not enough 'to make me change my whole life' (Wittgenstein 1967: 57).

On Certainty and the meaning of life

If we accept the significance of world-pictures in shaping our way of seeing the world, then the next question would be to enquire about the relation between one's world-picture and one's conception of life's meaning. Think of a militant atheist and a believer. They might be colleagues, share similar jokes, and eat the same food; they enjoy each other's company, and they learn from each other regardless of their disagreements. Every now and then, they might tease each other about their beliefs but only to show that having a sense of humour is helpful in these situations. It is true that in many respects not only they but all of us have a lot in common. So could we say the difference between the believer and nonbeliever is only about one's having an idea about a supernatural being, which is not shared by the other? No. The difference runs deeply. Though they have a lot in common there are also vast differences in the ways these common elements are manifested or perceived. A believer's attitude towards the world is different from that of the nonbeliever. The former might agree with the latter that our judgements of what makes a life virtuous or good are based on elements whose worth we can recognise in human terms, without any need for God's approval. However, the believer continues, religion gives a character of depth to our striving for the good; it transcends our tendency towards the good to something more than just a human disposition. Thus, Cottingham writes,

> The morally good life is indeed one which enables us to fulfil our human nature. But what the religious dimension adds is a framework within which that nature is revealed as more than just a set of characteristics that a certain species happens intermittently to possess, but instead as pointing to the condition that a Being of the utmost benevolence and care that we can conceive of desires us to achieve.... To act in the light of such an attitude is to act in the faith that our struggles mean something beyond the local expression of a contingently evolving genetic lottery. (2003: 72–73)

Whereas an objectivist is certain of the self-justificatory nature of intrinsic values, a supernaturalist views them as the necessary but not sufficient conditions of a meaningful life. An objectivist might say, human beings are able to make rational decisions and thus can ascertain what the elements of a good life are. In Metz's words, 'for all we know, nature, independently of God, could perform the functions of which God alone has been thought capable' (2013: 110). On the other hand, sympathising with all this, a believer might raise other concerns. For example, Cottingham suggests that this outlook, insightful as it might look, cannot remove the 'most fundamental aspect of the human condition', namely our mortality and finitude. 'Many philosophers', Cottingham writes, 'show a strange tendency to conceal this bleak reality from themselves by adopting, almost unconsciously, a kind of jaunty optimism about the power of human reason' (2003: 76–77). For believers, religion, unlike the secular moral outlook, provides an answer for the most fundamental fact of human life, their vulnerability. It gives an attitude, a certain orientation, to their moral life that a naturalist outlook fails to provide.

Now, mightn't we say this attitude is the same as the believer's world-picture? Mightn't we say the believer tries to defend a world-picture that, in Cottingham's words, 'is hard to describe in purely cognitive terms' (ibid.: 74)? It seems that the argument between believers and nonbelievers over the ultimate source of value is an instance of a situation 'where two principles really do meet which cannot be reconciled with one another' (Wittgenstein 1975: § 610). In this dispute the 'grounds' of the nonbeliever's claim might be 'well known' (ibid.: § 336) to the believer, and yet the latter might not be ready to 'give up' his world-picture. The believer says 'he has proof', and he might be willing to risk 'things on account of it which he would not do on things which are by far better established for him' (Wittgenstein 1967: 54). But is risking other things in life for one's belief a good reason? From an objectivist's perspective, the supernaturalist's belief in God is 'groundless', but the believer might say, so is the objectivist's trust in the power of human reason or 'history books'. Our lives show that we accept many things based on trust until we acquire a method of examining what we accept and take for granted. But we don't merely accept a set of disconnected ideas (such as where the human heart is or that 2 + 2 = 4); rather, we learn a 'whole system of propositions' (Wittgenstein 1975: § 141) or a 'whole system of verification' (ibid.: § 279). Life informs us with a whole way of seeing the world and acting in it based on trust, which makes any investigation unnecessary:

If the shopkeeper wanted to investigate each of his apples without any reason, for the sake of being certain about everything, why doesn't he have to investigate the investigation? And can one talk of belief here (I mean belief as in 'religious belief', not surmise)? (1975: § 459)

In ordinary circumstances the shopkeeper does not need to investigate every single item in his shop to ascertain that the delivered items are in good shape. The language-game of doubt is usually unnecessary here. Likewise, the believer stands fast in his belief and 'nothing in the world will convince [him] of the opposite.... He shall give up other things but not this' (ibid.: § 380). Naturalists object that the believer is 'in the grip of a delusion now' (ibid.: § 658) and that he will find this out if he thinks more objectively. The claims of naturalism, they suggest, are so well founded that no philosophy that rejects them can hope to survive. In Russell's words,

That man is the product of causes which had no prevision of the end they were achieving; that his origins, his growth, his hopes and fears, his loves and his beliefs, are but the outcome of accidental collocations of atoms; that no fire, no heroism...can preserve an individual life beyond the grave; that all the labours of the ages...all the noonday brightness of human genius, are destined to extinction in the vast death of the solar system,...all these things, if not quite beyond dispute, are yet so nearly certain that no philosophy which rejects them can hope to stand. (1957: 56)

So, a naturalist not only believes in her world-picture but also is certain that her belief is in conformity with objective reality. Russell's point is that the naturalised world is altogether different from the world of believers. It would be odd, I submit, to think that the whole conflict between believers and nonbelievers is over evidence. What is at stake in the conflict is a whole way of seeing the world and living in it. From a naturalist perspective, conversion to supernaturalism might be similar to questioning the incontrovertibility of 'multiplication table' (Wittgenstein 1975: § 658) because the truth of naturalism is 'quite beyond dispute' whereas supernaturalists believe in something the existence of which is 'disputable' (Russell 1957: 56).

On the other hand, a believer might say believing in God is not only about believing in a set of disputable claims. For example, Cottingham writes, with a Wittgensteinian tone, that 'belief, in the sense of subscribing to a set of theological propositions, is not in fact central to what it is to be religious' (2003: 88).[5] Rather, what is central is the adoption of 'a framework of understanding and praxis' (ibid.: 90). This approach to religion is in sharp contrast with those supernaturalist accounts of life's meaning that are as absolutist as naturalists, such as Russell, in their descriptions of the human condition. 'If theism is true and there is a benevolent supreme being governing the universe', Pojman writes, the following eight theses are true:

> 1. We have a satisfying explanation of the origins and sustenance of the universe.... 2.... The universe is suffused in goodness... 3. God loves and cares for us.... 4. Theists have an answer to the question why be moral.... 5. Cosmic justice reigns in the universe.... 6. All persons are of equal worth.... 7. [There exists] grace and forgiveness – a happy ending for all.... 8. There is life after death. (2002: 27–29)

A naturalist might sincerely try to see 'cosmic justice' and 'happy ending' in the universe that is suggested to be 'suffused in goodness', but the more she searches, the less she sees these conditions. She watches some history channels, hears some news and sees things with her own eyes, and then one day she might knock the table in frustration and loudly utter that what happens in this world is a 'matter of complete indifference for what is higher' (Wittgenstein 1966: § 6.432). And then in due time words such as 'justice', 'goodness', 'grace' and 'happy ending' to her might sound devoid of meaning or even 'obscene' beside the concrete ordinary names that don't try to aspire to anything transcendental.[6]

What calls for attention here is not whether or not theism is true but is the question how one might arrive at this picture of the world. A believer hasn't acquired the language-game of doubting his world-picture, but 'certain events' *might* put him in a position in which he can no longer go on with the old language-game (Wittgenstein 1975: § 617). Only then the naturalist or pessimist world-picture might begin to *dawn* on him. Consequently, he might be able to find his feet with a nonbeliever who questions the belief that the world is 'suffused in goodness':

> There are two things which make it impossible to believe that this world is the successful work of an all-wise, all-good, and, at the same time, all-powerful Being; firstly, the misery which abounds in it everywhere; and secondly, the obvious imperfection of its highest product, man, who is a burlesque of what he should be. These things cannot be reconciled with any such belief. (Schopenhauer 1851: 51)

In short, the disagreements between the ones who see the world 'suffused in goodness' and the ones who see it abounded in misery seem categorical and not hypothetical, and thus the chance of their arguments having an effect is low. The believer might refer to the '*accessibility conditions*' of religion and suggest that the truth of religion is accessible 'only on condition that there is some kind of transformation in the subject' (Cottingham 2008: 255). But it is not clear what this transformation consists of, and surely, this is not something philosophical argument alone can lay a hand on. I think what Cottingham means by 'transformation' is very close to Wittgenstein's key idea that 'life can educate one to a belief in God' (1980: 86). As I said in Chapter 3, sometimes there is a life behind the dawning of an aspect, and that is usually the key in understanding a religious world-picture. Furthermore, unlike Cottingham, I submit that believers and nonbelievers alike can appeal to the accessibility condition in defence of their claims. If a believer can claim that the truth of religion is accessible only if certain requirements, things like receptivity and openness and humility, are met, so can a nonbeliever.

So much for the disputes between believers and nonbelievers from the standpoint of *On Certainty*. The other key facet of the text is that it tries to go beyond a naturalism/supernaturalism debate to show how, regardless of our differences, we are in many respects the same. It wants to show the limits of theory and the 'primacy of praxis'. As D. Z. Phillips suggests, 'one of the achievements of *On Certainty*, is to get us to look at our world in a new way; a way which is often impeded by our philosophisings' (2005: 16). And in this new way of looking at the world, we see that long before our search for an intellectual answer for the meaning of life we acquire a way of living and assessing the world. That is, we live, and with the act of living, some meaning is obtained. People have lived 'unexamined' lives since time immemorial, and, to say the least, their lives have not been utterly worthless, partly because most of what we do in life does not stand in need of examination and justification and partly because meaning is not totally absent.

Life, according to this view, does not stand in need of justification unless 'certain events' make us realise that we can no longer go on with our old way of seeing the world. Shopkeepers open their shops in the morning; children come back from school; we all gather around the fire when it is cold; we respond to people's pain; and most of us take care of our children like the way *all* elephants do. And if we are not 'doing philosophy'[7] for none of these activities, do we need a conception of a meaningful life? Believers and nonbelievers alike bury or burn the dead; *the sun also rises.* Believers and nonbelievers alike come to understand the concept of loss and come to find different ways of expressing their feelings, like the way the Portuguese invented the word *saudade* in the 13th century to describe the sadness they felt about those who departed on journey to unknown seas and never returned; the word conveys a delicate but potent longing for something or someone while you have a notion that the object of your longing may never return. The sea people didn't need a justification for the use of this word. They lived by the sea, and the sea took care of justification. Life can educate you to the use and thus to the meaning of words.

There is a limit to justification. While Moore was busy proving that there was a tree over there, other people were taking a nap under its shade or climbing it to steal juicy fruits. Wittgenstein's question is: as long as we enjoy its shade and its fruits, what difference does it make to know whether it is real? Philosophers who detach themselves from the stream of life 'engage in all manner of conceptual acrobatics' (Plant 2005: 84) but will ultimately return to the ordinary life because 'justification comes to an end' somewhere (Wittgenstein 1975: § 192).[8]

In a sense, *On Certainty* is a text on the pathology of philosophical detachment from the ordinary. It shows how our world-picture, our whole way of seeing the world, meshes with our life, and it shows that a fundamental trust runs through most actions that we usually undertake. Any account of life's meaning, which overlooks or trivialises the 'givenness' of life, fails to the same extent to go right to the foundations; it fails to 'put the question marks *deep* enough down' (Wittgenstein 1980: 62). In the next section, I show that Nagel's solution to the problem of the absurdity of life is one such account. Nagel makes a distinction between 'the absurd' and 'meaninglessness' and suggests that the sense of the absurd arises because we fail to justify our actions in life which are meaningless from an objective point of view, and yet we consider them meaningful from our subjective point of view. However, I argue that, contrary to what Nagel claims, some meaning is obtained with the act of living, one that does not stand in need of justification.

Nagel, irony and its limits

Traditionally, nihilism is associated with the idea that upon a detached contemplation and observation we fail to find an overarching purpose for life. Instead, what one observes in this process is the overwhelming abundance of pain and harm in the world. In Schopenhauer's words,

Unless *suffering* is the direct and immediate object of life, our existence must entirely fail of its aim. It is absurd to look upon the enormous amount of pain that abounds everywhere in the world, and originates in needs and necessitates inseparable from life itself, as serving no purpose at all and the result of mere chance. (1851: 45)

That is, a key feature of most works on nihilism is unfolding the tragic, and yet pointless, sense of life. On the other hand, there is the view that life is absurd because we fail to justify our actions and that there is an incongruity between the meaning we ascribe to them and the meaning they actually have from an objective point of view. Nagel makes a distinction between 'the absurd' and 'meaninglessness' and suggests that the sense of the absurd arises because we see the gap between the meaninglessness of life *sub specie aeternitatis* and its apparent meaningfulness *sub specie humanitatis* (Nagel 1986: 216, 218; 1987: 101).

We might try to orient all our life to something bigger than us, like 'justice', the 'glory of God' or the 'advance of science'. However, 'any such larger purpose can be put in doubt in the same way that the aims of an individual life can be, and for the same reasons' (1971: 147). Nagel goes so far as to claim that in every 'conceivable' world that contains us these 'unsettlable doubts' will ultimately arise (ibid.: 148). But in spite of these doubts, Nagel has it, we continue taking our lives and day-to-day strives seriously, 'as we must'. Something more fundamental than reason keeps us going. Our life cannot entirely rely on reason; otherwise, 'our lives and beliefs would collapse' (ibid.: 150).

Nagel's emphasis on the precedence of life over rational justification is strikingly similar to Wittgenstein's views in *On Certainty*. Both emphasise that the chain of justifications comes to an end somewhere. However, what separates them is the level of significance each ascribes to the role of certainty in our lives. Whereas Wittgenstein is more concerned with showing how certain aspects of our lives are not the subject of any doubt, Nagel suggests that a certain mode of viewing life – that is, viewing life *sub specie aeternitatis* – would lead to scepticism about life's meaning. For Nagel, we have the capacity to come out of the grip of life's 'inertial force' and view its contingencies from above. This unique capacity enables us to see the 'groundlessness' of our beliefs.[9] In other words, our capacity to detach ourselves from our everyday lives enables us to see the 'fundamentally correct' position of nihilism: The key to nihilism is detachment. That is, as long as one is involved in the course of everyday life, one fails to see the insignificance of one's concerns and commitments from a broader perspective (ibid.: 146). In other words, in becoming the observer of (our) life we see the absurdity of human endeavours since we fail to give a justificatory reason for our actions but act from a subjective standpoint as if everything is well justified.

Nagel claims that we can doubt everything and that there is a correlation between epistemic scepticism and the absurd. He writes,

> Both epistemological scepticism and a sense of the absurd can be reached via initial doubts posed within systems of evidence and justifications that we accept, and can be stated without violence to our ordinary concepts. (1971: 149)

We all have the capacity to ask not only why we consider something to be significant, but also why our reasons and justifications for its importance are enough to assure us of its importance. And when we do so, we realise that we cannot move without circularity or begging the question.

But, I wonder how often do we attend to this game of justification in everyday life. Or, if the absurdity of our situation depends on our recognition that we fail to provide enough justifications for what we deem important, then, in Michael Smith's words, 'does it follow that individuals who do not realise that their beliefs require such a justification have beliefs that are nonabsurd?' (2006: 96) According to Smith, 'For Nagel the absence of justificatory reason for certainty is the key and not one's recognition that the justificatory reasons are absent' (ibid.). But Nagel actually acknowledges that the only way to avoid the absurd would be either 'never to attain it or to forget it – neither of which can be achieved by the will' (1971: 151). What is problematic, however, is the assumption that our stepping back necessarily leads to the sense of the absurd.

Put differently, what would I be missing if I lived with certainty and not doubt? Nagel might reply that in that case I would remain blind to the ultimate truth of human life. The truth is that human beings are on a journey, and they have been told that there is a glorious carnival at the destination. However, if they step back and view the road from above, they will realise that there is no destination, no carnival; the whole 'journey fever' is a sham, and the road of life leads them to only a dead-end. There is no journey; there are only people on the road. The person who is enlightened by this truth would still be on the same road with other people. The only difference, Nagel might say, is that now she has an attitude towards people's sweating and struggling on the road ('irony'). He is delighted now, as Lucretius writes in *On the Nature of*

Things, that he 'may look down from on high upon others and behold them all astray, wandering abroad and seeking the paths of life' ([50 BC] 1982: Book II, 7).

Interestingly, it seems that in Nagel's scepticism certain things are exempt from doubt, and he is certain about them: He doesn't doubt (1) that there is a way to understand the ultimate nature of reality, (2) that the truth of his philosophical doubts can be expressed meaningfully and that people can understand it, (3) that irony is preferred over heroism or despair, (4) that he is proposing a world-picture which has to be lived with certainty, and so on. In other words, Nagel's scepticism is indeed defending a whole way of seeing the world and living in it.

In sum, whereas Wittgenstein highlights the 'groundlessness of our believing' (1975: § 166) to show the priority of praxis over theory and the fact that life equips us with a 'definite world-picture' (ibid.: § 167), Nagel uses it as a premise to prove that the chain of justifications for our beliefs comes to an end and that we realise that our whole system of justification 'rests on responses and habits that we never question, that we should not know how to defend without circularity, and to which we shall continue to adhere even after they are called into question' (Nagel 1971: 146). For Nagel, the starting point of scepticism is the fact that the things we do and the things we want are not justified by reason – that is, the absurdity of life lies in the fact that realising the arbitrariness of our beliefs does not 'disengage us from life' (ibid.).

What separates Nagel from most nihilists is the way he responds to the absurd. Pessimists have given two types of responses to the problem of the absurd. I call these responses 'inflationary' and 'deflationary'. The 'inflationary' responses are the ones that ask for extreme measures to solve or at least mitigate the problem of the absurd. Schopenhauer's 'negation of the will' (1818), Nietzsche's '*amor fati*' (1882), Camus' 'heroism' (1955) and Benatar's 'antinatalism' (2006) are among the inflationary responses to the problem of the absurd. The 'deflationary' responses, on the other hand, are not concerned with what Nagel calls the 'romantic' and 'self-pitying' solutions and rest content with the view that the absurd 'need not be a matter for agony unless we make it so' (1971: 152). Smith's 'suspension of belief' (2006), Feinberg's 'self-fulfilment' (1992) and Nagel's 'irony' are examples of a deflationary approach.[10]

Whereas most inflationary responses strongly support the idea of withdrawal from the ordinary forms of life, Nagel's deflationary approach acknowledges the 'givenness' of life and the significance of appreciating the ordinary (Nagel 1971: 150). The absurdity of life, Nagel has it, does not present us with a problem to which some 'solution' must be found. Unlike most nihilists, what Nagel advises with regard to the absurd is neither heroic affirmation of life nor despair but 'irony' (ibid.: 152). Having the capacity to step back and see the insignificance of life, one realises that nothing is as serious as it appears, and even the fact that nothing matters is not very serious. The ironist views the hurly-burly of life and the way people sweat over insignificant things and suggests that we develop a light-hearted, humorous kind of outlook. ('Isn't it ironic that as he was being knighted, his pants fell down?' the ironist would say (ibid.: 145).)

Thus, in Nagel's view, realising the absurdity of life leads only to a change of attitude but not more. He invites us to keep living our everyday life, but he wants us to add an *attitude* to it, which helps us go along with the absurd as we continue living, a Woody Allenian mode of being. But, I submit, here lies a tension which is overlooked in Nagel's account. If, as Nagel says, after encountering the absurd we return to the ordinary life, we should be able, then, to live the ordinary life with certainty. But how can I live my ordinary life with certainty and at the same time give an ironic attitude to everything I do? It seems to me that a large portion of our lives is immune from irony. We do not respond to the human pain with irony. We didn't seek shelter and warmth with irony. Usually when love begins, irony ends. The language-game of expressing one's love is played by betraying one's vulnerability; irony tries to hide it. What Wittgenstein calls 'primitive behaviour' (1958: § 99) or 'natural history of human beings' (ibid.: § 415), cannot be undertaken with an ironic attitude, like the way you cannot sneeze and keep your eyes open at the same time. They do not stand in need of justifications, because they are neither rational nor irrational; they are, rather, 'pre-rational' (Wittgenstein 1967: 58).

What is puzzling about Nagel's theory is that he is well aware of the limits of justification and reasoning, which makes his theory more interesting than his rivals' theories. He warns us that we cannot rely entirely on reason, and yet this is exactly what he is doing when he suggests that life could be meaningful only on condition that a rational justification for our beliefs and actions is obtained. I might contemplate whether it is worth changing my car or house, but when I choose a name for my baby, the need for a justificatory reason doesn't arise. I do not choose a name for the newborn because I have found that it 'pays'.[11] 'Nothing could induce me to put my hand into a flame' not because I have ascertained a justificatory reason not to do so but because I am certain that 'I shall get burnt if I put my hand in the fire: that is certainty' (1958: § 474). If these behaviours and countless others are usually performed with certainty, and if none of them stands in need of justification, then, it seems that irony, as a solution to the problem of the absurd, is a viable option only if and to the extent that we are in the sceptic's favourite mode of being – that is, detachment. But this, in turn, leads to a key question: how often do we actually see the world *sub specie aeternitatis*, and when was the last time you did so? (This is not meant to be a rhetorical question.)

Nagel's objection to the inflationary responses is that they have an exaggerated conception of the self and its significance in the world, whereas, viewing the world from a broader perspective, one realises that nothing is as serious as it first appears to be. In Nagel's view, absurdity is nothing to be ashamed of or to feel distressed about. Instead, 'at the risk of falling into romanticism by a different route', he would argue that 'absurdity is one of the most human things about us: a manifestation of our most advanced and interesting characteristics' (ibid.: 152). Thus, irony is considered to be an interesting characteristic of the people who are done with sensationalism of 'masochists of meaning' (Marquard 1991: 46). Irony is seen as a *cool* way of approaching life, without betraying our vulnerabilities and our 'longing for the transcendent' (Wittgenstein 1980: 15). We should gradually learn how to move away from the tragic sense of life and see the ironic side of the human condition since, after all, what Nagel's view implies is that there is no tragedy in life – there is a correlation between tragedy and one's conception of the significance of life.

According to Nagel's account, irony acts as an alternative to the extreme measures of philosophers who, in Hume's words, 'from reasonings purely philosophical ran into as great extravagancies of conduct as any *Monk* or *Dervise* that ever was in the world' ([1738] 1968: Book I, Part 4: § 7). However, even if we agree with him on discarding the inflationary approaches, one might still ask why we should limit ourselves to his favourite alternative. For one thing, it is quite possible to imagine someone who denies the availability of justifying reasons for our actions in life, and yet whose approach is that of wonder and awe at the existence of the world as a whole. Note that here I don't want to defend the idea that wonder is a better alternative option to that of Nagel's, though I am sympathetic to it. My point is that we can transcend ourselves and view the world from above, as Nagel suggests, but instead of seeing the absurd, we might experience awe and wonder at seeing life as a whole without any supernatural feelings attached to it. Wittgenstein refers to the same feeling, which is worth quoting at length:

> Nothing could be more remarkable than seeing a man alone in a room, walking up and down, lighting a cigarette, sitting down, etc. so that we are suddenly observing a human being from outside in a way that ordinarily we can never observe ourselves; it would be like watching a chapter of biography with our own eyes, – surely this would be uncanny and wonderful at the same time. We should be observing something more wonderful than a playwright could arrange to be acted or spoken on the stage: life itself. – But then we do see this every day without its making the slightest impression on us! ... But it seems to me too that there is a way of capturing the world *sub specie aeterni* other than through the work of artist. Thought has such a way – so I believe – it is as though it flies above the world and leaves it as it is – observing it from above, in flight. (1980: 4–5)

In other words, it is possible to view the world objectively from above and see the insignificance of our life as a whole and yet 'leave it as it is' without trying to add an ironic or tragic flavour to it. Irony, then, is not the only deflationary option in facing the absurd, and Nagel has not exhausted other possibilities. One might wonder at a world in which tragedy and irony meet under the same sun. One might wonder at the sun that is burning the edge of a little cloud over a little town, while the latter is engulfing the former with a stubborn grace. One might view life 'as a gift, as the coming to presence of what is mysterious' (Cooper 2005: 137). Viewing the world from above, one might seize, in Hadot's words, 'the hidden correspondence in things' (1995: 248):

> In the morning, his thoughts, in their freedom
> Soar up to the heavens like larks.
> – He sails over life, understanding with ease
> The language of flowers and voiceless things.[12]

The pessimistic background of Taylor's subjectivism

So much for Nagel's account of the absurd. In this section, I focus on Taylor's subjectivist view of life's meaning and show its connection to pessimism. Interestingly, most scholars in the literature downplay or ignore the background against which Taylor arrives at his subjectivist theory. It seems that we can make a distinction between two types of subjectivism: pessimist subjectivism like Taylor (2000) and optimist subjectivism like Frankfurt (2004). In this section, I focus on only the former, but some of my arguments against it apply to the latter as well. Taylor's theory feeds on mostly the same assumptions that Nagel's theory of the absurd does. We may use Isaiah Berlin's distinction between the fox and the hedgehog to explain Taylor's answer to the question of life's meaning. Berlin writes of two ways of experiencing and seeing the world: like a fox or like a hedgehog. The fox knows many little things, but the hedgehogs knows a single big one (Berlin 1978). A translation of this distinction in the literature on life's meaning would be like this: The hedgehog in his search for meaning usually wants to find, in David Cooper's words, what is 'beyond human' (2005: 126) or beyond the individual, but the fox is content with the little answers.[13] With regard to meaning in life, the foxes search for meaning in the lives of the individuals. The hedgehogs, on the other hand, search for meaning outside the 'hurly-burly' of life and believe that for life to be meaningful the human life in general or universe as a whole has to have an overarching ultimate point and purpose.[14] The hedgehog believes that it doesn't make sense to talk of meaning in life in its individualist sense if life as a whole is meaningless and that individual lives can be meaningful if only they are 'answerable' to something beyond human. On the other hand, a fox might say that there are many ways in which a life can be meaningful and that it is a mistake to make the affirmation of life depend on a universal proof of meaning. As I explain below, Taylor enquires about the meaning of life like a hedgehog, but he ends up with a, so to speak, foxian answer to the problem of life. That is, he starts off by claiming that life as a whole, 'from a distant' is devoid of meaning (Taylor 2000: 139). He appeals to several pictures and analogies to portray life's meaninglessness. One major picture, which is discussed the most in the literature, is the picture of life as the story of Sisyphus and his rolling stone. For Taylor, these pictures lead one 'to wonder what the point of it all is' (ibid.: 138). Here is another picture of life: two groups of prisoners, one group digging a hole that is 'no sooner finished than it is filled in again by the other group' and so on (ibid.). Taylor, like Nagel, claims that we have the capacity to step outside the hurly-burly of life and realise the pointlessness of everything that we consider to be the symbol of purpose in life. Think of all the poor birds that 'span an entire side of the globe each year and then return, only to insure that others may follow the same incredibly long path again and again' (ibid.). As a principle, Taylor has it, 'all living things present essentially the same [meaningless] spectacle' (ibid.).

This way of appraising life as a whole bears striking resemblances to that of the Iranian poet Omar Khayyám (1048–1131). In both appraisals we notice an overemphasis on the destructive power of time. According to both thinkers, there is a burning urge to portray the transient nature of things which in themselves carry a sense of sadness, and both try to show the absence of meaning in the cherished phenomena of life. Khayyám writes,

آورد به اضطرارم اول به وجود
جز حیرتم از حیات چیزی نفزود
رفتیم به اکراه و ندانیم چه بود
زین آمدن و بودن و رفتن مقصود.[15]

Khayyám and Taylor search for the meaning of life in its 'cosmic sense' (Edwards 1967: 124). That is, they want to find out 'what is the point of it all'. And the more they search, the less they see any overarching purpose that could give a sense of direction to our lives. We are like sparrows over a raging sea, facing storms and our wings are bound to break one way or another. From the standpoint of eternity we are insignificant as a little cloud in the infinite space. Words and deeds disappear and, in Kafka's dark observation, our 'written kisses never reach their destination; the ghosts drink them up along the way'.[16]

Whereas Khayyam's solution to the problem of life can be summarised in the principle of 'carpe diem',[17] Taylor's suggestion is that the point of life is nothing but living, and if one has the 'interest', 'passion' and 'the will' to live life to the same extent, his life would be meaningful. 'The meaning of life', Taylor suggests, 'is from within us, it is not bestowed from without' (2000: 142). In other words, from an objective point of view, one fails to find a cosmic meaning and purpose for life, but from an individual point of view, one's activities in life can be meaningful as long as, and to the extent that, there is a level of engagement, commitment and strong desire to undertake them. From a cosmic point of view, Sisyphus' life is meaningless, but from the point of view of Sisyphus, he is living a meaningful life in its particular sense as long as he is interested in stone rolling.

What is puzzling in this line of thought is the assumption that people can simply move away from the meaninglessness of life in its cosmic sense by orienting themselves towards the particular meaning. But it seems to me that such meaning is more like anaesthetic, something that temporarily keeps you away from the ultimate truth of life, which is supposedly its meaninglessness from an objective view. Taylor's view reminds me of Hans Schnier, the main character in Heinrich Boll's novel, *The Clown*, where he writes of different remedies to the problem of his life: 'There is one temporarily effective remedy: alcohol; there could be a permanent cure: Marie. Marie has left me' (2002: 2). Likewise, Taylor wants to say there is no permanent remedy and solution for life; everything is temporary. Marie is gone, hold unto alcohol, that is to temporary solutions, like being passionate about something in life.

The myth of Sisyphus is overrated. The significance of viewing the world *sub specie aeternitatis* is overrated. Nihilists talk about Sisyphus, the hero, who looks the absurd in the eyes and says yes to life. He is the creation of a tormented soul who longs for an extraordinary, superlative and transcendental solution to the problem of life. But, what do we know about Sisyphus? We know that gods punished him, but what kind of knowledge is that? In the literature we see only Sisyphus the symbol, the concept, the icon of a mode of being. His sole concern is facing the absurd by rolling stones. But he must have had a few friends. There must have been a shelter, a family maybe, with some children. He would have toothache now and again; winter would come, and he would need to store food for the family, and for storing food and taking care of his children, he didn't stand in need of any justification. Sisyphus was ordinary in many respects. He was one of us. Camus and Taylor made an idol out of him because they thought in the 'absence of an idol', we stand in need of another one, an earthly one.

Taylor and Camus would say the stone rolling is just an analogy for the absurdity of life, but I think this analogy doesn't do justice to the way most of us experience life. The analogy is based on an unrealistic inflationary picture of life and the way we experience it. It is important to be aware of the fictionality of the myth of Sisyphus and the scope of its effects on the factuality of life. In our involved journeys in search for meaning, telling the difference between fact and fiction is important.

Recalling the 'strange atmosphere' in which *The Sorrows of Young Werther* was written, Goethe writes in his autobiography of the therapeutic effects of transforming the turmoil in his inner life into a work of art and the way after finishing the work he was 'once more free and happy, and justified in beginning a new life' ([1833] 1913: Part III, Book XIII). However, Goethe notes, 'while I myself felt eased and enlightened by having turned fact into fiction, my friends were demoralised by my work, for they thought that fiction should be turned into fact' (ibid.).

And it appears that so is the lot of the myth of Sisyphus in the literature. A fiction is considered to be a fact about human life in general. A susceptible mind, craving a convincing answer for the problem of life, comes across the myth of Sisyphus and his never ending suffering, never ending perseverance and determination to do something in a world defined by injustice and absurdities, and an image, an idea, of a way of life forms in his mind based on these 'gloomy reflections'. Being a spectator of the vicissitudes of life with such detachment, Goethe observes, 'inspires seriousness; and to what can such serious thought lead us if not to the contemplation of the transitoriness and worthlessness of all earthly things?' (ibid.). It is from this vantage point that we might see, á la Camus, something heroic in Sisyphus's affirmation of life, something to which we relate: the realisation that we all can close the fifth act of the tragedy of our lives when we please and that yet we choose life. But here we are not talking about heroes and extraordinary people who look the absurd in the eye; we are talking about ordinary people whose life, in Goethe's words, 'is embittered in the most peaceful circumstances by want of action and by the exaggerated demands they make upon themselves' (ibid.).

There is a similarity between Taylor and Nagel in the significance each attributes to the problem of the absurd. Nagel doesn't see any reason for being distressed about the absurdity of life, and Taylor's motto is that 'the point of any living thing's life is, evidently, nothing but life itself' (2000: 138). Birds migrate every year because 'it is the doing that counts for them, and not what they hope to win by it' (ibid.: 141). Likewise, humans do what they do because 'it is the doing that counts for them' and because they have a will, passion and desire to do all these things, and that would give their lives meaning and purpose.

Taylor's theory can also be criticised apart from its pessimistic background; that is, it can be criticised as a subjectivist theory in general. One counterintuitive feature of subjectivist theories of meaning is the idea that the more I show commitment to something, the more meaningful my life becomes. But, I am not sure my life will become more meaningful if I commit myself to any random thing, say, playing computer games, collecting autographs of celebrities, or counting leaves of a tree. The idea that life's meaning is a function of one's subjective desires and passions is incoherent since it is bound to make judgements that are contradictory to its own claims. The subjectivist claims that the source of life's meaning is not supernatural or based on some features of the natural world, which are objectively valuable and that when someone judges her life to be meaningful, what we see in her life is nothing but the fulfilment of a subjective passion about something. Now, think of an agnostic who comes to accept Pascal's wager and decides to regulate his life as if God as the ultimate source of meaning exists. That is, he finds meaning not in his subjective attraction to the idea of betting over the existence of God but in virtue of a desperate leap of faith. In this situation, if the subjectivist is right, the agnostic's 'passionate commitment' to the idea of living in accordance to the will of assumed God should naturally confer meaning on his life. But if the subjectivist accepts that the agnostic's life is meaningful, he denies one of the premises of his argument for subjectivism of meaning, which states that the source of meaning is not supernatural. On the other hand, if he claims that the agnostic's life is meaningless, he undermines his own claim that meaning is subjective.

In the next and final section, I draw a distinction between two kinds of doubts. Philosophical scepticism might seem of interest to only philosophers, but losing one's certainty in life and doubting the meaning of life is not an anomaly. Some people are indeed prone, albeit provisionally, to what Tolstoy calls 'the arrest of life' (1905: 7). We all might go through experiences that affect the way we evaluate things and relate to them. 'Experience', James Joyce writes, 'had embittered his heart against the world' ([1914] 1995: 53). That is to say, certain experiences might put us in a situation in which we cease to trust the world. Consequently, we 'cannot go on with the old language-game any further' (Wittgenstein 1975: § 617). I think this type of doubt is categorically different from the armchair scepticism of the type Wittgenstein criticises in *On Certainty*. I examine three views about philosophical scepticism as discussed by Wittgenstein, Franz Rosenzweig and Cavell. I think Wittgenstein's idea of 'indifference'; Rosenzweig's notions of the 'sick', the 'healthy' and the 'fear to live'; and Cavell's distinction between 'knowledge' and 'acknowledgement' provide fresh insights into the nature of philosophical scepticism and thus enable us to distinguish it from existential doubts.

Indifference, fear and failure: Wittgenstein, Rosenzweig and Cavell on philosophical scepticism

In *A Treatise of Human Nature*, and at the end of his discussion of what justifies belief, David Hume describes his own experiences in dealing with the effects of scepticism on his life. The similarity between Hume and Wittgenstein on the significance of appreciating the ordinary life is striking.[18] Hume writes,

Most fortunately it happens, that since reason is incapable of dispelling these clouds, nature herself suffices to that purpose, and cures me of this philosophical melancholy and delirium, either by relaxing this bent of mind, or by some avocation, and lively impression of my senses, which obliterates all these chimeras. I dine, I play a game of backgammon, I converse, and am merry with my friends; and when after three or four hours amusement, I would return to these speculations, they appear so cold, and strained, and ridiculous, that I cannot find in my heart to enter into them any farther. ([1738] 1968: Book I, Part 4: § 7)

Philosophical scepticism is seen here as an illness that can be cured not in the realm of theory but in the 'stream of life'. Intellectually, Hume feels that he urgently needs to find a ground for his beliefs; otherwise, his belief would be groundless. However, as soon as he returns to his day-to-day life, such an 'urge' (Wittgenstein 1958:§ 109), a 'disquietude' (ibid.: § 111), and a 'mental cramp' (Wittgenstein 1969: 1) disappear. In other words, in ordinary circumstances his attitude towards life is of certainty and not of doubt because in ordinary life the 'absence of doubt belongs to the essence of the language-game' (Wittgenstein 1975: § 370). It is in these situations that Hume finds himself absolutely 'determined to live' and participate in the 'common affairs of life'. In his solitude, the philosopher searches for justifying reasons for his belief, but it might also dawn on him that by distracting himself from this disposition and participating in the countless modes of living, the need for justification disappears. The sense of excitement and relief as a result of such realisation is so tense that 'I am ready to throw all my books and papers into the fire, and resolve never more to renounce the pleasures of life for the sake of reasoning and philosophy' (Hume [1738] 1968: Book I, Part 4: § 7). From this vantage point, we would like to throw ourselves, along with Goethe, 'into living knowledge, experience, action,...with all the more zeal and ardour' ([1833] 1913: Part III, Book XI).

Likewise, in *On Certainty* doubt is seen as an anomaly in the stream of life. Humans are not sceptical animals; they are 'primitive beings' to whom one 'grants instinct but not ratiocination' (1975: § 475). In such a naturalistic account of life and meaning, certainty is not contingent upon a rational justification; rather, it is a distinctive feature of being human. 'The squirrel does not infer by induction that it is going to need stores next winter as well. And no more do we need a law of induction to justify our actions or our predictions' (ibid.: § 287). It is from this perspective that Wittgenstein criticises scepticism, especially with regard to our interactions with others – as something 'foreign' (1990: § 566) or 'perverse' (1975: § 524). We do not infer that someone is in pain; we simply react. In some aspects of life the need for inference doesn't arise. You do not infer that you have a toothache; you experience it. When it comes to the pain of others, it would be helpful to 'remember that it is a primitive reaction to tend, to treat, the part that hurts when someone else is in pain; and not merely when oneself is' (Wittgenstein 1990: § 540). It would be strange to watch someone writhing in pain and merely contemplate whether his pain is identical with the kind one feels oneself. In specific circumstances, such as when a patient pretends to have more pain than what he actually does in order to get more doses of morphine, doubt makes sense,

> But the philosophical question whether someone else is in pain is completely different; it is not doubt about each individual in a particular case.... Do we encounter this doubt in everyday life? No. But maybe something which is remotely related: indifference toward other people's expression of pain. (Wittgenstein 1998a: §§ 239–240)

A sceptic's statement that 'his pains are hidden from me' is as awkward as saying that 'these sounds are hidden from my eyes' (ibid.: § 888). The point here is that scepticism might emerge as a result of 'indifference' towards, or aloofness from, the surrounding circumstances of one's life. In this view, the problem of scepticism has less to do with the 'intellect' and more with 'the will' (Wittgenstein 1980: 17). It refers to a mode of being in the world or, rather, a mode of failing to be present in the world.

However, even a sceptic hopes, fights, believes or seeks shelter without thinking that they stand in need of justification. In other words, the certainty of life is there; the sceptic only tries to give an attitude to it by adopting a 'way of speaking' (1975: § 524). That is, even a sceptic's or nihilist's life consists in her 'being content to accept many things' even though she doesn't *acknowledge* it (§ 344).

The sceptical positions about life's meaning might appear 'queer', but they get their force from a strong tendency, especially among philosophers, to view the world *sub specie aeternitatis*. As Hadot has shown, our tendency to see the world from above is a pervasive tendency throughout the history of philosophy. In ancient philosophy, all philosophical schools dealt with this tendency but, according to Hadot, it had the most significance in the Cynic tradition. For Cynics, 'the view from above was intended to denounce the absurdity of human life'

(1995: 247). For them, 'to observe human affairs from above means, at the same time, to see them from the point of view of death' (ibid.). The Cynic thinks if we are to '*see things as they really are*', we must provide the required distance, which enables us to fly over the contingencies of our desires and localities. Likewise, a pessimist, in his search for seeing life as it is, cannot help seeing the human frailty and the more he searches the less he sees any purpose or point. He might then conclude that the vicissitudes of life happen without any 'rhyme or reason' and that in his search for justifiable value the best response to the human predicament is to distract himself, like the way Hume did.[19] The pessimist might also remind us, 'unfortunately...when it comes to the pursuit of value, that really does seem to be all that there is' (Smith 2006: 105–106). Certainty in action, doubt in theory.

On the other hand, a person who is not 'in the grip' of this picture of the world might find these 'speculations' very melancholic. To use Hume's expressions quoted above, an ordinary person would react not only to the 'philosophical melancholy' of the sceptic or nihilist but also to the anti-sceptic's 'strained' and 'ridiculous' way of arguing against scepticism. Wittgenstein alludes to this when he writes,

> I am sitting with a philosopher in the garden; he says again and again 'I know that that's a tree', pointing to a tree that is near us. Someone else arrives and hears this, and I tell him: 'This fellow isn't insane. We are only doing philosophy'. (1975: § 467)

In ordinary circumstances this kind of philosophising stands in need of justification because in everyday life we don't see the point of doing philosophy the way it is described above. Ordinary people do not say 'the tree exists'; they sit under its shade. They don't say 'other minds exist'; they talk to the people who have those minds. But the philosopher is taught not to be put off by the prejudices of the common and to follow the leads of independent reason, no matter where those leads take one. Philosophy has something to do with the ability to come out of the grip of commonly held beliefs, traditions or sometimes even what common sense holds.

Franz Rosenzweig's little book, *Understanding the Sick and the Healthy*, precisely targets this view about philosophy.[20] He draws a distinction between 'common sense' and 'philosophy' and views philosophy as a deviation from 'common sense'. Most of us, for Rosenzweig, every now and again wonder at life as a whole but our wonder is 'finally enveloped in the stream of time', and 'it vanishes as naturally as it appeared'

(1999: 40). To wonder, we have to 'pause'. But we can't remain 'still'; we are 'adrift on the river Life'. We wonder at the world, but afterwards we go on living, and hence the 'numbness' caused by our wonder passes (ibid.).

The philosopher, however, 'is unwilling to accept the process of life and the passing of the numbness that wonder has brought', and 'he insists on a solution immediately.... He separates his experience of wonder from the continuous stream of life' (ibid.). In other words, he doesn't 'permit' his wonder to vanish into the flow of life but tries to continue viewing the world from above. In this process, the whole world becomes the object of a thinking subject that is the philosopher. From this stance the philosopher asks, 'What then actually is?'

Rosenzweig warns us that we all have such philosophical tendencies and that we all might 'trip over' ourselves and follow the trial of philosophy. 'No man is so healthy', Rosenzweig has it, 'as to be immune from an attack of this disease' (ibid.). In other words, every man's common sense can become crippled by the stroke of doing philosophy. He compares the philosopher who is struck by essential questions with a 'bedridden patient' who is unable to attend to the necessities of life. 'What happened to him?' Rosenzweig asks. Yesterday he was walking and enjoying fruits of the tree that lined his way, 'exchanging friendly words with comrades on his journey' (ibid.: 43). Then suddenly bewilderment seized him.

There is a striking affinity between Wittgenstein's and Rosenzweig's methods of providing a 'therapy' to 'cure' the sceptic. Wittgenstein's therapy consists of attention to the ordinary language and searching for the grammar of propositions in everyday life, and Rosenzweig suggests that we should return to 'common sense' and the ordinary. Moreover, both philosophers insist that their therapy cannot be forced. As Rosenzweig says, if we want the therapy 'to be effective, it must be part of living experience' (ibid.: 56). According to both philosophers, 'everyday life...cannot possibly be ignored; one cannot exist entirely in the sublime realm of theory, no matter how "essential" it may seem when compared to dull, tedious reality' (ibid.). We might be able to get onto 'slippery ice where there is no friction', and we might think this condition is 'ideal', but we should also bear in mind that 'just because of that, we are unable to walk'. If we want to walk, we need *friction* of ordinary reality. 'Back to the rough ground!' (Wittgenstein 1958: § 107).

Philosophers, in Rosenzweig's view, have sought an imaginary position, a standpoint outside the stream and flow of life. But our tendency to seek a view of the world and life from above, as if we are only spectators of and not participants in it, stems from something deeper than a mere search for essence; it is related to our 'fear to live':

> We have wrestled with the fear to live, with the desire to step outside of the current; now we may discover that reason's illness was merely an attempt to elude death. Man, chilled in the full current of life, sees, like that famous Indian Prince, death waiting for him. So he steps outside of life. If living means dying, he prefers not to live. (1999: 102)

A therapeutic philosophy such as Rosenzweig's can only save the sceptic from his paralysis, but it is 'unable to prevent his death'. Thus, teaching him to live is indeed equal to teaching him to move towards death. Anyone who 'withdraws from life' might think that he has renounced death. But by doing so he has only 'foregone life'. And 'death, instead of being avoided, closes from all sides and creeps into one's very heart, a petrified heart' (ibid.: 103). Therefore, the only way to restore life is to recognise the 'sovereignty of death' and yet to have the strength to meet the 'small things' that Goethe once called the 'demand of the day' (ibid.: 18), which reminds us of Marquard's 'little delaying factors' (1991: 44).

Whereas Rosenzweig talks of fear to live, Stanley Cavell talks of the sceptic's failure to 'acknowledge' and recognise the other in our daily interactions. According to Cavell, the truth of sceptical claims concerning the existence of the world and of the other minds cannot be denied, but not because we actually 'don't know', for example, that the external world exists or that someone is in pain. In everyday life, Cavell has it, our relation to other people and to the surrounding circumstances of our lives is not about 'knowing' or 'not knowing'. Rather, in everyday life we 'acknowledge' other people and the world. Our duty is not to provide arguments or theories, as Moore does, to prove the existence of other minds or the world but to acknowledge them in the way we live. And this acknowledgement is not something one can theorise. It is a way of seeing the world; it is a matter of aspect-seeing. In this view, the sceptic is suffering from a grave aspect-blindness towards the other's existence and not from an epistemic lacuna. Cavell follows Wittgenstein in asserting that scepticism might be the function of 'indifference' towards the existence of the other:

> The block to my vision of the other is not the other's body but my incapacity or unwillingness to interpret or to judge it accurately, to

draw the right connection. The suggestion is: I suffer a kind of blindness, but I avoid the issue by projecting this darkness upon the other. (1979: 369)

This kind of blindness is a case of 'soul-blindness' (ibid.: 378) or a kind of 'illiteracy' (ibid.: 369). The sceptic fails to acknowledge and to see an aspect of human life because he hasn't acquired the necessary 'education' for it:

Aspect-blindness is something in me failing to dawn. It is a fixation. In terms of the myth of reading the physiognomy, this would be thought of as a kind of illiteracy; a lack of education. (ibid.)

In our everyday life what is called for is not knowing the truth of scepticism but acquiring the education to acknowledge the presence of the world and the other. The problem of scepticism is that it doubts our knowledge of the world where what matters the most is the acknowledgement of it.

Rosenzweig compares scepticism to 'paralysis', and Cavell compares it to 'fixation', and by these comparisons they both try to highlight something crucial about scepticism: scepticism ultimately interrupts the course of everyday life.

As we see now, one can find overlapping similarities between the three philosophers I discussed in this section. They show, I think, what could be at stake when one philosophises. In Cavell's words, 'philosophers, being human beings, fail to recognise the bits of madness or emptiness they are subject to under the pressure of taking thought' (ibid.: 336). Whether scepticism has something to do with 'indifference' (Wittgenstein), 'fear to live' (Rosenzweig) or 'incapacity' to acknowledge the other (Cavell), there is a point that all three philosophers try to highlight, namely that there is a connection between cutting ourselves from the stream of life and leaning towards a sceptical attitude. This, in turn, shows in an important sense the difference between philosophical scepticism and existential doubts. We should keep in mind that not all types of doubts are philosophical. 'Sufferings of various sorts' (Wittgenstein 1980: 86) can lead one to a position where one ceases to trust the world. But, certainly, in this situation one's doubts are not concerned with the existence of the external world or other minds; rather, what is at stake is one's world-picture. If a person constantly fails in his relationships, no matter how much he tries, he might come to believe, like Virginia Woolf did, that human experiences are incommunicable, and that's the reason for human loneliness, but it is unlikely that he will doubt whether the other's pain is as genuine as his. Or, a war survivor might doubt whether the world is a safe place to bring a child into, but it is unlikely that he will become an antinatalist.

Conclusion

In this chapter, I focused on sceptical theories of life's meaning. I argued that Nagel's nihilism feeds on the assumption that we can step outside of life and see it from above. But what he fails to address is the implications of such a view on one's relation with others in life. If I have the capacity to realise that life as a whole is 'insignificant', then by the same token, I should have the capacity to believe the other's suffering is, after all, insignificant – a position that I find morally questionable. In our interactions with others what is called for is not reminding oneself that human life is absurd or insignificant but seeing a human being as a human being and cultivating the capacity to acknowledge the other. In Cavell's words, 'if it makes sense to speak of seeing human beings as human beings, then it makes sense to imagine that a human being may lack the capacity to see human beings as human beings' (1979: 378). What is called for is the cultivation of the capacity to see 'human beings as human beings'.

In Nagel's view, human beings can 'trip over' themselves and view life from above and then throw away the ladder with which they have climbed up to the ideal position. He acknowledges that one advantage of his view, as compared to the inflationary approaches, is that we return to ordinary life after encountering the absurd and seeing the world aright, but I argued that the idea of returning to the stream of life is incompatible with his suggestion of taking an ironic stance towards it.

There is a 'home' for the question of life's meaning. That is, no one asks it out of the blue. The question 'How shall one live?' emerges in the midst of life. When someone writes about his 'frustrated longing' (Wittgenstein 1980: 44), when a young girl feels that 'all the seas of the world tumbled about her heart' (Joyce [1914] 1995: 37) or when a believer confesses that 'Our hearts are restless till they find rest in Thee' (Augustine [398] 1966: 32), they all, in a sense, try to give a sense to their lives in their 'original homes'. In the next chapter, I propose an alternative, or a supplementary, approach to the current approaches in the literature. I mean that I want to move away from the 'metaphysical voice' (Cavell 1994: 59) and return to our 'clear and ordinary' voice (Wittgenstein 1975: § 347). I want to talk about an often missing voice. I want to talk about 'the human voice' (Cavell 1994: 58).

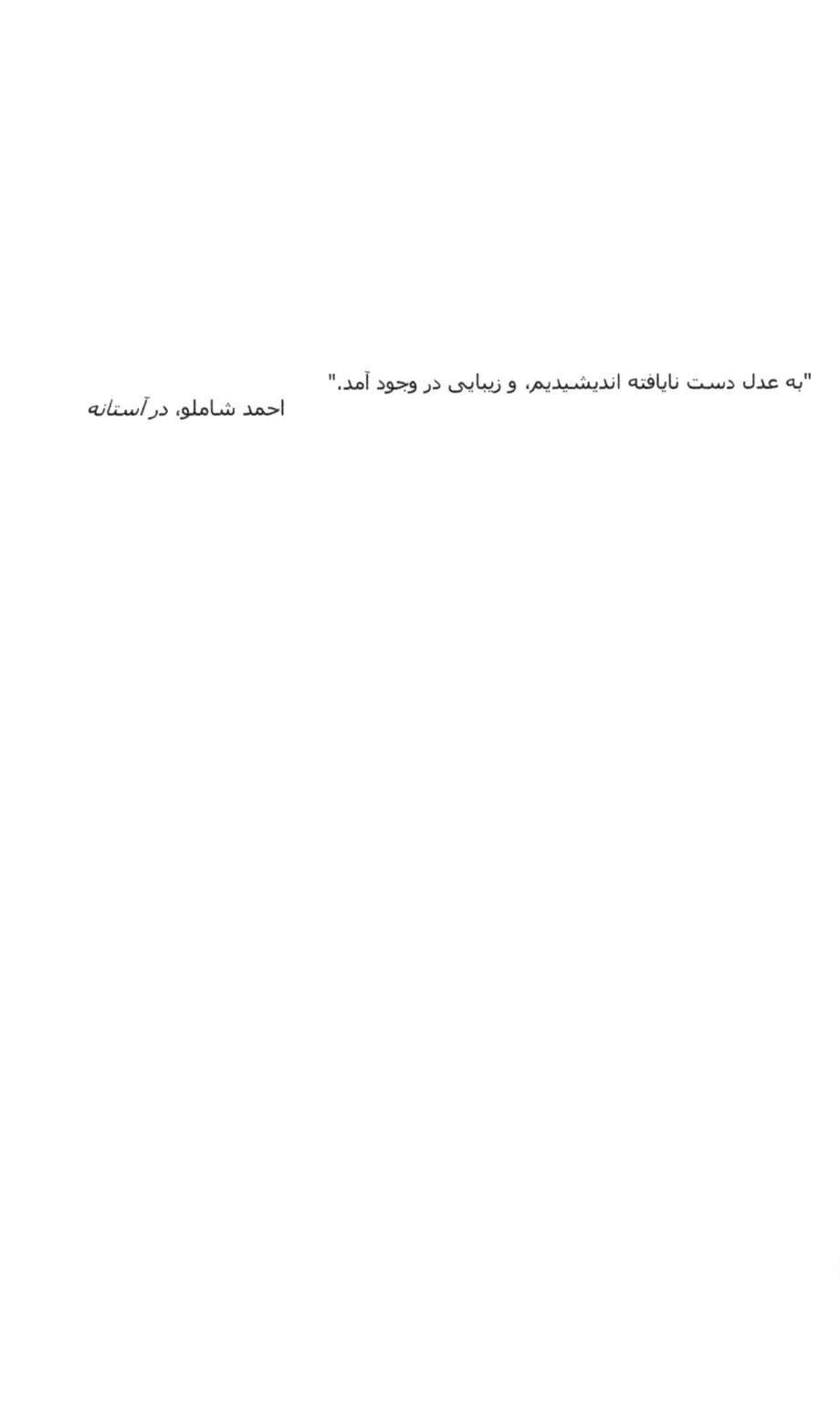

"به عدل دست نایافته اندیشیدیم، و زیبایی در وجود آمد."

احمد شاملو، در *آستانه*

6
The Human Voice: The Confessional Nature of Enquiring into Life's Meaning

'In the same town were two men, one rich, the other poor. The rich man had flocks and herds in great abundance; the poor man had nothing but a ewe lamb, only a single little one, which he had bought. He fostered it and it grew up with him and his children, eating his bread, drinking from his cup, sleeping in his arms; it was like a daughter to him. When a traveller came to stay, the rich man would not take anything from his own flock or herd to provide for the wayfarer who had come to him. Instead, he took the poor man's lamb and prepared that for his guest'.

— 2 Samuel, 12: 1–5

Introduction

My discussions so far, from the fact/value dichotomy to the implications of aspect-seeing for one's understanding of life's meaning, from the elusive boundaries between great and ordinary meaning to the fundamentality of our world-pictures in shaping our conception of life's meaning, have been variations of a single theme: the limits of theory. The common, underlying theme in previous chapters is a non-theoretical examination of the way we deal with the question of life's meaning. It is clear by now that the absence of Wittgenstein in the literature has to do with the nature of his philosophy. His philosophy does not offer a general theory of life's meaning. It only proposes alternative ways of approaching the question. In this regard, my approach towards the conventional theories of the meaning of life is negative in that I am not trying to refute those theories by providing yet another theory. Rather, the aim is to bring about a change in our 'way of looking at things' (Wittgenstein 1958: § 144).[1] In the literature on life's meaning we are often forced to look at the concept of a meaningful life in certain ways. But what I want to do is 'suggest...other ways of looking at it' (cf. Malcolm 1972: 50).

Thus, in this chapter my aim is to draw attention to a key aspect of our enquiry into the meaning of life which is often neglected in the literature. I argue that an alternative way of enquiring into life's meaning is to enquire about 'the grammar' of the meaning of life and not its 'essence', and I suggest that in our everyday life the grammar of the question of life's meaning is most often *confessional*. In the next section, I explain and defend the idea of confessionality as the grammar of our enquiry into life's meaning. I establish the differences between theoretical and confessional approaches by juxtaposing them and showing how the latter would lead to a more 'perspicuous representation' of the ways we experience the phenomenon of life's meaning and, arguably, of the way we understand the standard theories of life's meaning. Afterwards, I address possible objections to my view and try to clarify my position in the light of raised objections. Then, I will analyse two examples of a confessional approach: Joyce's description of the life of Mr Chandler in one of his short stories in *Dubliners* and Wittgenstein's 'private conversations'. Furthermore, I show that a confessional approach can provide a plausible account of the apparent inconsistency in Wittgenstein's reflections on the 'problem of life' in his diaries.

Grammar of the question

In *Philosophical Investigations*, Wittgenstein writes of the ordinary life as the benchmark with which we are to evaluate concepts and words. 'When philosophers use a word', Wittgenstein writes, 'and try to grasp the essence of the thing, one must always ask oneself: is the word ever actually used in this way in the language-game, which is its original home?' (1958: § 116). And the 'original home' of words is their 'everyday use' and not their 'metaphysical' applications. What Wittgenstein calls the 'grammar' of a word or a language-game, refers to the applications and uses of them in ordinary language and everyday life.

Imagine a game that you know well or play well and then try to describe it. Your description of the game is the grammar of the game (cf. Wittgenstein 1974: 40). Grammar determines the meaning of a word. Wittgenstein goes so far as to suggest that 'Essence is expressed by grammar' (1958: § 371). One of the main sources of our philosophical confusions, Wittgenstein has it, is that we don't have a clear view of the grammar of our language. The aim of doing philosophy, then, is to provide that clear view through conceptual analysis. Having a clear view of the grammar is significant because it makes us see how things are; 'Grammar tells what kind of object anything is. (Theology as grammar)' (1958: § 373).

I would like to suggest a corresponding shift from essence to grammar in our approach towards the issue of life's meaning. So, instead of asking 'what, if anything, makes life meaningful?' we ask, 'What is (are) the grammar(s) of the question of life's meaning?' That is, in what circumstances does our enquiry into the meaning of life arise? What do we talk about when we talk about the meaning of life in everyday life?

In what follows, I propose that in our everyday life the grammar of the question of life's meaning is most often *confessional*. I take confession here to be an *activity* in which one shares or describes one's understanding of life, whether it is directed at life as a whole or only an aspect of it.

But, how are we to understand the grammar of the question of life's meaning? The answer is straightforward: 'Look and see' how in everyday life people enquire about life's meaning. In other words, by a close attention to the contexts in which we contemplate life, we hope to gain insights into the grammar of the meaning of life. In this approach, we do not 'look for anything behind the phenomena', because we believe, in Goethe's words, 'they themselves are the theory'.[2] This, in turn, leads to yet another question: What do we observe when we examine the contexts in which we reflect on the meaning of life? In this chapter, I refer to various literary and philosophical works in search of an answer to this last question.

When I suggest that our enquiry into life's meaning is most often confessional, I am referring to neither a Christian nor a Freudian conception of confession. Freud, for example, talks of the 'curative effect' of confession and the way it 'brings to an end the operative force of the idea which was not abreacted in the first instance, by allowing its strangulated effect to find a way out through speech' (Freud & Breuer 1974: 68). Or, Erik Berggren refers to the 'cathartic element' involved in confession and suggests that this element has been the forcing power behind 'all literary confessions since Saint Augustine's *Confession*' (1975: 3). These views of confession take it to be a way of coming to terms with oneself (cf. Brown 1967: 165). That is, in both Christian and Freudian conceptions, one resolves a conflict either in the soul or in the psychological self.

Although in Christianity the word 'confession' is sometimes used as a statement of beliefs and not for admission of guilt, the latter plays a central role in the Christian sense of confession.[3] That is, in this view no one confesses that she has a great and prosperous life filled with love and surrounded by grandchildren. In the Christian tradition one confesses one's sins, frailty and shortcomings and thus submits oneself to the will of God. Wittgenstein, for example, alludes to this conception of confession when he writes,

> Anyone...who has the gift of opening his heart, rather than contracting it, accepts the means of salvation in his heart.... Someone who in this way penitently opens his heart to God in confession lays it open for other men too. In doing this he loses the dignity that goes with his personal prestige and becomes like a child. (1980: 46)

From this perspective, one might say, confession is akin to psychoanalysis.[4] Both would lead to the disappearance of the problem. But, by suggesting that contemplating the meaning of life is most often confessional, neither am I specifically concerned with the spiritual or psychological cathartic elements of our enquiry, nor am I suggesting that the aim of our confessional enquiry is to make the problem of life disappear.

One might raise a concern here and say that using religiously loaded concepts such as confession is risky because it imply that one is appealing to religious concepts without committing oneself to the metaphysical package attached to them. However, I think this can be avoided by clarification. I use this concept because in confession, taken religiously or nonreligiously, one narrates how things are with oneself. So, I am primarily concerned with confession as a *narrating activity*. One might contemplate and narrate the meaning of (one's) life in one's diaries, through an artwork or in the midst of everyday activities, like when the children are in bed and while you are turning the lights off one by one, you remember something of the past, or like when Goethe would think of summer seasons in his childhood and the way watching the sun set and 'neighbours wandering about in their gardens', 'children playing' and 'parties of friends enjoying themselves', would awake within him 'a feeling of solitude, and thence a vague sense of longing' ([1833] 1913: Book I). In these situations, one usually enters into a state of receptivity and introspection.

A confessional approach, properly understood, differs from a theoretical approach for various reasons. Firstly, in this approach the aim is not to prove something or to defend a theory against its rivals; rather, the aim is to describe or share an understanding of life, knowing that one cannot prove it and hoping that one will be believed based on 'trust' and 'charity'. Augustine's *Confessions* is an exemplary work in this regard:

> Charity believes all things – all things, that is, which are spoken by those who are joined as one in charity – and for this reason I, too, O Lord, make my confession aloud in the hearing of men. For although I cannot prove to them that my confessions are true, at least I shall be believed by those whose ears are opened to me by charity.
> ([398] 1966: Book X: III)

That is, the context of confession and the context of theory differ. Whereas the former, to use Augustine's words, relies on trust and 'charity', the latter is based on the authority and force of reasoning and argument. When, for example, Kurt Baier rejects God's purpose theory[5] by arguing that fulfilling the purpose of God reduces us to mere tools and that 'it is degrading for a man to be regarded as merely serving a purpose' (1957: 101), his argument takes its strength from the authority of reason. On the other hand, when a person confesses that she no longer sees the world religiously and 'the eternal silence of these infinite spaces' begins to terrify her, as it did Pascal once, she arrives at a different understanding of God's purpose. That is, they arrive at the same conclusion from two different routes. The point is that in the course of our lives we have these confessional experiences and awareness of meaning arises from them. It appears that some experiences in life force a picture of the world upon us, and we *narrate* it. It emerges from within; we do not think of proving it. Put differently, I submit, no confessional approach towards the meaning of life can be apologetic. 'But man exists in this world, where things break, slide about, cause every imaginable mischief. And of course he is one such thing himself' (Wittgenstein 1980: 71). Things break in this world: bicycles, bones, branches, bonds and wings, among others; and it is in these contexts that people think of the meaning of life. Or, it is in the context of a family, a reunion, a healing wound, 'an understanding heart',[6] a commitment, an open arm and an open door that people think of the world they grew up in and its meaning.[7] That is, *the act of life forces meaning upon us*.

Wittgenstein writes, 'Children do not learn that books exist, that armchairs exist, etc. etc., – they learn to fetch books, sit in armchairs, etc. etc.' (1975: § 476). By the same token, I suggest, we don't learn the meaning of life in theory; we live, and within the act of living, meaning emerges.[8] In James Joyce's short story 'Two Gallants', he describes the lives of two young men on the streets of Dublin, one of whom thinks about his life:

> He was tired of knocking about, of pulling the devil by the tail, of shifts and intrigues. He would be thirty-one in November. Would he never get a good job? Would he never have a home of his own? He thought how pleasant it would be to have a warm fire to sit by and a good dinner to sit down to. He had walked the streets long enough with friends and with girls. He knew what those friends were worth: he knew the girls too. Experience had embittered his heart against the world. ([1914] 1995: 53)

Lenehan is contemplating his life, and the story describes where he stands in life. He is completely aware of 'his own poverty of purse and spirit' (ibid.). The way Joyce presents Lenehan's contemplations on Lenehan's life is akin to the way most of us think of our lives, namely through a *dialogue* with ourselves. Sometimes our contemplation, to use Cavell's words, is a dialogue between the 'voice of temptation' and the 'voice of correctness' (1976: 71). While Lenehan realises that experience has 'embittered his heart against the world' (voice of correctness), he still fancies he 'might yet be able to settle down in some snug corner and live happily if he could only come across some good simple-minded girl with a little of the ready' (voice of temptation) ([1914] 1995: 53). We think of a whole range of different things, such as memories and experiences: these are the materials with which, for which, we contemplate life. 'One by one,' Joyce writes at the end of 'The Dead', 'they were all becoming shades. Better pass boldly into that other world, in the full glory of some passion, than fade and wither dismally with age' (ibid.: 213). These remarks, as they stand in the context of a specific life, do not need any justification, because they are not meant to be philosophical claims about life. The grounds of these remarks are in the lives vividly described by Joyce, which we read with 'charity'. When Mr Duffy in another Joyce's stories felt that 'he was outcast from life's feast' (ibid.: 109), we understand his point easily as if we have lived it with him. Anyone who thinks these remarks are metaphorical and artistic and, thus, devoid of any truth-value is among those 'people ... [who] think that scientists exist to instruct them, poets, musicians etc., to give them pleasure. The idea that these have something to teach them – That does not occur to them' (Wittgenstein 1980: 36).

Thus far, I have discussed three aspects of a confessional approach towards the meaning of life, namely description instead of explanation, trusting instead of reasoning and narrating instead of claiming. Interestingly, these three elements shape, to a large extent, the later Wittgenstein's conception and way of doing philosophy. That is, the confessional method, I think, informs much about Wittgenstein's ideal way of doing philosophy.

> And we may not advance any kind of theory. There must not be anything hypothetical in our considerations. We must do away with all *explanation*, and description alone must take its place. And this description gets its light, that is to say, its purpose, from the philosophical problems. (1958: § 109)[9]

A number of philosophers have addressed the affinity between *Philosophical Investigations* and the confessional tradition.[10] What is common in these readings is that they take confession to be a matter of describing and sharing one's way of life. In Thompson's reading of Cavell's reading of Wittgenstein, 'in talking about ordinary language, in talking about what we say, I am inevitably saying something about myself, about what I say' (2000: 3). Likewise, Rowe suggests, 'a confession is not...a work of reasoning, but of memory, self-scrutiny and interpretation' (1994: 328), and this is what *Investigations* is about. The purpose of confession is not to justify one's belief but to describe one's own particular way of seeing the world. In Cavell's words,

> In confessing you do not explain and justify, but describe how it is with you. And confession, unlike dogma, is not to be believed but tested, and accepted or rejected. Nor is it the occasion for accusation, except of yourself, and, by implication, those who find themselves in you. There is exhortation...not to belief, but to self-scrutiny. (1976: 71)

The grammar of confession, in this view, is to 'describe' one's deeds and one's beliefs, and the grammar of the question of life's meaning is confessional because we describe how things are with us. In this line of enquiry my concern is 'to speak to your whole being, and to write from mine' (Nozick 1989: 17). The confessional method presents us with a '*portrait*, not a theory' of life's meaning (ibid.: 12), and as a result we arrive at an understanding of life which is different from what we arrive at by the aid of theoretical enquiry.

Furthermore, by its attention to the details of a life, by its emphasis on description instead of explanation and by its narrating instead of claiming, a confessional approach bears a strong resemblance to the methods of enquiry in literary works, exemplified in the works of Tolstoy, Dostoyevsky, Proust and Henry James, among many others. In *Love's Knowledge*, Martha Nussbaum argues that for a more in-depth understanding of moral life, literature can be of significant help since it familiarises us with the complexities involved in a moral situation. Some moral truths, Nussbaum has it, consist of subtleties and complications which 'the plainness of traditional moral philosophy lacks the power to express' and which literature can express (1990: 142). Literature can provide us with a different way of approaching the complexities of life. In literary works, we examine the surrounding circumstances of a life not with a set of pre-established principles but with an unadulterated look to see a 'complexity, a many-sidedness, a temporally evolving plurality' that is often missing in 'explicit theories' (ibid.: 283).[11] Likewise, the confessional approach, exemplified in the narrative contemplations of Augustine, Goethe, Tolstoy, John Stuart Mill, Dostoyevsky, Wittgenstein, Nozick, and so on can show us aspects of human life which are absent in the conventional theories of life's meaning. In confession we see a life; we don't speculate about it. In confession we arrive at a knowledge of the human heart which cannot possibly be acquired in the speculative study of philosophers. A confessional literature can deepen our understanding of the ways the phenomenon of life's meaning is experienced in everyday life – it can show how the phenomenon of life and the phenomenon of meaning are intertwined.[12] For example, in Tolstoy's works, our understanding of people's conception of life's meaning is arrived at the background of a detailed description of their lives. As Alice Crary notes, 'Tolstoy repeatedly suggests that there is a kind of understanding of human life that neither comes in the form of nor is reducible to knowledge of plain doctrines' (2009: 154). The aim of a confessional approach is precisely to gain access to this kind of understanding of the human life.

One might raise another concern here and rightly suggest that a theoretical work is categorically different from a literary one, and preferring one over the other doesn't undermine the merits each work has. I agree; the scope of these two approaches are different. But I am not claiming that one should be overruled in favour of the other. Instead, I am more interested in exploring how these two different approaches can benefit from each other. Let me elaborate this in detail by discussing a theory of life's meaning. James C. Klagge in his paper 'From the Meaning of

Life to a Meaningful Life' suggests that meaningful lives consist of 'three normative conditions', which are as follows:

1. 'Enough activities must be engaged in for their own sake, or as an ends in themselves'.
2. 'The life must make enough contribution to something outside of itself'.
3. 'The life must have enough intentional structure' (1985: 7–8).

Klagge's approach is minimalist in that his work enquires about the minimum positive conditions a life should have in order to be considered meaningful. One advantage of this position is that it only tries to establish a broad framework within which a meaningful life is usually acquired. The first condition refers to activities we undertake because we are subjectively interested in them and not because they are means to something else. The second condition refers to the importance of involvement in activities that have some value beyond self-interest. And the third condition refers to the idea that some degree of autonomy is necessary in order to have a meaningful life. As we will see shortly, this view bears some resemblance to Susan Wolf's theory of life's meaning. According to Klagge, these three conditions are the 'necessary' and 'sufficient' conditions for a meaningful life. These conditions are presented in a 'vague' manner to cover a wide range of lives because what people consider as 'enough' in the above conditions varies. An implication of this theory is that many lives can be meaningful. He then applies his theory to several examples and tries to see whether his theory can *explain* why they are meaningless. For example, a sacrificing mother who gets no joy from her life may fail to satisfy the first condition. The child of a doctor who goes to college and becomes a doctor like his father without giving a thought whether this is the life he wants may fail to meet the third condition because his life's plan is not intentional and voluntary.

Let us focus on the first example, the sacrificing mother, to see how a theoretical approach can benefit from a confessional approach. What do we know about her, except knowing that she doesn't enjoy her life and that she puts her family first? In this example, the background against which she chooses, or happens, to be a sacrificing mother is not addressed. One might wonder how a person can sacrifice her needs and preferences for the sake of someone else and yet be 'pleased' with herself about it.[13] But a perspicuous representation of her life might bring about an understanding 'which consists precisely in the fact that we see the connections' between her sacrifices and her life as a whole (Wittgenstein 1996: 89). That is, we arrive at a different understanding of Klagge's theory upon attention to the particularity of mother's life. In this case, the main concern in a confessional approach would be to find the 'connecting links' between the mother's self-sacrifice and her life. A confessional approach does not dispute Klagge's insightful theory but only asks what this theory can tell us about the *particular* aspects of a life. We need the particular aspects of a life to understand clearly the meaning of that life. Wouldn't it make a difference if we knew that the mother is doing so because she wants to compensate for her shortcomings in the past? Wouldn't it be different if we knew that she does so because her husband is in war and she has to keep the family together? In a theoretical approach, the distinctive particularity of a life is not of central significance because the aim is to find the universal condition(s) of the meaningful lives.

We might see the difference between a confessional and a theoretical approach in a remark Wittgenstein once made to his sister Hermine. In a conversation, she expresses her inability to understand why a person such as Wittgenstein, who is talented in philosophy, would prefer to work as a teacher or a gardener rather than a philosophy professor. As she recalls, 'Wittgenstein replied with an analogy that reduced me to silence. He said, "You remind me of somebody who is looking out through a closed window and cannot explain to himself the strange movements of a passer-by. He cannot tell what kind of storm is raging out there or that this person might only be managing with difficulty to stay on his feet". Then I understood the state of mind he was in' (Wittgenstein 1984: 4). Hermine was of the *opinion* that her brother had exceptional talents in philosophy, and that anyone who is so, should naturally pursue a philosophical career so as to flourish this talent. But Wittgenstein's analogy shows the difference between two ways of appraising a human life, a view that is attentive to the particularity of a life and a view that is detached from it. I suggest that any theoretical perspective probably runs the risk of neglecting the storms that are raging out in the particularity of every person's life. Theorists of life's meaning in the examples they offer see ordinary people through a closed window and conclude that they meet or do not meet the requirements of a meaningful life, but once, upon close attention to the details of their lives, more defining aspects are revealed, a different understanding of their lives might emerge as well.

A confessional approach accommodates precisely those aspects that a theoretical approach, in virtue of its abstractions, has to leave aside. That is, in this approach the surrounding circumstances of a life are crucial in determining the meaningfulness of that life or the lack thereof. In other words, the surrounding circumstances of one's life provide what Wittgenstein calls 'imponderable evidence'. As he writes,

> Imponderable evidence includes subtleties of glance, of gesture, of tone. I may recognise a genuine loving look, distinguish it from a pretended one (and here there can, of course, be a 'ponderable' confirmation of my judgment). But I may be quite incapable of describing the difference. And this is not because the languages I know have no words for it. (1958: 228)

Think of this: What do you see when you see hypocrisy or bravery in someone's face, and how could you prove it? Wittgenstein wants to know if there is 'such a thing as expert judgement about genuineness' of our behaviours, and he suggests that such knowledge can only be based on imponderable evidence. But is it possible to learn this knowledge? 'Yes; some can'. However, not 'by taking a course in it, but through "*experience*"' (ibid.: 227).

I would like to suggest that a confessional approach, in virtue of accommodating the particular aspects of a life, is more likely to provide us with 'imponderable evidence' for our judgement of the life in question. It sheds light precisely on those aspects of a life that are crucial in our judgement of the life in question. Here is an example: think of the life of a person who is compulsively addicted to gambling to the extent that he pawns the jewellery of his pregnant wife. Most of us tend to characterise this person's life as anything but meaningful. In fact, we might characterise it as what Metz aptly calls 'anti-matter', those aspects of one's life that are not only meaningless but also disvaluable (2013: 64).

But here is some more information that might change our way of looking at the gambler's way of life. This person is not fictional. His name was Feodor Dostoyevsky, and he did exactly this in 1867, the same year he wrote *The Idiot*.[14] Now, one might suggest that Dostoyevsky's life was a life of anti-matter to the extent that he wasted it on gambling and other destructive behaviours. But these kinds of divisions are misleading. When we appraise people's lives, as Murdoch aptly noted, we consider their 'total vision of life', the 'texture' of their beings (1997: 80–81), and this texture acts like an imponderable evidence that is shown in the subtleties of their behaviour – that is, in 'their mode of speech or silence, their choice of words, their assessment of others, their conception of their own lives' (ibid.). Dostoyevsky was Dostoyevsky *all the way down*; the same person who wrote *The Gambler* was a gambler. I wonder how someone can write so meticulously on gamblers' unconscious desire for losing and for self-annihilation without having gone through these kinds of experiences. In everyday life, we do not have a segregating view of people's lives; that is, we view their lives holistically, and we consider their total vision of life. We do not ask, for example, whether Dostoyevsky's life was meaningful when he was living with illiterate criminals in Siberia. It was the coldness of Siberia, the heat of gambling, the fragility of faith and the mightiness of 'eternal questions' that made Dostoyevsky who he was and that led him to his total vision of life, portrayed in his works. I agree with Metz. Anti-matter does exist. But by attention to the particularity of Dostoyevsky's life, I also see anti-matter in his life from a more informed perspective. It might dawn on us, then, that maybe it was only because of his struggle with anti-matter that he was able to explore the darkest nooks and crannies of the human heart in his individual search for what truly matters.

Objections and clarifications

So much for the difference between the confessional and the theoretical approaches towards the question of life's meaning. In this section, I address some of the objections against the former for further clarification of my suggestion. Firstly, one might object, if the grammar of the question of life's meaning is confessional, then it implies that all sorts of people can claim that they describe their way of living in their works. Yellow pages write about the meaning of life; movie stars feel entitled to lecture people about the meaning of life; people write 'silly books' (Wolf 2010: 10) on the meaning of life, which simplify the meaning of life for lay people (Positive thinking, power of love, and the likes), and none of these have to do with a revealing approach towards the question of life's meaning.

This is a bad comparison. A confessional approach doesn't offer a shortcut to happiness. It is not about a narcissistic celebration of ego and advertising a strategy to achieve a sense of happiness and well-being, which, according to these works, are often easily obtainable. Moreover, what a person claims is not as important as the relation between his claim and the life he is living. That is, in a confessional approach we see a self-examination of a life and, obviously, not everyone who writes about himself provides the audience with a revealing understanding of life's meaning.

The next objection questions the very distinction I make, claiming it to be dubious and that, just like theorists of life's meaning, I am also putting forward a theory about the meaning of life, and to that extent my confessional approach is an instance of a theoretical approach, too. One might also say, I have been contemplating the meaning of life the whole time without confessing anything, and thus, if I can do that, so can philosophers. Furthermore, while in a theoretical approach one should provide reasons and arguments for one's claims, a confessional approach is concerned with style and rhetoric, and neither the philosopher nor the artist needs to imitate the other. Therefore, a philosophical work on the meaning of life does not need to be confessional-literary. It enquires about the 'conditions' or the common element(s) between all meaningful lives; it is an enquiry about the 'universal' not the 'particular'.

In response, I would suggest that philosophy itself can lead us to the realisation that a confessional approach is more revealing than a mere theoretical approach in understanding a life. The very philosophy which suggests that the particular is of importance in our understanding of human lives would suggest that we would have a more perspicuous picture of the phenomenon of life's meaning if we were to take a confessional approach towards it. What separates a confessional approach from a theoretical approach is defined by the emphasis of the former on the particular. And these two approaches are different in that while a theoretical approach tries to set forth a theory to capture the essential elements of a meaningful life, a confessional approach does not have a theory of its own to refute other theories. It does not compete with other theories; it doesn't *deny* their significance either. It only tries to understand their applications in everyday life. Therefore, and concerning the theoretical aspect of the confessional approach, I provide a meta-theory about ways of approaching the question of life's meaning.

One might point out that a confessional approach doesn't add anything to our knowledge of the meaning of life, whereas the conventional theories of life's meaning strive to provide insights into the common elements between all the particular meaningful lives. For example, consider values such as benevolence, creativity and justice. Many people's lives are meaningful in virtue of orienting their lives towards these values. And this observation itself can be the foundation of a very plausible theory of life's meaning which is not confessional at all. In addition, if we agree that there are some meaningful lives, then the enquiry should focus on finding the underlying element(s) between them. We want to know in virtue of what, if anything, we consider the lives of some people more meaningful than others. A confessional approach, however, remains silent about this and doesn't address the whole story of our enquiry.

In response, I would suggest that attention to the particularity of a person's life gives sense to rather lifeless concepts. If at least one of the main purposes of enquiring into life's meaning is to get to know oneself, then why should we drive our attention away from the particular lives as they are lived? A confessional approach emphasises the particular and takes our quest for the meaning of life to be, in Matthew Arnold's words, 'a dialogue of the mind with itself' in the stream of life (1987: 654). Whereas the aim of a theoretical approach is to explain the meaning of life and provide a systematic account of it (affirmatively or negatively), the aim of a confessional approach is clarity; clarity in understanding one's life is an end in itself. The aim is not to build a theory but to have a clear view of it. In a confessional approach, 'clarity, perspicuity, are valuable in themselves'. We are not 'interested in constructing a building, so much as in having a perspicuous view of the foundations of possible buildings' (Wittgenstein 1980: 7). From this perspective, a confessional approach is not a rival to a theoretical approach; they can benefit from each other. They can be allies. Theory needs confession as a faithful ally and vice versa. A good theory confesses something fundamental about the human life.

A confessional method of describing one's life leads to a knowledge of human life that is usually different from that of a general theoretical approach. It 'leads to a piece of knowledge in life outside the laboratory' (Wittgenstein 2005: 95e), a knowledge that consists in 'seeing connections' *between* life and meaning. It tries to step 'outside the laboratory' to reach an understanding which is different from what a theoretical approach might provide. It aims at a 'holistic' understanding of life; it sees no harm in 'stepping outside the seminar room' for a while and reminding oneself that

> In our ordinary human life and experience, the characteristic way in which we normally achieve understanding within the domain of meaning, ... is not analytically but holistically: not by taking things apart but by reaching across and outwards. The significance of thoughts and desires and beliefs and intentions is typically revealed when they are located within a wider network, connecting up, both synchronically and diachronically, with the current actions and the continuing lives both of individual human beings and of the groups of which they are necessarily a part. (Cottingham 2009b: 11)

In the next two sections, I discuss two different cases in which two different persons think of their lives. The first one, Mr Chandler, is a fictional character, and the second one is real. However, both cases provide enough material with which we can see the connection between their lives and the meanings ascribed to them. I also discuss briefly Susan Wolf's influential theory of life's meaning and show its limit when we apply it to Mr Chandler's life. These case studies, in turn, highlight the difference between a confessional and a theoretical approach in a more vivid way.

A case study: Little Chandler against the world

Joyce's stories in *Dubliners* are narrated mostly in third-person; that is, the protagonists' reflections on their lives are narrated by a third person who acts like an invisible observer of life. However, and this is what makes the stories pertinent to my discussion, Joyce furnishes us with enough imponderable evidence so that we see the connections between the protagonists' lives and the meanings ascribed to them. Their reflections usually come after a detailed description of their lives. Eveline, Mr Duffy, Lenehan, Little Chandler, Maria and Gabriel have different lives, but the similar element between them is the narrative tone of their voice, searching for the sense of their lives. In this section, I focus on only Mr Chandler in 'A Little Cloud'.

'Little Chandler', an ordinary journalist in Dublin, is about to meet an old friend, Ignatius Gallaher, who has just come from London. Before and after the meeting, Chandler reflects on the past and compares his own quiet life with the wild life of his friend. They meet in a restaurant and talk about many things, past and present. Gallaher enlightens him about life outside Ireland, and Chandler thinks of his own 'inartistic sober' life. Eight years have passed since the two old friends last met, and now Chandler doesn't have any eye-catching story to share except telling him that he is married and that he has a child. Being in such a position, he would rather be a listener in that 'brief space' that the two meet. He invites Gallaher to his place so that Gallaher meets his family, but Gallaher refuses the invitation because he is going to a 'card-party' with another fellow. Joyce narrates,

> The adventure of meeting Gallaher after eight years ... of listening to Gallaher's stories and of sharing for a brief space Gallaher's vagrant and triumphant life, upset the equipoise of his sensitive nature. He felt acutely the contrast between his own life and his friend's and

it seemed to him unjust.... He was sure that he could do something better than his friend had ever done... if he only got the chance. What was it that stood in his way? His unfortunate timidity he wished to vindicate himself in some way, to assert his manhood. He saw behind Gallaher's refusal of his invitation. Gallaher was only patronising him by his friendliness just as he was patronising Ireland by his visit. ([1914] 1995: 74–75)

They part, and Chandler returns home and forgets to buy a 'parcel of coffee', which upsets his wife. She decides to go out and buy a 'quarter of a pound of tea and two pounds of sugar'. She gives him the baby and warns him not to wake it up. With the baby in his arms Chandler walks around the room, looking at the photograph of his wife, and he realises that there is 'something mean' in her face, and he asks himself, 'Why had he married those eyes in the photograph?':

A dull resentment against his life awoke within him. Could he not escape from his little house? Was it too late for him to try to live bravely like Gallaher? Could he go to London? There was the furniture still to be paid for.... The child woke up and began to cry. He... tried to hush it: but it would not be hushed.... It was useless.... He couldn't do anything. The wailing of the child pierced the drum of his ear. It was useless, useless! He was a prisoner for life. His arms trembled with anger and suddenly bending to the child's face he shouted: 'Stop!' (ibid.: 77–78)

Chandler's reflections is set against the background of some imponderable evidence for the misery of a life. What gives life to his reflections is the details or what Wittgenstein calls 'fine shades of behaviour' (1958: 204): his excitement at going to a famous restaurant for the first time; his reservations when Gallaher talks to him; his sensitive nature that could be upset by a cigar and a glass of whiskey; his 'fragile' frame; his 'childish white teeth'; his naïvely curious questions, such as asking Gallaher 'is it true that Paris is so... immoral as they say?'; his 'timid insistence' that his friend will marry too if he finds the right girl, while Gallaher is boldly reminding him that 'When I go about a thing, I mean business'; the outburst of anger at his own little child and his remorseful tears afterwards; his alien wife and her 'thin tight lips'; and so on. In sum, we see Chandler's 'totality of vision', but if you ask us what we actually perceive, we might fail to articulate it. As Peter Lamarque and S. Haugom Olsen argue in their study, *Truth, Fiction, and Literature*, 'literary works can contribute to the development and understanding of the deepest, most revered of a culture's conceptions without advancing propositions, statements, or hypotheses about them' (1996: 22). In the *Dubliners*, likewise, we come to know what it is like to be a Dubliner in the 1910s; it can educate us to understand the moral life of a people. Mr Chandler's reflections and recollections 'model for us our attentions to details of our own lives, as we too seem sometimes to haunt the world, from within our reserves of loneliness' (Eldrige 2008: 146).

Wittgenstein writes, 'An inner process stands in need of outward criteria' (1958: § 580). Throughout Joyce's story there is a parallel between the 'inner process' and 'outward criteria', and the latter betray or reveal the former. We understand why Chandler feels he is a 'prisoner for life' because we are shown the prison; we have seen him inside the prison. Put differently, a theory of life's meaning is like a house; just because you manage to build one doesn't necessarily mean that someone is living there.[15] If we consider reflection upon the meaning of life as an inner process, then we all need 'outward criteria' to find a sense for our contemplations. A confessional approach acknowledges the interconnection between the two and aims at investigating the connecting links, whereas in a theoretical approach this connection is, at the best, of a secondary significance. This capacity to find the connecting link or, in Stephen Mulhall's words, 'this capacity for right judgement involves being able to make the right connections – to see a particular expression as a manifestation of a precise state of mind, to link that inner state with something in the situation to which that person is responding' (2001: 261).

Consider, for example, Susan Wolf's influential theory of meaning in life. According to Wolf, meaning in life is a matter of loving objects worthy of love and engaging with them in a positive way. What is distinctive in Wolf's theory is that 'it involves subjective and objective elements, suitably and inextricably linked' (2010: 9). In this view, 'meaning arises when subjective attraction meets objective attractiveness' (ibid.). Someone, for example, might be passionately interested in solving puzzles, but his subjective interest in puzzle solving does not meet the objective attractiveness's requirement, and, thus, his life would be of no meaning.

Now, as far as Wolf's theory is concerned, Chandler's life doesn't seem like an interesting case. Apparently, his life lacks the element of 'depth' and 'subjective attraction' (ibid.: 7). His life consists of a constant remembrance of his crippling situation, of the gap between what he needs and what he gains in actual life. That is, the element of 'love' or subjective attraction is missing in his life. So, it seems safe to say Chandler's life lacks meaning. But, one might ask, is that all there is to Mr Chandler's life? After all, Chandler has a 'poet's soul' and usually goes through a 'poetic mood'.[16] He is a constant observer of his inner life. As a habit, he usually tries to 'weigh his soul to see if it was a poet's soul. Melancholy was the dominant note of his temperament...but it was a melancholy tempered by recurrences of faith and resignation and simple joy' ([1914] 1995: 68). Chandler is subjectively interested in the life of art, which is of objective worth in Wolf's account. But we are still reluctant to call his life meaningful because it seems that there are more elements which play significant roles in our judgement than the mere roles of 'subjective attraction' and 'objective worth'. Chandler lives in an alien world, and he painstakingly realises that he is too timid to come out of his surrounding circumstances in Ireland. He is a loser, although he has a job and a family. He is an ordinary fellow, but he doesn't want to be one; he wants to be Gallaher; he wants to be extraordinary. He needs to be spoken to; he needs to be invited, to be heard, to be taken seriously. He wants to be at the centre of conversations at the parties and the bars where he mesmerises a crowd with his poetic insights. But his weak body, his weak voice and his weak demeanour don't allow him bold assertions. He thinks he doesn't exist. To put it in Henry James's words, 'He had perhaps not had more losses than most men, but he had counted his losses more' (1993: 2). In light of these details we might arrive at an understanding of his life that goes beyond meaningfulness/ meaninglessness categories. And even if we call his life 'empty' or 'meaningless', we do so not merely because his 'subjective attraction' does not meet an 'objective worth'.

Wolf acknowledges that in offering a conception of meaningfulness she doesn't want to insist that 'the term is always used in the same way' (2010: 8). But, Wolf writes, 'whether or not my idea of meaningfulness captures what others mean when they use the term, it is an idea of philosophical interest, for it is an idea of a significant way in which a life can be good' (ibid.). Ironically, based on Wolf's account, Gallaher's life meets all the requirements of a meaningful life. He is a 'brilliant' journalist at the 'London Press', a player who cherishes life. But it strikes me that we are more willing to call his life 'happy' or 'a life of pleasure' than meaningful.

The problem with Wolf's account, I think, is that it overlooks the significance of *attitude*. Gallaher's subjective attraction to journalism and the objective worth of it might confer meaning on his life, but what we see in the story is not only Gallaher the journalist – we see in the story also his condescending attitude, his outspokenness when he trivialises the things that matter to Chandler, his vulgarity, his 'fearless accent' and his refusal of a friendly invitation. In fact, Gallaher is not concerned about his life's meaning at all, and yet, in Wolf's account, the meaningfulness probably would go to the opportunistic and arrogant Gallaher and not to the melancholic Chandler who sincerely suffers to find the *sense* of his life, which is falling apart.[17]

In sum, Wolf provides a general account of the constitutive elements of a meaningful life. But, if we were to appraise Mr Chandler's life based on her account, we would see that it fails to address certain aspects of his life which I think are crucial in our understanding of it. On the other hand, by focusing on the complexities involved in Chandler's life, the totality of his vision and his mode of being, we arrive at an understanding of his life which is informed by the complexities of his texture of being. Chandler is a fragile poet who knows in his heart that life is short, but for some reason the mortgage never ends. In spite of this, and by virtue of our awareness of the nature of his introspection, we can also hope that at the end of his sufferings, he might come to a sense of reconciliation and peace with the world. One day he might come to terms with his agony, and bit by bit life might introduce him to deeper poetic horizons, which in themselves carry the seeds of appreciation and confidence to his life. And then we might find him one day standing behind a window, smiling, as he just sees the glimpse of a sudden poetic notion arriving at him. And then he might whisper, 'We thought of unfulfilled justice, and beauty came into existence'. In that moment his solid voice will find a place for him in the world.

Wittgenstein's private conversations

Wittgenstein once wrote in his diaries that nearly all his writings are 'private conversations' with himself: 'Things that I say to myself tête-á-tête' (1980: 77). Throughout his philosophical career, the medium to record these private conversations was mainly his diaries.[18] In this section, I focus on some of Wittgenstein's notes on the 'problem of life' and his contemplations on his own moral life. The aim in this section is not to defend or to justify his statements. I view them as another case study pertinent to what I have discussed so far in this chapter. My aim is to say by the end of this section that this is how a person thought of his life. It is also important to bear in mind that in his diaries Wittgenstein doesn't talk about 'the meaning of life' or 'meaningful life'. Rather, he is more concerned with the 'problem of life' or 'sense of life', but that doesn't make these notes irrelevant to my discussion, as I believe they shed light, in an important sense, on the varieties of dealing with the question of life's meaning or 'how shall one live?' More importantly, as I will argue shortly, they reveal the intimate connection between the question of morality and the question of meaningfulness in everyday life.

One recurrent theme in Wittgenstein's diaries is the relation between one's way of living and the meaning ascribed to it. Even though he is more preoccupied with a religious solution to the problem of life and its implications for his life, his contemplations are an instance of a human's struggle to give a sense to his life and, thus, pertinent to the our discussion.[19] Wittgenstein writes,

> *A religious question is either a question of life or it is (empty) chatter, this language-game – one could say – gets played only with questions of life. Much like the word 'ouch' does not have any meaning – except as a scream of pain. I want to say: if eternal bliss means nothing for my life, my way of life,* then I don't have to rack my brain about it; if I am to rightfully think about it, then what I think must stand in a precise relation to my life. (2003: 211)

In other words, religious utterances and tendencies get their meanings from their connections to the believer's life. As James Conant puts it, 'whether someone's belief is (properly termed) religious will show up in the way it informs the entire character of that individual's life' (1995: 266). The life of the believer is the key to understanding his belief.[20] A believer might seem to provide arguments for her beliefs, but in fact she is offering a 'solution' to the problem of life as she lives it. This shows the connection between one's understanding of the meaning of life and its effects on one's way of living: 'if one lives differently, one speaks differently. With a new life one learns new language-games (2003: 169).

Note that Wittgenstein is not concerned with incoherence of the arguments for religious claims. He focuses on only their bearings on the lives of the believers and on himself. His 'struggle' and interest in moral and religious issues is only to the extent that they have a bearing on his own life. He would reject, for example, the traditional solutions to the problem of life, but he asks about the implications of this for his own life. In his words, 'I may well reject the Christian solution to the problem of life (salvation, resurrection, judgement, hell, heaven), but this does not solve the problem of my life, for I am not good and not happy. I am not saved' (2003: 169). His reflection on his relation to the religious solution goes like this: There is a religious solution to the problem of life. I may reject this solution but this does not change the fact that the problem of my life is still unsolved. My wisdom cannot save me: 'If I am to be REALLY saved – what I need is *certainty* – not wisdom, dreams or speculation – and this certainty is faith' (1980: 33).

A. M. S. Christensen argues, 'the fact that Wittgenstein thinks the problem of life could be given a Christian solution shows that he sees an intimate connection between the ethical and the religious' (2011: 209). In his diaries, both religious and ethical questions refer to a similar concern: the problem of life or how we are to live. That is, by asking religious or moral questions, one searches for a solution to the problem of one's own life. The Christian tradition offers a solution that he is unable to find his feet with:

> Let me confess this: After a very difficult day for me I kneeled during dinner today and prayed and suddenly said kneeling and looking up above: 'There is no one here.' That made me feel at ease as if I had been enlightened in an important matter. But what it really means I do not know yet. I feel relieved. But that does not mean, for example: I had previously been in error. (2003: 193)

He had not been in error with regard to his previous belief, because 'only an opinion can involve an error' (Wittgenstein 1996: 85). We are not in error when we wonder at the existence of the world. 'Was Augustine in error...when he called upon God on every page of the *Confessions*?' (ibid.: 82). We might be in error when we 'set forth a theory' about it (ibid.). When you realise that 'there is no one here', you don't state an opinion or a knowledge-claim; you express an attitude. And this attitude might remain with you: 'Now I often tell myself in doubtful times: "There is no one here" and look around' (2003: 207).

However, the striking realisation that no one is listening to his prayer doesn't stop him from 'buzz[ing] around the *New Testament*' like an 'insect' (ibid.: 177). His struggles with the Scriptures reminds me of the way Goethe 'constructed a Christianity' for his 'private use' ([1833] 1913: Part III, Book xv) because the love of the Scriptures could not be taken away from him. One might say, Wittgenstein's Christianity is also a Christianity constructed for a personal use. He sometimes accuses himself of not being 'serious' enough to deal with the problem of life. He does not want to brush aside a religious solution to the problem of his life just because he is of the opinion that it is incoherent. There is a strong urge to understand the language-game of belief because, as he wrote on another occasion, 'Only religion would have the power to destroy vanity and penetrate all the nooks and crannies' (1980: 48). That is, he needs to understand what it is in religion that changes one's whole way of being in the world. Consider the following:

> I believe: I understand that the state of mind of believing can make the human being blissful. For when people believe, *wholeheartedly* believe, that the perfect one has sacrificed himself for them, that he has therefore – from the beginning – reconciled them with God, so that from now on you shall simply live in a way that is worthy of this sacrifice, – then this must refine the whole person, elevate him to nobility, so to speak. I understand – I want to say – that this *is* a movement of the soul toward bliss. (2003: 227)

A believer would say someone has suffered for you, and this fact alone has to change the way you relate to that suffering; that is, you should 'change the way you live' (Wittgenstein 1980: 27). If I believe in providence, what effects would it have on my life? What would happen to my life if I knew that a human being had sacrificed his life for me? 'Mustn't this fact then be of "decisive significance" for you? I mean: mustn't it then have implications for your life, commit you to something? I mean: mustn't you enter into an ethical relation with him?' (2003: 223).

In all these remarks Wittgenstein is trying to find his own stance towards the Christian solution. In his approach, the bearings of a religious belief on one's way of life is more significant than its theological claims such as incarnation or providence. An alternative to this approach is to suggest that claims of theism cannot be verified or that these claims are irrational and should be discarded as metaphorical utterances, devoid of any truth-value.[21] In this approach it is against one's intellectual integrity to accept and believe the truth of something the existence of which cannot be rationally proved. But Wittgenstein doubts that a theological claim per se has the power to regulate one's whole life. Discarding a religious view does not necessarily amount to discarding 'a way of living, or a way of assessing life' (1980: 64).

Consider, for example, a religious text such as the New Testament. One might dispute it by questioning the authenticity of the text and asking how it is possible that God assigns four people to write about the life of his incarnated son and yet they write four different and even inconsistent texts. But refuting the Scripture in virtue of its inconsistency can undermine only its 'letter' and not its 'spirit'. Wittgenstein wonders, 'might we not say: it is important that this narrative should not be more than quite averagely historically plausible *just so* that this should not be taken as the essential, decisive thing? So that the *letter* should not be believed more strongly than is proper and the *spirit* may receive its due' (ibid.: 31). In other words, discarding the 'letter' of the New Testament does not destroy its spirit. Jesus of Nazareth, in this view, is not only a historical person; he is also the incarnated son of an idea: the possibility of hope – that is the spirit of Christianity. The spirit of a religion is its way of 'assessing life',[22] the solution that it offers to the problem of life. Christianity offers a solution by portraying a way of living in which the problem is solved; it presents a role model and says, 'Now, live like this, and the problem will be vanished!' However, the question is how one can adjust oneself to such a way of living:

> The horrible instant in an unblessed death must be the thought: 'Oh if only I had. ... Now it's too late.' Oh if only I had lived right! And the blessed instant must be: 'Now it is accomplished![23] – But how must one have lived in order to tell oneself this? I think there must be degrees here, too. *But, I myself, where am I? How far from the good and how close to the lower end!* (2003: 185)

Christianity offers a solution, and, Wittgenstein thinks, if he wants to accept it he has to change the way he lives: He might have doubts about everything but one thing cannot be doubted: 'That in order to live *right* I would have to live completely differently from what suits me' (ibid.). One might say, here Wittgenstein is searching for the dawning of an aspect on his life. He confesses his inability to see those aspects. In his diaries he looks, but he can't see those aspects:[24] 'In my soul there is winter (now) like all around me. Everything is snowed in, nothing turns green and blossoms. But I should therefore patiently await whether I am destined to see a spring' (ibid.: 205).

There is a single fundamental point, with far-reaching implications, that we can take away from these intensely idiosyncratic notes. They show that whether one is a believer or a nonbeliever, whether one is objectivist or subjectivist, whether one is indifferent to the problem of life or arrested by it, whether one is Chandler or Gallaher, whether one is a stranger in the world or at home with it, whether you are a bibliomaniac or graduated from the streets, whether you are familiar with the concept of loss or yet to be touched by it, whether you get moved by the silence of the wind that shakes the barley in the open or not, there is a question to be faced: 'How do you go through this life?' (ibid.: 217). What we can take away from Wittgenstein's diaries is that scrutinising the '*letter*' of the meaning of life, enquiring about the conditions of a meaningful life, is probably of little help when we go through life. There are promises to be kept out there, hands to be extended, glances to be exchanged, children to be born, silences to be heard, tables of brotherhood to be sat on, conversations to be animated, mouths to be fed, stars to be stared at and then to be imploded; there are snows to be fallen upon the dead and the living; there are words to be struck 'on the keyboard of imagination', and then to be loaded with life, and then to be hurled 'into the darkness of hearts', and then to be waited for an echo no matter how faint or mighty; there are hard works to be done always not by 'scheming speculators' but by men and women of 'endurance'[25]; and there will be feelings (care, confidence and the like) by the people, for the people; and there you are, the reader of these words, who walk on this third planet of the sun and somewhere down the line you begin to ask questions. These questions, and the answers given to them, are the manifestations of a long and involved education the lessons of which could be called 'lessons of life'.[26]

The other important element is what Christensen calls the essential link between 'self-assessment and normative obligation' (2011: 212). Wittgenstein's ethical reflections on the solutions to the problem of life call for a reflection on his own position with regard to these solutions. There are some demands that he needs to meet: 'I will either meet the demand or suffer from not meeting it, for I cannot prescribe it to myself and not suffer from not living up to it' (2003: 175). Thus, an ethical self-assessment has to lead to an ethical self-improvement. His reflections involve two normative demands. The first demand 'arises because we in ethical reflection must attempt to achieve a true view of our place in the world.... The second demand embedded in Wittgenstein's view of ethical reflection is the simple requirement to try to do better' in life (Christensen 2011: 212). Therefore, to contemplate the meaning of life, in Wittgenstein's diaries, is to contemplate the ways of moral improvement. Whereas in the literature a distinction is made between morality and meaningfulness (Metz 2002; Frankfurt 2004; Wolf 2010), Wittgenstein's reflections portray a life in which living morally and living meaningfully are intertwined.[27] His moral life, however, is not concerned with conventional theories of morality; it is concerned only with the ideals of authenticity and living without vanity.[28]

Before closing this chapter, let me briefly discuss the relation between morality and meaningfulness in the literature in order to highlight the difference between Wittgenstein's view of the relation between the two and that of most scholars in the literature. There are opposing views about the relation between morality and meaningfulness. Supernaturalists believe that a meaningful life is ultimately a moral life, and for there to be an objective foundation for morality, we need God to secure the objectivity, necessity and universality of morality and, consequently, meaningfulness of life (Cottingham 2003).

On the other hand, subjectivists and objectivists often attack this view for different reasons. For example, Frankfurt claims that 'morality can provide at most only a severely limited and insufficient answer to the question of how a person should live' (2004: 7). According to Frankfurt, normativity is not limited to morality or 'self-interest'. 'There are modes of normativity', Frankfurt claims, 'that are quite properly compelling but that are grounded neither in moral nor in egoistic considerations' (ibid.: 8).

Sympathetic to Cottingham's view of the necessity of having an objective morality for a meaningful life, Metz agrees that 'at least a necessary condition of a meaningful life is the existence of a suitably non-arbitrary moral system' (2013: 85). However, Metz has it, a moral life is only one source of a meaningful life among others. One might think of searching for 'the true' and 'the beautiful' as other compelling sources of a meaningful life. Wolf also shares a similar idea and suggests that at least some of what we do and pursue in life is not guided by our moral concerns (2010: 3). Enjoying cooking, friendly gatherings, sewing a scarf for one's child or learning Russian to read Dostoyevsky in his native language are not typically considered to be examples of moral actions, and yet they can plausibly contribute more or less to the meaningfulness of one's life. These are what we might do because we are attracted to them and judge them to merit attraction. They make us feel good and yet make our lives meaningful; that is, our subjective attraction to them meets the objective worth of doing them, unlike activities such as caring about a goldfish, typing Tolstoy's *War and Peace*, and solving Sudoku, which are devoid of objective value and worth (2010: 16).

I think clarifying the term 'morality' might be of help here. Traditionally, morality is considered to be something that has to do with our actions with regard to others. Morality, Frankfurt suggests, 'is more particularly concerned with how our attitudes and our actions should take into account the needs the desires, and the entitlement of other people' (2004: 7). Frankfurt and others treat morality and meaningfulness as if there is a clear distinguishing line between the two. But it appears that sometimes one might do something out of the reasons of morality and at other times do the same thing out of reasons of meaningfulness. In other words, it is not written in the face of our actions whether they are meaning-conferring or moral. Instead, our judgements about the nature of our actions are linked to the surrounding circumstances in which those actions are undertaken. Think of the following examples: a man who buys flowers for his wife might do this out of considering the needs of another person, but his action might as well be regulated by reasons of love. He has found a way to make her smile. Now, is buying flowers a moral or non-moral action? Is having a cheerful sense of humour and making people enjoy your company moral or non-moral? The answers to these questions depends on the context. Flowers that are bought for peace offering after an altercation do not smell the same as the ones that are bought because they match with the Persian carpet in the living room. A physicist's life, according to those who defend non-moral meaningfulness, would be meaningful in virtue of his intellectual engagement with 'projects of worth'. But, when we think of Robert Oppenheimer we also think of the Manhattan Project and his 'necessary evil' and not *merely* his intellectual activity during the 1930s.

It seems that one major problem of most accounts of the relation between morality and meaningfulness is that they offer, and appeal to, what I call a 'static picture of life'. Scholars such as Frankfurt and Wolf come to believe that not everything that confers meaning on life is pursued out of concern for morality, and they refer to activities that are non-moral but meaningful (loving someone, creating artworks, friendship, reading, travel, healthy adventures, etc.). Take the example of reading as a non-moral meaning-conferring activity. For a desperate housewife or a prisoner, discovering Dostoyevsky and Tolstoy and engaging with their works could be of high significance; these works might give them fresh insights into the nature of life, and they might find reading them very fulfilling. Our prisoner might contemplate the life of Raskolnikov in *Crime and Punishment* and identify with him; Dostoyevsky might give him a reason to find his 'Sonia'. But for a person who believes 'from life one can extract many books, but from books, so little, so very little, life', reading probably wouldn't be as fulfilling as for our prisoner. An intellectual academic person might realise that the poverty of her writings says something about the poverty of how much she has lived and that she needs to leave the study for a while. That is, the background against which an action takes place can affect our judgement of its capacity to confer meaning on a person's life. This is where a confessional approach can play a central role.

A final point that needs to be discussed is the way we relate to, or use, the notion of 'meaningfulness' in our lives. As I said in the Introduction, for most scholars in the literature, the notion of 'meaningfulness' is established as a distinct category that can account for a good life. But it seems to me that this term is not used very often in our everyday life. I think there are specific circumstances in which the need to use the term 'meaningful' is raised. We tend to refer to terms and expressions such as 'good', 'fulfilling', 'dignified', 'respectful', 'great', 'significant' or even 'happy' while what we mean by them might be 'meaningful'. In fact, in many respects, the term 'meaningful' sounds like an archaic word in our everyday lives. We don't say 'look how meaningful his life is!' or 'look how meaningful their relationship is!' But, that doesn't mean we never refer to 'meaningfulness' or 'meaninglessness' to describe our emotions or opinions. We do.

Let's imagine a person named R., who is sitting by the empty pool of his house on a Sunday afternoon. An old friend stops by and R., excited by the arrival of unexpected guest, opens up a conversation about his life. He talks about things he has achieved in his career: financial stability, independence and the like. He also talks about his wife, who is not happy around him, and his 'ungrateful' children, who have abandoned him, and then he says, 'There is nothing in my life that I'm proud of. My life is meaningless, and I don't know what to do about it'. Here, the more we know about R.'s life, the better we understand what he means when he says his life is meaningless. Would he consider his life to be meaningful if he had a more fulfilling relationship with his family? His life might have all the requirements of a meaningful life. He might be passionate about his job, and his job might add value to the world or might 'reduce some avoidable pain in the universe'. Yet upon close attention we might arrive at the conclusion that R. takes his life to be meaningless not because the conditions of meaningfulness are not obtained but because something more important is missing in his life. What if we find out that there is something wrong with, so to speak, his moral demeanour, his condescending attitude towards others and the way he thinks the head of the table is wherever he sits? Here talking about meaningfulness is shifting towards talking about morality because we find out the absence of meaning in R.'s life is actually the result of the absence of morality.

But, in due time, life might educate R. to values and attitudes that are not currently available to him. It might dawn on him one day that in life sometimes the door is short, and one has to be humble. He might learn one day from a book loaded with life or from life itself that 'Defect in manners is usually the defect of fine perceptions' (Emerson [1844] 1940: 392). He might learn to be patient. He might learn to 'open' his heart instead of 'contracting it' (Wittgenstein 1980: 46) and, by virtue of which, let people get close to him. He might learn one day that there is a difference between being straightforward and bold and being abrupt and rude, and he might learn how not to confuse the two. There is a hope here that life will smooth rough edges of his character. And if these things, along with many other things, happen, we might see R. years later on another Sunday afternoon by the same pool which is no longer empty, of the house that is animated with the human voice. 'Purged by suffering' (Cottingham 2005: 144), enlightened by endurance, he might look at his life with a sense of content and see something meaningful in it. In R.'s life, morality was the gateway to meaningfulness. It would be a grave mistake to separate the two here. They are intertwined.

A confessional approach, unlike a theoretical one, is mindful of the transitions and criss-crosses between morality and meaningfulness in a person's life and aims at providing a dynamic picture of it. In this approach, there is an acute awareness that 'the subtleties of a complex ethical situation', in Nussbaum's words, 'must be seized in a confrontation with the situation itself' (1990: 69). In virtue of such confrontation, we could arrive at a dynamic picture of life. A key feature of Wittgenstein's diaries is that here we are dealing with a dynamic portrayal of his life. We see Wittgenstein as a person and not merely as a philosopher; we see his fears, his struggles, his take on the events of the day, his openness to considering both the Christian solution to the problem of life and rejecting it, and so on. It is in virtue of these details that we can see the connection between morality and meaningfulness in his life. In light of my discussion of the relation between the two, now I am inclined to think meaningfulness and morality cannot be disjoined easily. In theory, we can separate them, but in life they are most often intertwined. Meaningfulness without morality is ultimately problematic. A life involved with merely pursuing meaning-conferring projects might look sophisticated, smart, progressive or sexy as it has been advertised nowadays (life of engaged commitments, busy schedule, cutting edge projects, multi-tasking, professionalism and casual flings on intercontinental business trips), but ultimately if we fail to recognise our interdependence with regard to others in our shared world, we might fail to the same extent to appreciate the significance of moral values of benevolence and care in transcending our lives to something beyond a life of subjective attraction to projects of objective worth.

In *Investigations*, Wittgenstein compared his work to 'a number of sketches of landscapes which were made in the course of these long and involved journeyings' (1958: viii). Likewise, his contemplations on the problem of life can be seen as various sketches of a landscape: a human life; a life in which there was a 'glorious sun' and a 'bad person' who couldn't help staring at it; a life in which values of modesty and 'living in agreement with the world' (1979a: 75) were equal and this identity had an 'absolute value'. He writes, 'God, what a blessing it is to be able to live without horrible problems!' (2003: 229). His reflections describe how a human being has dealt with the problem of life, but the *value* of those reflections, beyond its idiosyncratic nature, lies in the fact that they show how far an enduring soul can go down into 'the abyss in the human heart' (ibid.: 183) to discover the sources of its 'disquietudes'.

Into the abyss of life

On 16 June 1904, a young man and a young woman walked together through the suburb of Ringsend in Dublin. Eighteen years later the no longer young man published a novel, *Ulysses*, which was about the life of a Leopold Bloom in the course of an ordinary day, 16 June 1904.[29] Joyce's decision to set the events of the whole novel on this day was a unique way of confessing something about a shared life which began on that otherwise ordinary and obscure day. Joyce writes in *Ulysses*, 'Every life is in many days, day after day'.[30] Some days are longer than others, and a few days leave traces. But if a day remains, and when it remains, it remains with a human voice. Here are farmers, builders, teachers, gardeners and makers with common aspirations and similar dreams whose plain wisdom shies away from the speculations of theorists of superlative meaning; here is a person who buzzes around the New Testament. Here is the glorious sun, and here is a philosophy student. Here are quiet fishermen; here are butterflies flying over a minefield; here is a sea of words tumbling about a poet's mind, and here is an unconceived possibility in an exchange of glances. A siren echoes in your heart and a ship sails through the ocean: tell us more about the world you grew up in. These are all manifestations of modes of life, and they can all criss-cross, overlap and integrate in an inseparable way. The thief might be the philosopher, and the fisherman might be Stalin or St. Paul. The phenomenon of living and the phenomenon of meaning are intertwined. And to what can this intertwinement lead us if not to the realisation that only by attentiveness to life, to these 'wandering eye-beams', would we be able to understand, and to do justice to, the meanings ascribed to it? When I think of life's meaning, I must be, necessarily, in one of countless situations that, following James, we might call the varieties of life experience. We can't clearly think of the meaning of life without taking into consideration, first and foremost, these experiences.

A thief who comes to realise that he is an outcast from the feast of life might arrive at a different understanding of the grace of God from that of a theorist of God's purpose. God speaks to the thief differently, in a way the theorist wouldn't, or rather couldn't, hear. After all, 'You can't hear God speak to someone else, you can hear him only if you are being addressed' (Wittgenstein 1990: § 717).

A confessional approach, as an alternative way of approaching the question of life's meaning or a supplement to it is open to the endless varieties of human life; it is open to the way meaning 'meshes with our life' (Wittgenstein 1974: § 29). Since the aim here is to understand *a* life, all the concepts and conditions of a meaningful life are weighed against the particularity of that life. In other words, a confessional approach invests in the particular to gain something about our shared form of life. Thus, it is indeed a *method*, a way of seeing, and not a theory. In this view, the confessional approach is not opposed to the theoretical approach; it only tries to have a clear view of the life that is being examined in one's enquiry. Wittgenstein writes, 'Every sign *by itself* seems dead. *What* gives it life? – in use it is *alive*' (ibid.: § 432). Likewise, confession, properly understood, gives life to all the concepts of a meaningful life that are dead in themselves. Confession, as it were, breathes fire into the concepts and makes a life for them to describe.

Coda

In the preface to *Philosophical Investigations*, Wittgenstein writes about his 'several unsuccessful attempts' to bring all his ideas in a book with 'natural order and without breaks' (1958: ix). He alludes to the difficulty to impose an overall system or structure to the 'movements of his thoughts'. This difficulty is a defining element of his philosophy, which revolves around a resistance against theorisation and systematisation. Thus, one might be tempted to say, paradoxically, his philosophy aims at putting an end to philosophy the way it is traditionally pursued – with its imitation of the methods of science, its oversimplifications, its theorisation of the phenomena that escape systematisation. He targets a certain way of doing philosophy and tries to introduce a new method of doing philosophy. He writes,

> The real discovery is the one that makes me capable of stopping doing philosophy when I want to. – The one that gives philosophy peace, so that it is no longer tormented by questions which bring *itself* in question. – Instead we now demonstrate a method, by examples; and the series of examples can be broken off. – Problems are solved (difficulties eliminated), not a *single* problem. (ibid.: § 133)

The difficulty with which he was struggling was the difficulty of establishing a way of doing philosophy, which hopefully brings about a perspicuous understanding of things – that is, a method that would lead to a change in our *'way of looking at things'*. He firmly believed that philosophical problems will be resolved if we 'command a clear view' of the grammar of our language (ibid.: § 122). This, he thought, is possible by attention to the ordinary circumstances of the use of words. In a sense, Wittgenstein's philosophy is an invitation to rediscover and, thus, to recognise the significance of the *ordinary*: the ordinary uses of words, the ordinary life, the ordinary people, the ordinary rules and the way we follow them and the ordinary certainty of our world-pictures. He tried to show how extraordinary it is that we wonder at the ordinary (Wittgenstein 1980: 4–5). Embedded in such a view is a celebration of the ordinary. Let me write a few words, which were long overdue, about Wittgenstein's attraction to ordinary and non-philosophical life and the implications of such a tendency for our discussion.

Anyone who is familiar with Wittgenstein's works and his biographies can see what one might call a philosophy-bashing tendency, a certain way of speaking about philosophy that tries to utterly undermine it. This tendency is most vividly described in one of his notes in his diaries: 'It occurred to me today as I was thinking about my work in philosophy and said to myself: "I destroy, I destroy, I destroy"' (1980: 21). But what was it exactly that he wanted to destroy? It was the foundations upon which all the elaborate theories of philosophy are built, the way philosophical language imposes a certain way of approaching problems, which in his view was mostly alienated from the ordinary forms of experience.

Wittgenstein said that he didn't want to create new idols in the absence of those that he aims to destroy. However, it seems that in the process he actually did manage to create a new idol, which was the exaltation of the ordinary. The ordinary, one might say, was the holy grail of Wittgenstein's philosophy. It is beyond the scope of this work to examine the justifiability of this tendency in his philosophy. But as far as my discussions of life's meaning are concerned, I need to address the implications of such an attitude and to acknowledge its limits.

Let me reframe the question as follows: What were the reasons for Wittgenstein's fascination with the idea of ordinary life? Was it the realisation that in ordinary life he was no longer 'tormented' by the philosophical questions, as he mentioned in *Investigations*? Different speculations might be made to answer this question, but I want to focus on Wittgenstein's own need for attachment and communication, which he would usually experience when he was surrounded by what Goethe once called the 'healthiness of the moment', a lived life, not a philosophically examined one. The ideal of 'primordial life, wild life striving to erupt into the open' had a quite strong grip on him (Monk 1990: 490).

In Wittgenstein's note on the problem of life and in his conversations with friends, we notice time and again two kinds of longings: 'longing for the transcendent' and longing for attachment to others in everyday life (Cf. Eldrige 2008: 62). Von Ficker's impression of Wittgenstein in their first meeting was that 'he seemed possessed by a deep need for communication' (McGuiness 1988: 206). The joy of receiving a letter from an old friend, 'silly talks' with them, meeting new people and looking at their eyes and enjoying their company, watching American movies after his lectures and reading comic strips all had appealing effects on him (those philosophers who are usually more interested in what happens between the presentations in philosophy conferences are probably familiar with this).

I think Goethe's account of his shoemaker's life in his autobiography, *Poetry and Truth: From My Own Life*, aptly alludes to what Wittgenstein found most appealing about the common sense of ordinary life and ordinary people. Goethe writes about this shoemaker:

> He remained always the same, because there was but one source of all his conduct. He possessed sound common sense, based upon a cheerful disposition and he delighted in uniform accustomed activity. Incessant labour was a prime necessity to him; the fact that he regarded all else of secondary importance, preserved his peace of mind; and I felt bound to accord to him a high place in the class of those who are called practical philosophers, unconscious sages.
> ([1833] 1913: Part II, Book viii)

We might say, by undertaking various occupations, such as teaching, gardening, architecting and working as a technician in a hospital, he was searching for a 'peace of mind'. He would see labour as a cure for tormented souls. In a letter to Drury, Wittgenstein highlights the significance of Drury's work in a hospital and the way it can have a healing effect. Wittgenstein writes,

> Look at people's sufferings, physical and mental, you have them close at hand, and this ought to be a good remedy for your troubles.... Look at your patients more closely as human beings in trouble and enjoy the opportunity you have to say 'good night' to so many people. This alone is a gift from heaven which many people would envy you.... I think in some sense you don't look at people's faces closely enough.
> (Drury 1984: 95–96)

Having said that, I think that with a close attention to other aspects of his life we can also notice that his high regard for the ordinary and for non-philosophical life is only one side of the story. The same person who was in need of human contact and ordinary life also had a strong urge for detachment or in Louis Sass' words, 'a yearning for solitude and distant places' where he could work in peace and escape from the 'theatricality or inauthenticity' of urban life (2001: 111). In his diaries one can find every now and then a condescending attitude towards the ordinary. He writes in his diaries, 'a phenomenon that is extraordinarily characteristic of me: Unless their appearance or demeanour makes a special impression on me, I consider people lesser than myself: that is, I would be inclined to use the word "ordinary" about them' (2003: 161).

What can we make of these two extreme modes of being in Wittgenstein's life? Wittgenstein himself was acutely aware of this tension in his inner and social life. In his diaries he would sometimes blame it on his vanity. One of the recurrent themes in Koder diaries is his reflections on his moral inauthenticity. There is something inferior in being conceited about one's superiority, and he was deeply concerned about it. He writes in one of his demanding injunctions to himself, 'The edifice of your pride has to be dismantled. And that is terribly hard work' (1980: 26). One might say, Wittgenstein's reflections in his diaries is a manifestation of a hard work to reach an agreement with the world and with oneself, a sense of authenticity and freedom. A passage in Koder diaries gives an illuminating and, I should add, moving picture of his need to resolve deep conflicts in himself:

> Often I feel that there is something in me like a lump which, were it to melt, would let me cry or I would then find the right words (or perhaps even a melody). But this something (is it the heart) in my case feels like leather and cannot melt. Or is it just that I am too cowardly to let the temperature rise sufficiently? (2003: 11)

By paying close attention to the movements of his reflections, thus, we arrive at a multi-layered picture of Wittgenstein's life. As I have been saying throughout this work, there are insights and perspectives that we can take away from Wittgenstein's philosophy in general and from his reflections on the problem of life in particular. But we neither need to buy his idiosyncratic statements about his low regard for philosophy nor to romanticise the significance of ordinary life. There is something problematic, and potentially misguiding, in Wittgenstein's way of dismissing philosophy. After all, it was philosophy which led Wittgenstein to the realisation that attention to the ordinary and to the particular would result in more clarity in our enquiries. In fact, doing philosophy and writing was a central part of his life. Comparing Wittgenstein and Goethe, Eldrige suggests that Wittgenstein, like

Goethe, 'achieved through the act of writing, repeatedly and day to day, a kind of catharsis, some distance or perspective on his anxieties as a subject and some sense of himself as having a social identity as a writer' (2008: 68).

Time and again in this book I suggested that from Wittgenstein's corpus we can gather that he would advocate a certain way of approaching the question of life's meaning. In this approach the emphasis is on a faithful observation of the ordinary contexts in which we contemplate life's meaning. Embedded in such an approach is a sense of care or, one might even say, yearning for experiencing the genuineness and healthiness of a life that is not tarnished by cold detachment or alienation, reaching a 'certain coolness' without 'meddling with them' (1980: 2).

It is hard to miss the aesthetic tone of such an attitude in Wittgenstein's philosophy. But there is a limit to this non-interventional appreciative outlook, and it is important to be aware of it. Appreciation of the ordinary life is revealing in our enquiry into life's meaning, but it could also lead us to the realisation that some of the problems in our lives require action and intervention. The same faithful observation that Wittgenstein supports might as well lead us to the realisation that reaching a certain 'coolness' is a luxury that many people simply don't have. In particular, for many people the tendency to fly over themselves and view the world from above comes and goes, but it goes mostly. In the face of pressing problems such as poverty, systematic injustice and bio-environmental crises the simple philosophy of leaving 'everything as it is' wouldn't do. Understanding and appreciating the ordinary is important, but it might also compel us to do something to change it. For example, if ordinarily we tend to use generalisations in order to make our claims sound stronger ('these black people...', 'these white people...'), if ordinarily we don't care about the way we damage the environment, and so on, then the ordinary must be fixed. Leaving it as it is would be morally problematic. We should bear in mind that Wittgenstein tries to establish the idea that attention to the structure of our language would lead to discovering the source of our philosophical and conceptual confusions. And he hardly ever wrote about socio-political questions. But in dealing with Wittgenstein's approach to the question of life's meaning and philosophy in general, it is important to be mindful of the difference between what we can take away from his way of seeing and what we would be better off to leave aside. In our search for the former, we shouldn't be put off by the latter.

Notes

Introduction

1. See, for example, Wolf (2010); and Metz (2013).
2. The French painter (1864–1942).
3. Hereafter, I mostly refer to the literature on the meaning of life as 'the literature'.
4. For subjectivist theories of life's meaning, see Taylor (2000); Williams (1976); Frankfurt (1988); Trisel (2002) and for objectivist theories, see, for example, Nozick (1981); Singer (1995); Audi (2005); Wolf (2010); and Metz (2013).
5. Most anthologies on the meaning of life have similar classifications of the existing approaches to the question of life's meaning, with some slight differences between them. For example, while Klemke and Cahn (2008) refer to 'theistic' and 'nontheistic' approaches, Metz uses the terms 'supernaturalism' and 'naturalism' to describe the same approaches (Metz 2013). In this book, I mostly refer to Metz's classification.
6. Cf. Martin (1993: 556); Benatar (2006: 107); and Smith (2006).
7. See, for example, Feinberg (1992); Smith (2006); and Nagel (1971).
8. For works related to Wittgenstein and meaning in life, see Thomas (1995, 1997, 1999); Thompson (1997, 2000); Lurie (2006); Kishik (2008); and Arnswald (2009). There are also other works which address related issues to life's meaning, such as religion and value: Barrett (1991); Verbin (2000); and Litwack (2009). However, except for Lurie (2006); and Kishik (2008), none of these works engage with the literature on life's meaning.
9. I shall discuss the similarity between Cottingham's 'holistic' method and Wittgenstein's 'anthropological method' in more detail in Chapter 4.
10. John Cottingham alluded to this expression in his paper, 'Dignity, Autonomy, and Embodiment', which was presented at the 19th ESPR conference in Soesterberg, Netherlands, September 2012. Cottingham writes, 'On the Judaeo-Christian view...human beings, despite their frailty (formed of the 'dust of the earth'), are, as the Hebrew Bible has it, made in the image and likeness of God'.

1 Book of Facts, Book of Values

1. In Augustine's words, 'I was entangled in the life of this world, clinging to dull hopes, of a beauteous wife, the pomp of riches, the emptiness of honours, and the other hurtful and destructive pleasures' (Aug. De Util. Credendi, § 3).
2. The rest of his works were published posthumously.
3. See, Russell's introduction to the *Tractatus* (1966: xxi).
4. Galeb Thompson rightly suggests that there is a similarity between Tolstoy and Wittgenstein in seeing the solution to the problem of life in its disappearance. See Thompson (1997).

Notes   153

5. The vast discrepancy between the commentators over the last proposition of the *Tractatus* shows how equivocal this statement is. According to the 'resolute' reading of the *Tractatus*, proposed by Cora Diamond and James Conant, we shouldn't infer from the last proposition of the *Tractatus* that there are some 'important' things that cannot be said and with regard to which we have to be silent. Wittgenstein's allusion to silence refers to nothing; it doesn't allude to some 'infallible truths'. On the other hand, traditional commentators of the *Tractatus*, like P.S. Hacker, claim that the *Tractatus* draws a line between the things that we can speak about and a world of things of which we cannot speak. That is to say, according to Hacker's reading, the *Tractatus* offers a two-world metaphysics. What is interesting in the 'resolute vs. non-resolute' reading debate, I think, is the fact that both interpretations are grounded in good textual evidence. For example, Anscombe, as a traditional reader of the book, refers to § 6.432 and argues that God does not reveal himself in the world of accidental things. Because, if whatever is the case in the world is accidental, why does Wittgenstein mention the non-accidental (Anscombe 1959: 171)? However, referring to § 6.54, Diamond asks how seriously we can take that remark concerning the nonsensicality of the *Tractatus*'s propositions. She suggests that we should take Wittgenstein at his words and read him literally; otherwise, what we do is nothing but 'chickening out':

> That is what I want to call chickening out. What counts as not chickening out is then this, roughly: to throw away the ladder is, among other things, to throw away in the end to take seriously the language of 'features of reality'. To read Wittgenstein himself as not chickening out is to say that it is not, not really, his view that there are features of reality that cannot be put into words but show themselves. (1995: 181)

A resolute reader will take Wittgenstein's statements on the mystical and the problem of life to be inconsequential, whereas Hacker or Anscombe take them seriously. For more on the resolute reading, see also Conant (2000: 174–217). Recently, Hans Sluga disputed the 'interpretation business' that is running in the exegetical literature on Wittgenstein's philosophy. According to Sluga, it seems that we are caught in a spiral of 'increasing hyper-specialization of the exegetical type of philosophizing'. This process is in danger of 'losing view of the world'. The problem with much of the literature on Wittgenstein's philosophy, according to Sluga, is that it lacks precisely the passion with which Wittgenstein would struggle with his 'burning questions'. Sluga argues that 'the questions that preoccupied Wittgenstein are no longer so deeply burning to us' (Sluga 2012). The burning questions, in Sluga's view, are now those questions that are concerned with our social existence (the unstoppable growth of population, the unstoppable growth of technology and the environmental crises).

6. I do not want to imply here that according to Wittgenstein there are some nonsenses that are significant nonsenses. Instead, I'm focusing here on the limits of communicability of innermost emotions and experiences. James Conant and Cora Diamond claim that the idea that there are some profound nonsenses with regard to which we have to remain silent is in sharp contrast to the spirit of the *Tractatus*. Conant argues against those who claim that 'for the *Tractatus* the propositions of ethics and religion – as well as either

154 *Notes*

all or only the most important propositions of the *Tractatus* itself – are both nonsensical and deeply significant' (Conant 1989: 247).
7. Cf. the film *Waking Life* (2001), where Kim Krizan talks to the young man about intangibility of our innermost experiences:
What is 'frustration'? Or, what is 'anger' or 'love'? When I say 'love' – the sound comes out of my mouth and it hits the other person's ear, travels through this byzantine conduit in their brain, through their memories of love or lack of love, and they register what I'm saying...and they say yes they understand, but how do I know? Because words are inert. They're just symbols. They're dead – you know? And so much of our experience is intangible. So much of what we perceive cannot be expressed, it's unspeakable. And yet, you know, when we communicate with one another and we feel that we have connected – and we think we're understood, I think we have a feeling of almost spiritual communion...and that feeling may be transient, but I think it's what we live for. (Linklater 2001)
See also the film *Run Lola Run* by Tom Tykwer (1999). In one sequence, Lola interrogates Manni:
'Do you love me?' – 'Sure I do.' – 'How can you be so sure?' – 'I don't know. I just am.' – 'I could be some other girl.' – 'No.' – 'Why not?' – 'Because you are the best' – 'The best what? – The best girl of all the girls in the world.' – 'Sure.' – 'How do you know?' – 'I just do.' – 'You think so.' – 'Okay, I think so.' – 'You see?' – 'What?' – 'You aren't sure.' – 'Are you nuts or what?' – 'What if you never met me?' – 'What do you mean?' – 'You would be telling the same thing to someone else.' – 'Okay, if you want to hear it.' – 'I don't want to hear anything; I want to know how you feel.' – 'Okay, my feelings say that you are the best.' – 'Who is "your feeling" anyway?' – 'It's me. My heart.' – 'Your heart says "Hey Manni, she is the one"?' – 'Exactly.' – 'And you say, "Thanks for the information, see you around."' – 'Exactly.' – 'And you do what your heart says?' – 'Well, it really doesn't say anything. I do know. It just feels.' – 'So, what does it feel now?' – 'That someone is asking rather stupid questions.' – 'Man, you aren't taking me seriously.' – 'Lola, what is wrong? Do you want to leave me?' – 'I don't know. I think I have to make a decision.' (Tykwer 1999)
This dialogue is also quoted in Nordmann (2005: 206).
8. Cf. Wittgenstein's letter to his friend, Ludwig von Ficker in Wittgenstein (1996: 92).
9. Cf. Wittgenstein (2003: 133).

2   The Limits of Justification

1. Cf. The Qur'an XX, 12.
2. I am thankful to Seyyed Hossein Nasr who brought this into my attention in an interview with me. See also, Nasr (1976, 1989).
3. Cf. Wittgenstein (1966: § 6.43).
4. Process theologians raise similar kinds of questions. For example, Delwin Brown writes, 'if God, like the human mind, is a succession of occasions of experience, there seems to be no metaphysical guarantee that God preserves all values. That is, it is at least possible that some values become lost, even to God' (1967: 30). See also Trethowan (1983).

5. See Tolstoy (1905); Craig (1994); and Pojman (2002).
6. In the supernaturalist approach, there are also theories that take other attributes of God to be essential for meaning, attributes such as 'infinity' (Nozick 1981); 'unity' (Hartshorne 1984); 'redemption' (Davis 1987); and 'atemporality and simplicity' (Metz 2000). For example, Robert Nozick argues that elements of a meaningful life is a matter of relationship with something that is already meaningful. Empowering people, for example, is meaningful because it promotes autonomy and justice. But for justice to confer meaning on lives, it must have already obtained its meaning from something else. Similarly, this last element also have its meaning from somewhere else, as Nozick says:

> About any given thing, however wide, it seems we can stand back and ask what its meaning is. To find a meaning for it, then, we seem driven to find a link with yet another thing beyond its boundaries. And so a regression is launched. To stop this regress, we seem to need...something which is unlimited, from which we cannot step back, even in imagination, to wonder what its meaning is. (Nozick 1989: 167)

And this final element that confer meaning on all the other meaningful elements is nothing but God. For a brief discussion of two arguments against Nozick's arguments, see Metz (2013: 110).

7. However, one can also find exceptions who advise supernaturalists to 'epistemic modesty' with regard to the question of life's meaning. Phillip L. Quinn's approach is a good example. He writes:

> Christians [shouldn't] exaggerate the certainty about life's meanings to be derived from their narratives.... What is more, other religions have reasonable stories to tell about life's meanings, as do some nonreligious worldviews.... Christians ought to adopt an attitude of epistemic modesty when making claims about life's meanings. They can be, I think, entitled to believe that Christian Narratives provide the best story we have about life's meanings. But claims to furnish the complete story should, I believe, be advanced only with fear and trembling. (Quinn 1997: 40)

8. See Wittgenstein (1980: 86).
9. Despite their differences, one might see striking resemblances between Wittgenstein and Cottingham on various issues, including the 'primacy of praxis', limits of theory, regulatory effects of having a religious world-picture, etc. I shall discuss the resemblance between the two on various occasions in Chapter 2, Chapter 3, and Chapter 5.
10. The Euthyphro dilemma was first mentioned in Plato's dialogue, *Euthyphro*, where Socrates asks Euthyphro, 'Is the pious loved by the gods because it is pious, or is it pious because it is loved by the gods?' A modified version of the dilemma is as follows: 'Is the moral good commanded by God because it is morally good or is it morally good because it is commanded by God?' For an objectivist answer to this dilemma, see Scanlon (1998: 95); and Metz (2009: 205–224; 2013: 87–93). For a supernaturalist response to the question, see Cottingham (2005: 49–57; 2009a: 264–268).
11. For a strong rejection of evolutionary ethics, see Woolcock (1999: 276–306).
12. Note the Epicurean tone of this statement. Epicureanism shares the same view about death and asserts that death is not an event in life. In Epicurus'

words, 'Death does not concern us, because as long as we exist, death is not here. And when it does come, we no longer exist'. See Hadot (1995: 222).
13. For some fresh objections to the Tractarian philosophy of life, see Lurie (2006: 162–167), for example.
14. It is not clear when exactly Wittgenstein began to realise the problems in his Tractarian philosophy. It has been said that once in a conversation with Piero Sraffa about the *Tractatus*, Wittgenstein was insisting that any proposition and what it describes must have the same 'logical form'. Based on Norman Malcolm's report, 'Sraffa made a gesture ... of brushing the underneath of his chin with an outward sweep of the finger-tips of one hand. And he asked, 'What is the logical form of that?' (Malcolm 1972: 59). Sraffa's sarcastic gesture, I think, alludes to the fact that the ways we understand phenomena of everyday life and interact with them do not necessarily follow a predetermined set of logical rules, and this realisation had far-reaching implications for Wittgenstein.
15. See Rhees (1970).
16. See Putnam's introduction to Rosenzweig (1999: 11).

3 Aspect-Seeing and Meaning in Life

1. Other remarks on aspect-seeing appear in Wittgenstein (1990: §§ 155–225; 1988a: §§ 411–436, 505–546, 860–890, 952–1137; 1988b: §§ 355–391, 435–497, 506–557; 1998a: §§ 146–180, 429–613, 622–812; and 1998b: 12e–19e). Related remarks on this subject can also be found in Wittgenstein (1969, 1975, 1978, 1980). The substantial presence of this discussion in Wittgenstein's body of texts implies that aspect-seeing was not only a diversion from the main discussions of *Investigations*. As Day and Krebs suggest, Wittgenstein's notes on aspect-seeing are also 'the expression of a theme whose figures and turns we might have been hearing, however, faintly, all along' (2010: 5).
2. See, for example, Cavell (1979); Mulhall (1990, 2001); Verbin (2000); Monk (2001); Kellenberger (2002); Rhees (2003); Litwack (2009); and Day and Krebs (2010).
3. These films are directed, respectively, by François Truffaut (1959); Jean-Pierre Melville (1967); Jacques Audiard (2005); Marcel Carné (1945); Jules Dassin (1955); Jean-Luc Godard (1960, 1964); Krzysztof Kieslowski (1993); François Truffaut (1962); Albert Lamorisse (1956); and Eric Rohmer (1986). *A Moveable Feast* was Ernest Hemingway's last book, which is about his years as an expatriate in Paris in the 1920s, published posthumously in 1964.
4. Cf. John Berger's take on Paris:
   Every city has a sex and an age which have nothing to do with demography. Rome is feminine. So is Odessa. London is a teenager, an urchin, and in this hasn't changed since the time of Dickens. Paris, I believe, is a man in his twenties in love with an older woman. (Berger & Bielski 1987)
5. See also *Investigations*, Part II, 205.
6. For an insightful discussion about the concept of 'soul' in Wittgenstein's *Philosophical Investigations*, see E. B. Litwack, *Wittgenstein and Value: The Quest for Meaning* (2009).

7. Wittgenstein writes,
   We do not see the human eye as a receiver, it appears not to let anything in, but to send something out. ... One can terrify with one's eyes, not with one's ear or nose. When you see the eye you see something going out from it. You see the look in the eye. (1990: § 222)
8. Likewise, Wielenberg claims that it takes 'courage' to accept the truth of atheism and its implications (2005: 117).
9. Russell's account of the meaning of life, for example, is precisely founded upon the same picture of the world that Craig describes. See Russell (1957: 56).
10. See, for example, Taylor (2000); Wielenberg (2005); and Russell (1957).
11. In Cottingham's words, 'A religious outlook, it seems to me, is never, or at any rate not typically, adopted on the basis of an inference to the best explanation' (2005: 22).
12. See, for example, Wittgenstein (1980: 71): 'But man exists in this world, where things break, slide about, cause every imaginable mischief. And of course he is one such thing himself'.
13. Jennifer Faust makes a distinction between epistemic and non-epistemic uses of philosophical arguments for the existence of God and suggests that even though the standard arguments for the existence of God are unlikely to persuade nonbelievers, they have various other functions. For example, 'argumenta are often a part of doctrinal or theological training, they are often voiced during sermons, they serve as aids in exegetical work, and they are often aimed at increasing the understanding of those who already adhere to the beliefs stated in their conclusions' (Faust 2008: 83).
14. For criticism of expressivist readings of Wittgenstein's views of religion, see Barrett (1991); Schroeder (2007); and Cottingham (2009c: 203–227).

4 In Defence of the Ordinary

1. In fact, one of the objectives in the literature is to establish that meaningfulness is and should be considered a distinctive category that can account for a good life. See, especially, Wolf (2010: 1–34); and Metz (2013: 17–73).
2. As quoted in Hadot (1995: 220).
3. It refers to a verse of *Talmud*: 'Whoever destroys a soul, it is considered as if he destroyed an entire world. And whoever saves a life, it is considered as if he saved an entire world'. See, *Mishnah Sanhedrin* 4:5; *Babylonian Talmud Tractate Sanhedrin* 37a. Interestingly, the same verse with similar wording can be found in the Qur'an. The difference is that the Qur'an refers to 'mankind' instead of 'the world entire':
   > For this reason did we prescribe unto the children of Israel that he who slayeth anyone (man), without (that being for) murder, or for mischief on earth, (it shall be) as though he hath slain mankind as a whole; and he who saveth it (a human life), shall be as though he hath saved mankind as a whole. (The Qur'an, V: 32)
4. Cf. Wittgenstein (1969: 18).
5. See Wiggins (1998: 100).

6. Metz also raises another objection. According to Metz, the most important part of Levy's theory begs the question. That is, if we ask why it is that the pursuit of open-ended activities confers great meaning on life, the answer would be that these activities make progress toward 'supremely valuable' goals (Metz 2011: 398).
7. Cf. Metz (2013: 199–218).

5 On Detachment or Why the Shopkeeper Does Not Investigate his Apples

1. For example, Lurie (2006) focuses on only the early Wittgenstein's approach towards the 'problem of life', and Kishik (2008) tries to show the way our 'language meshes with life' by focusing on Wittgenstein's central ideas in his later works concerning the interwoven connection between words, life and meaning and compares them with the works of Augustine and Tolstoy. See also Thomas (1999); Thompson (2000); and Arnswald (2009). In general, most works written on Wittgenstein's views of value and the meaning of life to a large extent rely on the early Wittgenstein's writings on ethics and the nature of value.
2. Wittgenstein sometimes refers to world-picture as 'our frame of reference' (1975: § 83); a 'whole system of propositions' (§ 141); and a '*totality* of judgments' (§ 140).
3. Cf. Wittgenstein (1967: 57; 1975: § 262; 1980: 85).
4. In fact, some of Herzog's movies have been considered as paradigm cases in the analysis of incommensurable situations. See, for example, the movie *Where the Green Ants Dream* (1984). The movie portrays a dispute between Aborigines and a local mining company with regard to land ownership. In one of the scenes Aborigines present some 'sacred' wooden objects as 'evidence'. These objects, buried in the land, were the evidence of land ownership. B. Readings, in a philosophical engagement with the movie, analyses both parties' world-pictures and the 'injustices' that are done in this situation (1992). For another interesting example, see *Grizzly Man* (2005), which is about the life and death of a bear enthusiast, Timothy Treadwell, who was killed and eaten by a bear in 2003.
5. Cf. Wittgenstein (1980: 28).
6. Cf. Ernest Hemingway's take on this matter in *A Farewell to Arms* where the protagonist, Fredric Henry, describes how words lost their meanings during the World War I:
   > There were many words that you could not stand to hear and finally only the names of places had dignity. Certain numbers were the same way and certain dates and these with the names of the places were all you could say and have them mean anything. Abstract words such as glory, honor, courage, or hallow were obscene beside the concrete names of villages, the numbers of roads, the names of rivers, the numbers of regiments and the dates. ([1929] 2012: 184–185)
7. Cf. Wittgenstein (1975: § 476).
8. See also Wittgenstein (1975: § 204 ('Giving grounds... justifying the evidence comes to an end'), § 563; 1978: 342 ('Interpretation comes to an end'); 1990: § 301, 404 ('The chain of reasons comes to an end').).

9. Ironically, when Nagel criticises the 'standard arguments for absurdity' in order to then present his own, he appeals to Wittgenstein's idea of the limits of justifications. One of the standard arguments for the absurdity of life is that whatever we do in life is ultimately absurd because we are finite creatures. To this Nagel replies, 'chains of justification come repeatedly to an end within life, and whether the process as a whole can be justified has no bearing on the finality of these end-points. No further justification is needed to make it reasonable to take aspirin for a headache' (Nagel 1971: 144). This view is very similar to *On Certainty*'s recurrent theme, namely the limits of justifications. See Wittgenstein (1975: §§ 192, 204, 563).
10. Feinberg suggests that though our lives are pointless and tragic, they can be fulfilled at the same time. Fulfilment, in this view, has to do with exercising one's individual capacities (1992: 297–330). Likewise, by rejecting Nagel's claim that life is absurd because we fail to find justificatory reasons for our beliefs and actions, Smith suggests that we can suspend all our beliefs, and if we do so, 'we thereby remove all incongruity, for we no longer have any beliefs that lack justificatory relationships with other beliefs' (2006: 99).
11. Wittgenstein asks in *Investigations*, 'Does man think, then, because he has found that thinking pays? – Because he thinks it advantageous to think? (Does he bring his children up because he has found it pays?) (1958: § 467).
12. Charles Baudelaire, 'Élévation', as quoted in Hadot (1995: 248).
13. In a sense, the literature on life's meaning is divided between the foxes and the hedgehogs, and thus in the literature we mainly see two different ways of understanding the meaning of life. (Examples: Schopenhauer, Camus, Nagel and Cottingham are hedgehogs; Wolf, Frankfurt and Metz are foxes.)
14. It is beyond the scope of my research to discuss whether there is a way to reconcile the tension between these two ways of understanding meaning, and to my knowledge, this question has not been addressed in the literature, except in Cooper (2005).
15. A loose translation of the poem would be as follows: 'I was brought into existence with no choice/And life made me more perplexed/We parted from the world with reluctance/and we shan't get the point of it all'.
16. As quoted in Corngold and Wagner (2011: 3).
17. 'Seize the day', originally taken from a poem by Horace written in 23 BC.
18. Cf. Drury (1984: 95–96).
19. Most recently, R. J. Wallace in his book *The View from Here* has argued that many of us realise that our lives revolve around fairly expensive projects and activities, 'which would not be possible in their present form in a social world that did not involve massive deprivation and inequality in human life prospects' (2013: 7). Affirmation of our projects, in this view, entails affirming 'the social inequalities...even though we continue to view those inequalities as objectively lamentable' (ibid.). Wallace aptly calls this situation the 'bourgeois predicament'. In general, for Wallace, because of our attachments in life, we commit to affirm 'historical events and social structures' that from a broader perspective we cannot regard as 'worthy of affirmation' (ibid.: 8). This, in turn, involves some degree of absurdity, which he calls 'modest nihilism'. It is modest because absurdity, Wallace has it, is 'endemic' to the human condition.

20. Rosenzweig published his book in 1921, the year the *Tractatus* was published. The first philosopher who drew attentions to the affinity between the two philosophers, to my knowledge, was Hilary Putnam in his introduction to Rosenzweig's book. What is surprising is that both Wittgenstein and Rosenzweig appeal to very similar wordings and arguments to attack 'scepticism': notions such as the 'stream of life', 'therapy', philosophy as an 'illness', the significance of 'the ordinary' and 'everyday life'.

6 The Human Voice: The Confessional Nature of Enquiring into Life's Meaning

1. Cf. Shotter (1997: 1).
2. As quoted in Wittgenstein (1988a: § 889).
3. The older – that is, medieval – uses of the word 'confession' didn't necessarily carry an idea of guilt or sin. For example, one could confess to thy holy name in the Common Prayer Book. The same sense can be found in 'Heidelberg Catechism', written in 1563, which is a personal confession of faith. Thanks to David E. Cooper and James C. Klagge for bringing this into my attention.
4. For the relation between psychoanalytic practices and Christian confession, see Foucault (1980). For an in-depth philosophical study of confession, see Taylor (2009).
5. God's purpose theory is roughly the idea that one's life would be meaningful to the extent that one fulfils purposes assigned to human beings by God.
6. Quoted from the movie *The Philadelphia Story* directed by George Cukor (1940).
7. Cf. Coetzee (2004: 155).
8. Cf. Wittgenstein (1975: § 143).
9. See also, Wittgenstein (1980: 16 ('Working in philosophy...is really more a working on oneself'), 86; Wittgenstein 1958: §§ 109, 124, 126 ('Philosophy simply puts everything before us, and neither explains nor deduces. – Since everything lies open to view there is nothing to explain. For what is hidden, for example, is of no interest to us'), 128, 133, 309).
10. For example, Galeb Thompson highlights the similarities between Wittgenstein's *Investigations* and Augustine's *Confessions* in terms of their methods, and he defends the idea that 'what drives Wittgenstein to the confessional form in the *Investigations* is analogous to what drives Augustine to the confessional form in his *Confessions*' (2000: 4). Likewise, M. W. Rowe links Wittgenstein's later philosophy to the confessional aspects of 'German Romanticism' (1994: 327). To my knowledge, Cavell was the first philosopher who drew attention to the confessional dimension of *Investigations* (1976, 1979).
11. In a similar vein, D. D. Raphael suggests that works on literature can deepen the moral philosopher's understanding of moral conditions by focusing on particular cases and a detailed description of characters and their actions (cf. Raphael 1983).
12. For more interesting works on the way literature can deepen our understanding of the human forms of life, see Diamond (1995); Crary (2009); and Eldrige (2008).

13. In Wittgenstein's words, 'If you offer a sacrifice and are pleased with yourself about it, both you and your sacrifice will be cursed' (1980: 26).
14. For more on Dostoyevsky's addiction to gambling see *Dostoyevsky: The Miraculous Years 1865–1871* (Frank 1995: 426–427).
15. Cf. Virginia Woolf's criticism of Arnold Bennett's novel, *Hilda Lessways*. Woolf writes, Bennett 'is trying to hypnotise us into the belief that, because he has made a house, there must be a person living there' (1992: 80).
16. Wittgenstein suggests that having a 'poetic mood' is one thing, and being able to produce a good artwork is another. Chandler is fully aware of his poetic mood, but he is also aware of the fact that so far he hasn't produced anything worthwhile. Wittgenstein refers to Schiller's letter to Goethe in which he writes of a 'poetic mood', and comments,
    I think I know what he means, I believe I am familiar with it myself. It is a mood of receptivity to nature in which one's thoughts seem as vivid as nature itself. But it is strange that Schiller himself did not produce anything better (or so it seems to me) and so I am not entirely convinced that what I produce in such a mood is really worth anything. (1980: 65–66)
17. Wolf's book includes a separate section on comments and responses by other philosophers to her account and, further, Wolf's response to those comments and criticisms. See Wolf (2010: 67–92). For a criticism of Wolf' theory, see also Cahn (2008: 236–238); and Metz (2013: 180–184).
18. For an insightful study of the personal nature of Wittgenstein's philosophy, see Klagge (ed.) (2001).
19. In this section, I mostly refer to the so-named Koder diaries from the 1930s. The importance of Wittgenstein's diaries lies in the intimate connections between his philosophical thoughts and his life. Wittgenstein writes, 'The movement of thought in my philosophising should be discernible also in the history of my mind, of its moral concepts and in the understanding of my situation' (2003: 133). For more on the Koder diaries, see James C. Klagge's and Alfred Nordmann's preface in Wittgenstein (2003: 3–7).
20. For more on the relation between one's belief and one's life in Wittgenstein's diaries, see also (Wittgenstein 2003: 155, 212–213, 217, 223, 241).
21. Wittgenstein also speaks of the 'irritation of the intellect' when words, in religious contexts, are used inappropriately:
    I believe: the word 'believing' has wrought horrible havoc in religion. All the knotty thoughts about the 'paradox' of the *eternal* meaning of a *historical* fact and the like. But if instead of 'belief in Christ' you would say: 'love of Christ,' the paradox vanishes, that is, the irritation of the *intellect*. What does religion have to do with such a tickling of the intellect? (2003: 247)
22. We might say another aspect of a confessional approach is that it views our enquiry into the meaning of life as a way of 'assessing life'.
23. It refers to Christ's last words. See John 19: 30.
24. Wittgenstein's inability to participate in a religious life is captured in Wittgenstein (2003: 219: 'Kneeling means that one is a slave. (Religion might consist in this.) Lord, if only I knew that I am a slave!').
25. Cf. Emerson's reflections on farming: 'This hard work will always be done by one kind of man; not by scheming speculators, nor by soldiers, nor professors,

nor readers of Tennyson; but by men of endurance – deep-chested, long-winded, tough, slow and sure, and timely.' ([1858] 1940: 750)
26. Cf. Cottingham (2009c).
27. For an insightful discussion on the relation between meaning and morality, see Wolf (2010: 53–63).
28. A recurrent theme in Wittgenstein's personal notes is his evaluation of his 'vanity' and his difficulty in overcoming it; see Wittgenstein (2003: 23, 93, 97, 113, 139, 193, 207, 213). For an analysis of Wittgenstein's preoccupation with perfectionism and authenticity, see Sass (2001: 98–155).
29. This day has come to be known as Bloomsday which is named after the central character in *Ulysses*. For more on the importance of this day for Joyce, see Ellmann (1983).
30. (Joyce [1922] 2002: § 9; Scylla and Charybdis).

Bibliography

Adams, E. M. (2002). The Meaning of Life. *International Journal for Philosophy of Religion* 51, 71–81.
Anscombe, G. E. (1959). *An Introduction to Wittgenstein's Tractatus*. London: Hutchinson.
Arnold, M. (1987). Preface to the First Edition of Poems (1853). In K. Allot & M. Allot (eds), *Arnold: The Complete Poems*. London: Longman.
Arnswald, U. (2009). The Paradox of Ethics – 'It Leaves Everything as It Is'. In U. Arnswald (ed.), *In Search of Meaning: Ludwig Wittgenstein on Ethics, Mysticism, and Religion*. Karlsruhe: Universitätsverlag, pp. 1–24.
Atkinson, J. R. (2009). *The Mystical in Wittgenstein's Early Writings*. New York: Routledge.
Audi, R. (2005). Intrinsic Value and Meaningful Life. *Philosophical Papers* 34, 331–355.
Augustine, S. ([398] 1966). *The Confessions of St Augustine*. E. Pusey (trans.), London: Everyman's Library.
Ayer, A. J. (1952). *Language, Truth and Logic*. New York: Dover Publications.
Baier, K. (1957). The Meaning of Life. Repr. in E. D. Klemke & S. M. Cahn (eds), *The Meaning of Life: A Reader*. Oxford: Oxford University Press, 2008, pp. 82–113.
Barrett, C. (1991). *Wittgenstein on Ethics and Religious Belief*. Oxford: Basil Blackwell.
Bauer, N. (2005). On Human Understanding. In K. Nielsen & D. Z. Phillips (eds), *Wittgensteinian Fideism*. London: SCM Press, pp. 203–214.
Benatar, D. (2006). *Better Never to Have Been: The Harm of Coming into Existence*. New York: Oxford University Press.
Berger, J. and Bielski, N. (1987). *A Question of Geography: Play*. London: Faber & Faber.
Berggren, E. (1975). *The Psychology of Confession*. Leiden: E. J. Brill.
Berlin, I. (1978). The Hedgehog and the Fox. In I. Berlin, H. Hardy & A. Kelly (eds), *Russian Thinkers* New York: Viking, pp. 22–81.
Blackburn, S. (1999). *Think*. Oxford: Oxford University Press.
Boll, H. (2002). *The Clown*. L. Vennewitz (trans.). London: Marion Boyars.
Bouveresse, J. (2007). Wittgenstein's Critique of Frazer. *Ratio* (XX), 357–376.
Bouwsma, O. K. (1986). *Wittgenstein's Conversations 1949–1951*. Indianapolis, IN: Hackett Publishing Company.
Brown, D. (1967). Recent Process Theology. *Journal of the American Academy of Religion* 35, 28–41.
Brown, P. (1967). *Augustine of Hippo: A Biography*. Berkeley: University of California Press.
Burnett, W. (1958). *The Spirit of Man; Great Stories and Experiences of Spiritual Crisis, Inspiration, and the Joy of Life*. New York: Hawthorn Books.
Cahn, S. M. (2008). Meaningless Lives? In E. D. Klemke & S. M. Cahn (eds), *The Meaning of Life: A Reader*. Oxford: Oxford University Press, pp. 236–237.

Bibliography

Camus, A. (1955). *The Myth of Sisyphus.* Repr. in E. D. Klemke & S. M. Cahn (eds), *The Meaning of Life: A Reader.* Oxford: Oxford University Press, 2008, pp. 72–81.
Cavell, S. (1976). *Must We Mean What We Say? A Book of Essays.* Cambridge: Cambridge University Press.
Cavell, S. (1979). *The Claim of Reason: Wittgenstein, Scepticism, Morality, and Tragedy.* New York: Oxford University Press.
Cavell, S. (1994). *A Pitch of Philosophy: Autobiographical Exercises.* Cambridge, MA: Harvard University Press.
Child, W. (2011). *Wittgenstein.* London: Routledge.
Christensen, A. M. (2011). 'A Glorious Sun and a Bad Person', Wittgenstein, Ethical Reflection, and the Other. *Philosophia* 39, 207–223.
Churchill, J. (2009). The Convergance of God, the Self, and the World in Wittgenstein's *Tractatus.* In U. Arnswald (ed.), *In Search of Meaning: Ludwig Wittgenstein on Ethics, Mysticism and Religion.* Karlsruhe: Universitatsverlag Karlsruhe, pp. 113–130.
Coetzee, J. M. (2004). *Elizabeth Costello.* London: Vintage.
Conant, J. (1989). Must We Show What We Cannot Say? In R. Fleming & M. Payne (eds), *The Senses of Stanley Cavell.* Lewisbury, PA: Bucknell University Press.
Conant, J. (1995). Putting Two and Two Together: Kierkegaard, Wittgenstein and the Point of View for Their Work as Authors. In T. Tessin & M. von der Ruhr (eds), *Philosophy and the Grammar of Religious Belief.* New York: St. Martin's Press.
Conant, J. (2000). Elucidation and Nonsense in Frege and Early Wittgenstein. In A. Crary & R. Read (eds), *The New Wittgenstein.* London: Routledge, pp. 174–217.
Cooper, D. E. (2005). Life and Meaning. *Ratio* XVIII, 125–137.
Corngold, S. & Wagner, B. (eds) (2011). *Franz Kafka: The Ghosts in the Machine.* Evanston, IL: Northwestern University Press.
Cottingham, J. (2003). *On the Meaning of Life.* London: Routledge.
Cottingham, J. (2005). *The Spiritual Dimension: Religion, Philosophy, and Human Value.* Cambridge: Cambridge University Press.
Cottingham, J. (2007). What Difference Does It Make? The Nature and Significance of Theistic Belief. In J. Cottingham (ed.), *The Meaning of Theism.* Oxford: Blackwell, pp. 19–38.
Cottingham, J. (2008). The Self, the Good Life, and the Transcendent. In N. Athanassoulis and S. Vice (eds), *The Moral Life: Essays in Honour of John Cottingham.* New York: Palgrave Macmillan, pp. 231–274.
Cottingham, J. (2009a). *Why Believe?* London: Continuum.
Cottingham, J. (2009b). What is Humane Philosophy and Why is It at Risk? In A. O'Hare (ed.), *Conceptions of Philosophy, Royal Institute of Philosophy Supplement* 65, pp. 1–20. Cambridge: Cambridge University Press.
Cottingham, J. (2009c). The Lessons of Life: Wittgenstein, Religion and Analytic Philosophy. In H. J. Glock and J. Hyman (eds), *Wittgenstein and Analytic Philosophy: Essays for P.M.S. Hacker.* Oxford: Oxford University Press, pp. 203–227.
Cottingham, J. (2012). Introduction. In J. W. Seachris (ed.), *Exploring the Meaning of Life: An Anthology and Guide.* Malden, MA: Willey-Blackwell, pp. 115–120.

Craig, W. L. (1994). The Absurdity of Life Without God. Repr. in J. W. Seachris (ed.), *Exploring the Meaning of Life: An Anthology and Guide*. Malden, MA: Wiley-Blackwell, 2012, pp. 153–172.
Crary, A. & Read, R. (eds) (2000). *The New Wittgenstein*. London: Routledge.
Crary, A. (ed.) (2007). *Wittgenstein and the Moral Life: Essays in Honor of Cora Diamond*. Cambridge, MA: MIT Press.
Crary, A. (2009). *Beyond Moral Judgment*. Cambridge, MA: Harvard University Press.
Day, W. & Krebs, V. (eds) (2010). *Seeing Wittgenstein Anew*. Cambridge: Cambridge University Press.
Davis, W. (1987). The Meaning of Life. *Metaphilosophy*, 18, 288–305.
Diamond, C. (1995). *The Realistic Spirit: Wittgenstein, Philosophy, and the Mind*. Cambridge, MA: MIT Press.
Drury, M. O. (1984). Conversations with Wittgenstein. In R. Rhees (ed.), *Recollections of Wittgenstein*. Oxford: Oxford University Press.
Edwards, P. (1967). The Meaning and Value of Life. Reprinted in E. Klemke & S. M. Cahn (eds), *The Meaning of Life: A Reader*. Oxford: Oxford University Press, 2008, pp. 114–133.
Edwards, J. C. (1982). *Ethics Without Philosophy: Wittgenstein and the Moral Life*. Tampa: Florida University Press.
Eldrige, R. (2008). *Literature, Life, and Modernity*. New York: Columbia University Press.
Ellmann, R. (1983). *James Joyce*. Oxford: Oxford University Press.
Emerson, R. W. (1940). *The Selected Writings of Ralph Waldo Emerson*. B. Atkinson (ed.), New York: The Modern Library.
Engelmann, P. (1967). *Letters from Ludwig Wittgenstein, with a Memoir*. B. F. McGuinness (ed.), L. Furtmuller (trans.), Oxford: Basil Blackwell.
Faust, J. (2008). Can Religious Arguments Persuade? In E. T. Long & P. Horn (eds), *Ethics of Belief: Essays in Tribute to D. Z. Phillips*. Claremont, CA: Springer, pp. 71–86.
Feinberg, J. (1992). Absurd Self-Fulfilment. Repr. in E. D. Klemke & S. M. Cahn (eds), *The Meaning of Life: A Reader*. Oxford: Oxford University Press, 2008, pp. 153–183.
Fischer, J. M. (1994). Why Immortality Is Not So Bad. *International Journal of Philosophical Studies* 2, 257–270.
Foucault, M. (1980). The Confession of the Self. In C. Gordon (ed.), *Power/Knowledge: Selected Interviews and Other Writings, 1972–1977*. New York: Pantheon Books, pp. 194–228.
Frank, J. (1995). *Dostoyevsky: The Miracoulous Years 1865–1871*. Princeton: Princeton University Press.
Frankfurt, H. G. (1988). The Importance of What We Care About. In H. G. Frankfurt (ed.), *The Importance of What We Care About*. New York: Cambridge University Press, pp. 80–94.
Frankfurt, H. G. (2004). *The Reasons of Love*. Princeton: Princeton University Press.
Frege, G. (1980). *Foundations of Arithmetic*. J. Austin (trans.), Evanston: Northwestern University Press.
Freud, S. & Breuer, J. (1974). *Studies on Hysteria*. New York: Pelican.
Gellner, E. (2005). *Language and Solitude, Wittgenstein, Malinowski and the Habsburg Dilemma*. Cambridge: Cambridge University Press.

Bibliography

Genova, J. (1995). *Wittgenstein: A Way of Seeing*. London: Routledge.
Gewirth, A. (1998). Ultimate Values, Rights, Reason. In A. Gewirth (ed.), *Self-Fulfillment*. Princeton: Princeton University Press, pp. 159–228.
Goethe, J. W. von. ([1833] 1913). *Poetry and Truth: From My Own Life*. M. S. Smith (trans.), London: G. Bell and Sons, LTD.
Goodman, R. (2004). *William James and Wittgenstein*. Cambridge: Cambridge University Press.
Hacker, P. M. S. (2001). *Wittgenstein: Connections and Controversies*. Oxford: Clarendon Press.
Hacker, P. M. S. (2000). Was He Trying to Whistle It? In A. Crary & R. Read (eds), *The New Wittgenstein*. London: Routledge, pp. 353–388.
Hadot, P. (1995). *Philosophy as a Way of Life*. Malden, MA: Blackwell Publishing.
Hagberg, G. L. (2008). *Describing Ourselves: Wittgenstein and Autobiographical Consciousness*. Oxford: Oxford University Press.
Hanfling, O. (ed.) (1987). *Life and Meaning: A Philosophical Reader*. Cambridge: Basil Blackwell.
Hare, R. M. (1981). Nothing Matters. In E. D. Klemke (ed.), *The Meaning of Life*. Oxford: Oxford University Press, pp. 241–248.
Hartshorne, C. (1984). God and the Meaning of Life. In L. S. Rouner (ed.), *On Nature 6*, 154–168. Notre Dame: University of Notre Dame Press.
Heidegger, M. (1977). *The Questions Concerning Technology and Other Essays*. W. Lovitt (trans.), New York: Harper & Row.
Hemingway, E. (1964). *A Moveable Feast*. New York: Simon & Schuster.
Hemingway, E. ([1929] 2012). *A Farewell to Arms*. New York: Scribner.
Hepburn, R. W. (1966). Questions About the Meaning of Life. *Religious Studies* 1, 125–140.
Hick, J. (1964). Sceptics and Believers. In J. Hick (ed.), *Faith and the Philosophers*. London: Macmillan, pp. 235–250.
Hick, J. (2004). *An Interpretation of Religion: Human Response to the Transcendent*. New Haven, CT: Yale University Press.
Hughes, L. (2009). 'If There is Any Value that Does have Value, it Must Lie Outside the Whole Sphere of What Happens and is the Case' (TLP 6.41). In U. Arnswald (ed.), *In Search of Meaning: Ludwig Wittgenstein on Ethics, Mysticism, and Religion*. Karlsruhe: Universitätsverlag, pp. 51–66.
Hume, D. ([1738] 1968). *A Treatise of Human Nature*. Oxford: Clarendon Press.
Insole, C. (2006). *The Realist Hope: A Critique of Anti-Realist Approaches in Contemporary Philosophical Theology*. Farnborough: Ashgate.
James, H. (1993). *The Beast in the Jungle and Other Stories*. New York: Dover Publications, Inc.
James, W. (1987). The Varieties of Religious Experience. In B. Kuklick (ed.), *William James Writings: 1902–1910*. New York: Literary Classics of the United States, pp. 1–471.
Janouch, G. (2012). *Conversations with Kafka*. G. Rees (trans.), New York: New Directions Publishing.
Johnston, P. (2003). *The Contradictions of Modern Moral Philosophy, Ethics after Wittgenstein*. London: Routledge.
Joyce, J. ([1914] 1995). *Dubliners*. A. Goodwyn (ed.), Cambridge: Cambridge University Press.
Joyce, J. ([1922] 2002). *Ulysses*. New York: Dover Publications.

Kass, L. R. (2001). L'Chaim and Its Limits: Why Not Immortality? *First Things* 113, 17–24.
Kekes, J. (2000). *Pluralism in Philosophy: Changing the Subject.* Ithaca, NY: Cornell University Press.
Kellenberger, J. (2002). 'Seeing-as' in religion: discovery and community. *Religious Studies* 18, 1, 101–108.
Kelly, J. C. (1995). Wittgenstein, the Self, and Ethics. *The Review of Metaphysics* 48, 567–590.
Kerr, F. (2008). *Work on Oneself: Wittgenstein's Philosophical Psychology.* Arlington, VA: The Institute for Psychological Sciences Press.
Kishik, D. (2008). Wittgenstein on Meaning and Life. *Philosophia* 36, 111–128.
Klagge, J. C. (1985). From the Meaning of Life to a Meaningful Life. In *James C. Klagge Homepage.* http://www.phil.vt.edu/JKlagge/MEANING.pdf
Klagge, J. C. (ed.) (2001). *Wittgenstein: Biography and Philosophy.* Cambridge: Cambridge University Press.
Klagge, J. C. (2011). *Wittgenstein in Exile.* Cambridge, MA: MIT Press.
Klemke, E. D. & Cahn, S. M. (eds) (2008). *The Meaning of Life: A Reader.* Oxford: Oxford University Press.
Kober, M. (2006). Wittgenstein and Religion. In M. Kober (ed.), *Deepening Our Understanding of Wittgenstein.* Amsterdam: Rodopi, pp. 87–116.
Labron, T. (2009). *Wittgenstein's Religious Point of View.* London: Routledge.
Laing, R. D. (1960). *The Divided Self: An Existential Study in Sanity and Madness.* London: Penguin Books.
Lamarque, P. & Olsen, S. H. (1996). *Truth, Fiction, and Literature.* Oxford: The Clarendon Press.
Levy, N. (2005). Downshifting and Meaning in Life. *Ratio* XVIII, 176–189.
Lewis, S. C. (2012). On Living in an Atomic Age. In J. W. Seachris (ed.), *Exploring the Meaning of Life: An Anthology and Guide.* Malden, MA: Wiley-Blackwell, pp. 133–138.
Litwack, E. B. (2009). *Wittgenstein and Value: The Quest for Meaning.* London: Routledge.
Lucretius. (1982). *De rerum natura (On the Nature of Things).* In W. H. D. Rouse (ed.), *Lucretius, De rerum natura.* London: Cambridge University Press.
Lurie, Y. (2006). *Tracking the Meaning of Life: A Philosophical Journey.* Columbia, MO: University of Missouri Press.
Malcolm, N. (1972). *Ludwig Wittgenstein: A Memoir.* Oxford: Oxford University Press.
Malcolm, N. (2002). *Wittgenstein: A Religious Point of View?* London: Routledge.
Markus, A. (2012). Assessing Views of Life: A Subjective Affair? In J. W. Seachris (ed.), *Exploring the Meaning of Life.* Malden, MA: Wiley-Blackwell, pp. 95–111.
Marquard, O. (1991). On the Dietetics of the Expectation of Meaning: Philosophical Observations. In O. Marquard, *In Defence of the Accidental.* Oxford: Oxford University Press, pp. 29–49.
Martin, R. (1993). A Fast Car and a Good Woman. In D. Kolak & R. Martin (eds), *The Experience of Philosophy* (ch. 67), Belmont, CA: Wadsworth Publishing Co.
McGuinness, B. (1988). *Wittgenstein: A Life: Young Ludwig 1889–1921.* London: Duckworth.
Mersch, D. (2009). 'There Are Indeed Things that Cannot Be Put Into Words' (TLP, 6.522) Wittgenstein's Ethics of Showing. In U. Arnswald (ed.), *In Search*

Bibliography

of Meaning: Ludwig Wittgenstein on Ethics, Mysticism, and Religion. S. Kirgbright (trans.), Karlsruhe: Universitätsverlag Karlsruhe, pp. 25–50.

Metz, T. (2000). Could God's Purpose Be the Source of Life's Meaning? *Religious Studies* 36, 293–313.

Metz, T. (2001). The Concept of a Meaningful Life. *American Philosophical Quarterly* 38, 137–153.

Metz, T. (2002). Recent Work on the Meaning of Life. *Ethics* 112, 781–814.

Metz, T. (2003). The Immortality Requrement for Life's Meaning. *Ratio* 16, 161–177.

Metz, T. (2007). New Developments in the Meaning of Life. *Philosophy Compass* 2, 1–22.

Metz, T. (2008). God, Morality, and the Meaning of Life. In N. Athanassoulis & S. Vice (eds), *The Moral Life, Essays in Honour of John Cottingham*. New York: Palgrave Macmillan, pp. 201–227.

Metz, T. (2009). Happiness and Meaningfulness: Some Key Differences. In L. Bortollotti (ed.), *Philosophy and Happiness*. New York: Palgrave Macmillan, pp. 3–20.

Metz, T. (2010). The Meaning of Life. D. Pritchard (ed.), Oxford Bibliographies Online. Philosophy. http://oxfordbibliographiesonline.com/display/id/obo-9780195396577-0070.

Metz, T. (2011). The Good, the True, and the Beautiful: Toward a Unified Account of Great Meaning in Life. *Religious Studies* 47, 389–409.

Metz, T. (2012). Introduction. In J. W. Seachris (ed.), *Exploring the Meaning of Life: An Anthology and Guide*. Malden, MA: Willey-Blackwell, pp. 23–28.

Metz, T. (2013). *Meaning in Life: An Analytic Study*. Oxford: Oxford University Press.

Monk, R. (1990). *Ludwig Wittgenstein: The Duty of Genius*. London: Vintage.

Monk, R. (2001). Philosophical Biography: The Very Idea. In J. C. Klagge (ed.), *Wittgenstein: Biography and Philosophy*. Cambridge: Cambridge University Press, pp. 3–15.

Moore, G. E. (1994a). A Defence of Common Sense. In R. Ammerman (ed.), *Classics of Analytic Philosophy*. Cambridge, MA: Hackett, pp. 47–67.

Moore, G. E. (1994b). Proof of an External World. In R. Ammerman (ed.), *Classics of Analytic Philosophy*. Cambridge, MA: Hackett, pp. 68–84.

Moreland, J. P. (1987). God and the Meaning of Life. In *Scaling the Secular City: A Defense of Christianity*. Grand Rapids, Mich.: Baker Book House.

Morris, T. (1992). *Making Sense of It All: Pascal and the Meaning of Life*. Grand Rapids, Mich.: William B. Eerdmans Publishing Co.

Moyal-Sharrock, D. (2004). *Understanding Wittgenstein's On Certainty*. New York: Palgrave Macmillan.

Mulhall, S. (1990). *On Being in the World: Wittgenstein and Heidegger on Seeing Aspects*. London: Routledge.

Mulhall, S. (2001). Seeing Aspects. In H. J. Glock (ed.), *Wittgenstein: A Critical Reader*. Oxford: Blackwell, pp. 246–267.

Murdoch, I. (1970). *The Sovereignty of Good*. London: Routledge.

Murdoch, I. (1997). Vision and Choice in Morality. In I. Murdoch, *Existentialists and Mystics: Writings on Philosophy and Literature*. London: Chatto & Windus, pp. 76–98.

Nagel, T. (1971). The Absurd. Reprinted in E. Klemke & S. M. Cahn (eds), *The Meaning of Life: A Reader*. Oxford: Oxford University Press, 2008, pp. 143–152.
Nagel, T. (1979). *Moral Questions*. Oxford: Oxford University Press.
Nagel, T. (1986). *The View from Nowhere*. New York: Oxford University Press.
Nagel, T. (1987). *What Does It All Mean?* New York: Oxford University Press.
Nasar, S. (1998). *A Beautiful Mind*. New York: Simon & Schuster.
Nasr, S. H. (1976). *Man and Nature: The Spiritual Crisis in Modern Man*. London: Unwin Paperbacks.
Nasr, S. H. (1989). *Knowledge and the Sacred*. New York: State University of New York Press.
Nielsen, K. (1964). Linguistic Philosophy and 'The Meaning of Life'. In E. D. Klemke & S. M. Cahn (eds), *The Meaning of Life: A Reader*. Oxford: Oxford University Press, 2008, pp. 203–219.
Nielsen, K. & Phillips, D. Z. (2005). *Wittgensteinian Fideism*. London: SCM Press.
Nietzsche, F. W. ([1901] 1968). *The Will to Power*. W. Kaufmann & R. Hollingdale (trans.), New York: Vintage Press.
Nietzsche, F. W. ([1882] 1974). *The Gay Science*. W. Kaufmann (trans.), New York: Vintage.
Nordmann, A. (2005). *Wittgenstein's Tractatus: An Introduction*. Cambridge: Cambridge University Press.
Nozick, R. (1981). *Philosophical Explanations*. Cambridge, MA: Harvard University Press.
Nozick, R. (1989). *The Examined Life*. New York: Simon & Schuster.
Nussbaum, M. (2001). *The Fragility of Goodness: Luck and Ethics in Greek Tragedy and Philosophy*. Cambridge: Cambridge University Press.
Phillips, D. Z. (1970). *Death and Immortality*. London: Macmillan, St. Martin's Press.
Phillips, D. Z. (1999). *Philosophy's Cool Place*. Ithaca: Cornell University Press.
Phillips, D. Z. (2004). *The Problem of Evil and the Problem of God*. London: SCM Press.
Phillips, D. Z. (2005). *Wittgenstein's On Certainty*: The Case of the Missing Propositions. In D. Moyal-Sharrock & W. H. Brenner (eds), *Readings of Wittgenstein's On Certainty*. New York: Palgrave Macmillan, pp. 16–29.
Plant, B. (2005). *Wittgenstein and Levinas, Ethical and Religious Thought*. London: Routledge.
Pojman, L. P. (2002). Religion Gives Meaning to Life. Reprinted in E. D. Klemke & S. M. Cahn (eds), *The Meaning of Life: A Reader*. Oxford: Oxford University Press, 2008, pp. 27–30.
Putnam, H. (1994). *Words and Life*. Cambridge, MA: Harvard University Press.
Putnam, H. (2004). *Ethics Without Ontology*. London: Harvard University Press.
Quinn, P. L. (1997). The Meaning of Life According to Christianity. Repr. in E. D. Klemke & S. M. Cahn (eds), *The Meaning of Life: A Reader*. Oxford: Oxford University Press, 2008, pp. 35–41.
Raphael, D. D. (1983). Can Literature Be Moral Philosophy? *New Literary History* 15, 1–12.
Readings, B. (1992). Pagans, Perverts, or Primitives? Experimental Justice in the Empire of Capital. In A. Benjamin (ed.), *Judging Lyotard*. London: Routledge, pp. 168–191.

170 Bibliography

Rhees, R. (1965). Some Developments in Wittgenstein's View of Ethics. *Philosophical Review* 74, 17–26.
Rhees, R. (1970). *Discussions of Wittgenstein*. London: Routledge.
Rhees, R. (2003). *Wittgenstein's On Certainty: There Like Our Life*. Malden, MA: Blackwell.
Rorty, R. (1979). *Philosophy and the Mirror of Nature*. Princeton: Princeton University Press.
Rosenzweig, F. (1999). *Understanding the Sick and the Healthy: A View of World, Man, and God*. N. N. Glatzer (ed.), Cambridge, MA: Harvard University Press.
Rowe, M. W. (1994). Wittgenstein's Romantic Inheritance. *Philosophy* 69, 327–351.
Rozema, D. (2002). 'Tractatus Logico-Philosophicus': A Poem by Ludwig Wittgenstein. *Journal of the History of Ideas* 63, 345–363.
Ruse, M. (1986). Evolutionary Ethics: A Phoenix Arisen. *Zygon* 21, 95–112.
Russell, B. (1957). A Free Man's Worship. Repr. in E. D. Klemke & S. M. Cahn (eds), *The Meaning of Life: A Reader*. Oxford: Oxford University Press, 2008, pp. 55–61.
Sartre, J. ([1946] 1973). *Existentialism and Humanism*. J. Kulka (ed.), London: Methuen.
Sass, L. (2001). Deep Disquietudes: Reflections on Wittgenstein as an Antiphilosopher. In J. C. Klagge (ed.), *Wittgenstein, Biography and Philosophy*. Cambridge: Cambridge University Press, pp. 98–155.
Scanlon, T. (1998). *What We Owe to Each Other*. Cambridge, MA: Harvard University Press.
Schopenhauer, A. ([1818] 1966). *The World as Will and Representation*. E. F. Payne (trans.), New York: Dover.
Schopenhauer, A. ([1851] 2008). On the Suffering of the World. Repr. in E. D. Klemke & S. M. Cahn (eds), *The Meaning of Life: A Reader*. Oxford: Oxford University Press, pp. 45–54.
Schroeder, S. (2007). The Tightrope Walker. *Ratio* XX, 442–463.
Shields, P. R. (1993). *Logic and Sin in the Writings of Ludwig Wittgenstein*. Chicago: Chicago University Press.
Shotter, J. (1997). Wittgenstein in Practice: From 'The Way of Theory' to a 'Social Poetics'. In C. W. Tolman, F. Cherry, R. van Hezewijk, & I. Lubek (eds), *Problems of Theoretical Psychology*. York: Captus Press, pp. 3–12.
Sidgwick, H. (1907). *The Methods of Ethics*. Chicago: Chicago University Press.
Singer, P. (1995). *How Are We to Live? Ethics in the Age of Self-interest*. Amherst, NY: Prometheus.
Sluga, H. D. (2011). *Wittgenstein*. Malden, MA: Willey-Blackwell.
Sluga, H. D. (2012). Beyond 'Resolute', and 'New' Wittgenstein: The Heyek's Error. In M. G. Weiss & H. Grief (eds), *'Ethics, Society, Politics' The Proceedings of the 35th International Ludwig Wittgenstein Symposium XX*. Kirchberg am Wechsel: Antos Verlag.
Smith, M. (2006). Is That All There Is? *The Journal of Ethics* 10, 75–106.
Stern, D. G. (2004). *Wittgenstein's Philosophical Investigations: An Introduction*. Cambridge: Cambridge University Press.
Stevenson, C. L. (1963). *Facts and Values*. New Haven, CT: Yale University Press.
Stratton-Lake, P. (ed.) (2002). *Ethical Intuitionism*. Oxford: Clarendon Press.

Taylor, C. (2009). *The Culture of Confession from Augustine to Foucault: A Genealogy of the 'Confessing Animal'*. London: Routledge.
Taylor, R. (1999). The Meaning of Life. *Philosophy Now* 24, 13–14.
Taylor, R. (2000). The Meaning of Life. Repr. in E. D. Klemke & S. M. Cahn (eds), *The Meaning of Life: A Reader*. Oxford: Oxford University Press, 2008, pp. 134–142.
Taylor, R. (2012). Time and Life's Meaning. In J. W. Seachris (ed.), *Exploring the Meaning of Life: An Anthology and Guide*. Malden, MA: Wiley-Blackwell, pp. 296–303.
Thomas, E. V. (1995). Wittgensteinian Perspectives (*sub specie aeternitatis*). *Religious Studies* 31, 329–340.
Thomas, E. V. (1997). Wittgenstein and Tolstoy: The Authentic Orientation. *Religious Studies* 33, 363–377.
Thomas, E. V. (1999). From Detachment to Immersion: Wittgenstein and 'the Problem of Life'. *Ratio* XII, 195–209.
Thompson, G. (1997). Wittgenstein, Tolstoy and the Meaning of Life. *Philosophical Investigations* 20, 97–116.
Thompson, G. (2000). Wittgenstein's Confessions. *Philosophical Investigations* 23, 1–25.
Tolstoy, L. (1905). My Confession. Repr. in E. D. Klemke & S. M. Cahn (eds), *The Meaning of Life: A Reader*. Oxford: Oxford University Press, 2008, pp. 7–16.
Trethowan, I. (1983). The Significance of Process Theology. *Religious Studies* 19, 311–322.
Trisel, B. A. (2002). Futility and the Meaning of Life Debate. *Sorites* 14, 70–84.
Tykwer, T. (Writer) & Tykwer, T. (Director) (1999). *Run Lola Run* [Motion Picture].
Tyler, P. (2011). *The Return to the Mystical: Ludwig Wittgenstein, Teresa of Avila and the Christian Mystical Tradition*. London: Continuum.
Verbin, N. K. (2000). Religious Beliefs and Aspect Seeing. *Religious Studies* 36, 1–23.
Waismann, F. (1965). Notes on Talk with Wittgenstein. *Philosophical Review* 74, 12–16.
Wallace, R. J. (2013). *The View from Here: On Affirmation, Attachment, and the Limits of Regret*. Oxford: Oxford University Press.
Wielenberg, E. J. (2005). *Value and Virtue in a Godless Universe*. Cambridge: Cambridge University Press.
Wiggins, D. (1998). Truth, Invention, and the Meaning of Life. In *Needs, Values, Truth*, (3rd ed.). Oxford: Oxford University Press, pp. 87–138.
Wiggins, D. (2004). Wittgenstein on Ethics and the Riddle of Life. *Philosophy* 79, 363–391.
Williams, B. (1976). *Moral Luck, Philosophical Papers 1973–1980*. Cambridge: Cambridge University Press.
Williams, B. (1985). *Ethics and the Limits of Philosophy*. Cambridge, MA: Harvard University Press.
Williams, M. (2005). Why Wittgenstein Isn't a Foundationalist. In D. Moyal-Sharrock & W. H. Brenner (eds), *Readings of Wittgenstein's On Certainty*. New York: Palgrave Macmillan, pp. 47–58.
Wittgenstein, H. (1984). My Brother Wittgenstein. In R. Rhees (ed.), *Recollections of Wittgenstein*, 2nd ed. New York: Oxford University Press, pp. 158–199.

Bibliography

Wittgenstein, L. (1958). *Philosophical Investigations*. G. E. Anscombe (trans.), Oxford: Basil Blackwell.
Wittgenstein, L. (1965). A Lecture on Ethics. *The Philosophical Review* 74, 3–12.
Wittgenstein, L. (1966). *Tractatus Logico-Philosophicus*. D. F. Pears & B. F. McGuiness (trans.), London: Routledge.
Wittgenstein, L. (1967). *Lectures and Conversations on Aesthetics, Psychology and Religious Belief*. C. Barrett (ed.), Berkeley: University of California Press.
Wittgenstein, L. (1969). *The Blue and Brown Books*. Oxford: Basil Blackwell.
Wittgenstein, L. (1974). *Philosophical Grammar*. R. Rhees (ed.), A. Kenny (trans.), Oxford: Basil Blackwell.
Wittgenstein, L. (1975). *On Certainty*. G. E. Anscombe & G. H. von Wright (eds), D. Paul & G. M. Anscombe (trans.), Oxford: Basil Blackwell.
Wittgenstein, L. (1978). *Remarks on the Foundations of Mathematics*. G. H. von Wright, R. Rhees & G. E. Anscombe (eds), G. E. Anscombe (trans.), Oxford: Basil Blackwell.
Wittgenstein, L. (1979a). *Notebooks 1914–1916*. G. H. von Wright & G. E. Anscombe (eds), G. E. Anscombe (trans.), Oxford: Basil Blackwell.
Wittgenstein, L. (1979b). *Wittgenstein and the Vienna Circle, Conversations Recorded by Friedrich Waismann*. B. McGuinness (ed.), J. Schulte & B. McGuinness (trans.), Oxford: Basil Blackwell.
Wittgenstein, L. (1979c). *Wittgenstein's Lectures, Cambridge, 1932–1935*. A. Ambrose (ed.), Oxford: Basil Blackwell.
Wittgenstein, L. (1980). *Culture and Value*. G. H. Nyman (ed.), P. Winch (trans.), Oxford: Basil Blackwell.
Wittgenstein, L. (1988a). *Remarks on the Philosophy of Psychology: Volume I*. G. E. Anscombe & G. H. von Wright (eds), G. E. Anscombe (trans.), Oxford: Basil Blackwell.
Wittgenstein, L. (1988b). *Remarks on the Philosophy of Psychology: Volume II*. G. H. von Wright & H. Nymann (eds), C. G. Luckhardt & M. A. Aue (trans.), Oxford: Basil Blackwell.
Wittgenstein, L. (1990). *Zettel*. G. E. Anscombe & G. H. von Wright (eds), G. E. Anscombe (trans.), Oxford: Basil Blackwell.
Wittgenstein, L. (1996). Letters to Ludwig von Ficker. In C. G. Luckhardt (ed.), *Wittgenstein: Sources and Perspectives*. B. Gillette (trans.), Bristol: Thoemmes Press, pp. 82–98.
Wittgenstein, L. (1996). 'Remarks on Frazer's Golden Bough'. In C. G. Luckhardt (ed.), *Wittgenstein: Sources and Perspectives*. J. Beversluis (trans.), Bristol: Thoemmes Press, pp. 82–98.
Wittgenstein, L. (1998a). *Last Writings on the Philosophy of Psychology* I, G. H. Von Wright & H. Nyman (eds), C. G. Luckhardt & M. A. Aue (trans.), Oxford: Basil Blackwell.
Wittgenstein, L. (1998b). *Last Writings on the Philosophy of Psychology* II, G. H. von Wright & H. Nyman (eds), C. G. Luckhardt & M. A. Aue (trans.), Oxford: Basil Blackwell.
Wittgenstein, L. (1998c). *Philosophical Remarks*. R. Rhees (ed.), R. Hargreaves & R. White (trans.), Oxford: Basil Blackwell.
Wittgenstein, L. (2003). *Public and Private Occasions*. J. C. Klagge & A. Nordmann (eds), Lanham, MA: Rowman and Littlefield.

Wittgenstein, L. (2005). *The Big Typescript: TS 213*. C. G. Luckhardt & M. A. Aue (eds), C. G. Luckhardt & M. A. Aue (trans.), Malden, MA: Blackwell.

Wohlgennant, R. (1987). Has the Question about the Meaning of Life Any Meaning? In O. Hanfling (ed.), *The Quest for Meaning*. New York: Basil Blackwell, pp. 34–38.

Wolf, S. (2010). *Meaning in Life and Why it Matters*. Princeton: Princeton University Press.

Wolgast, E. (2004). A Religious Point of View. *Philosophical Investigations* 27, 129–147.

Wong, W. (2008). Meaningfulness and Identities. *Ethics Theory Moral Practice* 11, 123–148.

Woolcock, P. G. (1999). The Case against Revolutionary Ethics. In P. G. Woolcock (ed.), *Biology and the Foundation of Ethics*. Cambridge: Cambridge University Press, pp. 276–306.

Woolf, V. (1992). *A Woman's Essays*. London: Penguin.

Young, J. (2003). *The Death of God and the Meaning of Life*. Oxford: Oxford University Press.

Index

400 Blows, The (François Truffaut), 52
absurd, the, 62, 85, 96–114, 159
  deflationary responses to, 11, 99, 102
  inflationary responses to, 11, 99, 101, 114
  as opposed to meaningless, 97
Adams, E. A., 1, 67
Allen, Woody, 100
Anscombe, Elizabeth, 153
anti-matter, 81, 127–128
anti-natalism, 11, 99
Arnold, Matthew, 130
Arnswald, Ulrich, 152, 158
aspect
  change of, 50, 10, 49, 55
  continuous seeing of, 49, 56
  dawning of an, 9, 40, 49, 55, 56, 62, 63, 95, 139
  history behind seeing an, 65
Audi, Robert, 152, 156
Augustine, Saint, 14, 114, 119, 121, 124, 137, 152, 158, 160

Baier, Kurt, 121
Bande à part, (Jean-Luc Godard), 52
Barrett, Cyril, 152, 157
Baudelaire, Charles, 102, 159
Bauer, Nancy, 55, 60–61
A Beautiful Mind (Nasar, Sylvia), 62
Beethoven, Ludwig von, 30
belief
  groundlessness of, 88, 92, 97, 99, 108
Benatar, David, 99, 152
Bennett, Arnold, 161
Berger, John, 156
Berggren, Eric, 119
Berlin, Isaiah, 103
Blackburn, Simon, 58
Bloomsday, 145, 162
Boll, Heinrich, 105

Bouwsma, O. K., 76
Breathless, (Jean-Luc Godard), 52
Brown, Delwin, 119, 154

Cahn, Steven, M., 3, 152, 161
Camus, Albert, 11, 21, 68, 99, 105, 106, 159
Cavell, Stanley, 11, 21, 68, 99, 105, 106, 159
Child, William, 31
Christensen, A. M. S., 137, 140
Christianity, 29, 64, 120, 137, 139
Churchill, John, 43
Citizen Cane (Orson Welles), 14
common sense, 86, 110, 111, 149
Conant, James, 136, 153–154
confession, 11, 85, 107, 112–115, 130, 146, 160
  Christian conception of, 119–120, 160
  Freudian conception of, 119–120
  as a narrating activity, 120
conversion, 85, 88, 89, 93
Cooper, David, E., 102, 103, 159, 160
Cottingham, John, 1, 3, 7, 25, 26, 31–34, 37, 58, 65, 68, 79, 91–95, 130, 141, 144, 152, 155, 157, 159, 162
Craig, William, Lane, 3, 29, 31, 59, 155, 157
Crary, Alice, 124, 160

Dachau, 34
Day, William, 47–48
De battre mon coeur s'est arrêté, (Jacques Audiard), 52
death, 15, 17, 25–27, 34, 42, 58, 60, 61, 68, 70, 73, 81, 93, 94, 110, 112, 139, 155, 156, 158
Descartes, Renè, 87
detachment, 9, 10, 42, 45, 54, 84, 85, 96–97, 101, 106, 149, 151
Diamond, Cora, 153, 160

dichotomy
  fact/value, 5, 15, 25, 117
  ordinary meaning/great meaning, 2, 69, 72, 74
  showing/saying, 8
Dostoevsky, Feodor, 124, 127, 128, 141, 142, 161
downshifting, 75
Drury, M. O., 149, 159
Dubliners, (James Joyce), 11, 118, 131, 133

Edwards, Paul, 104
Eldrige, Richard, 133, 148, 150, 160
Elephant Man, (David Lynch), 51
Emerson, Ralph, Waldo, 56, 67, 143, 161
Enfants du Paradis, Les (Marcel Carné), 52
Engelmann, Paul, 20
Euthyphro dilemma, 36, 155
evidence, 23, 33, 51, 86, 93, 98, 153
  of God's existence, 32, 34, 58, 64
  imponderable, 32, 127, 131, 132
exclusivism, 10, 33, 75
extra-terrestrials, 62

A Farewell to Arms, (Ernest Hemingway), 158
Faust, Jennifer, 157
Feinberg, J., 99, 152, 159
Fischer, John, Martin, 3
forest roads, 51
Foucault, Michel, 160
Frankfurt, Harry, 33, 103, 140–142, 152, 159
Freud, Sigmund, 119
fundamentality theory, 10, 69, 80–83, 117

Gauguin, Paul, 78–80
Gellner, Ernest, 24, 43–44
Gewirth, Alan, 3
God, 3, 9, 14, 25–37, 56–65, 73, 88–97, 120, 137, 138, 141, 145, 146, 152–157
  purpose theory, 6, 22, 31, 121, 160
  as a simile, 64
  as the ultimate source of life's meaning, 10, 25, 107

Goethe, Johann, Wolfgang von, 7, 71, 105, 106, 108, 112, 119, 120, 124, 137, 148–151, 161
Goodman, Russell, 44
Green Ray, The (Eric Rohmer), 52
Grizzly Man, (Werner Herzog), 158
Gulag, 34

Hacker, P. S., 153
Hadot, Pierre, 22, 43, 102, 109, 156, 157, 159
happiness, 1, 2, 22, 52, 70, 75, 128
Hartshorne, Charles, 3, 28, 31, 155
Hegel, George, Wilhelm Friedrich, 70
Heidegger, Martin, 68
Hepburn, Ronald, W., 29
Herzog, Werner, 90, 158
Hick, John, 64
history, 13, 14, 42–44, 50, 52, 58, 63, 65, 87, 88, 92, 94, 100, 109
  nightmare of, 42
Hughes, Liam, 42
human condition, the, 24, 36, 58, 82, 94, 159
Hume, David, 101, 107–110
Husserl, Edmund, 7

Ida (Pawel Pawlikowski), 84
Insole, C., 65
Ireland, 16, 131–134
irony, 2, 11, 40, 96–102

James, Henry, 124
James, William, 16, 145
Jesus, 29, 59, 88, 139
Johnston, Paul, 38, 78
Joyce, James, 11, 107, 114, 118, 122, 131, 133, 145, 162
Jules et Jim, (François Truffaut), 52
justification, 8, 37, 40, 47, 86, 95–101, 105, 108–110, 122, 159
  limits of, 100

Kafka, Franz, 104
Kekes, John, 79
Kellenberger, J. 156
Kelly, John, C., 45
Khayyám, Omar, 104
Kishik, David, 52, 153, 158

Index 177

Klagge, James, C., 90, 124–126, 160, 161
Klemke, E. D., 3, 152
Kober, M., 5
Koder diaries, 150, 161
Krebs, Victor, J., 47, 48, 156

Lamarque, Peter, 132
language, 8, 9, 15–20, 25, 28, 41, 44, 46, 47, 51, 53, 56, 64, 102, 111, 119, 123, 127, 141, 147, 148, 151, 153, 158
  picture theory of, 15
A Lecture on Ethics, 19–23, 45
Lessways, Hilda, 161
Levy, Neil, 10, 69, 74–78, 82, 158
life
  arrest of, 54, 71, 85, 107
  autistic conception of, 24
  form of, 7, 23, 45, 51, 57, 146
  givenness of, 99
  good, 1, 37, 80, 91, 92, 143, 157
  stream of, 46, 86, 96, 108, 110, 111, 113, 130, 160
  unexamined, 95
Litwack, Eric, B., 152, 156
loneliness, 9, 44, 114, 133
love, 3, 14, 21, 23, 28, 30, 31, 52, 57, 76, 81, 93, 94, 100, 120, 128, 133, 137, 142, 154, 156, 161
Lucretius, 98
Lurie, Yuval, 152, 156, 158
Lynch, David, 51

McGuiness, Brian, 149
Macintyre, Alasdair, 85
Malcolm, Norman, 118, 156
Mandela, Nelson, 80
Manhattan Project, 142
Marquard, Odo, 10, 68–72, 82, 101, 112
meaning (fullness), 1–3, 10, 26, 38, 40, 61, 74, 97, 127, 134–136
  aiming directly at, 70–71
  anti-theoretical approach toward, 6–7
  the confessionality of enquiring into life's, 10, 11, 46, 66, 118–130, 142, 144, 146, 161
  dietetics of expectations of, 10, 69, 70
  holist questions about, 13, 79, 130, 152
  individualist questions about, 13, 69, 103
  and morality, 140, 141–144, 162
  ordinary, 2, 69, 72–76, 113
  superlative, 2, 69, 72, 75, 83, 145
  theoretical approach toward, 6, 7, 10, 125–133
Mersch, Dieter, 42, 43, 168
Metz, Thaddeus, 1, 3, 4, 6, 10, 13, 27, 31, 63, 67, 69, 80–83, 92, 127, 128, 140, 141, 152, 155, 158, 159, 161
Mill, John Stuart, 124
Mohammad, Prophet, 59
Monk, Ray, 19, 20, 30, 41, 44, 55, 148, 156
Moore, J. E., 45, 86, 88, 96, 112
moral
  objectivism, 4
  subjectivism, 4
Moreland, James, P., 31
Moses, 58
A Movable Feast, (Ernest Hemingway), 52
Moyal-Sharrock, Daniele, 86
Mulhall, Stephen, 133, 156
Murdoch, Iris, 2, 10, 45, 63, 79, 127

Nagel, Thomas, 5, 10, 11, 53, 84, 85, 96–103, 106, 114, 152, 159
Nash, John, 62
Nasr, Seyed Hossein, 154
New Testament, the, 137–139
Nielsen, Kay, 61
Nietzsche, Fredrick, 11, 68, 73, 99
nihilism, 4, 5, 68, 85, 96–97, 114, 159
Nordmann, Alfred, 16, 21, 22, 154, 161
Nozick, Robert, 3, 26, 31, 69, 123, 124, 152, 155
Nussbaum, Martha, 11, 124, 144

Olsen, Haugom, S., 132

Paris, 51, 52, 132, 156
particularity, 72–78, 126, 128, 130, 140
Pascal, Blaise, 13, 107, 121
persuasion, 85, 89, 90

pessimism, 62, 69, 85, 99, 102, 103, 106, 110
Philadelphia Story, The (George Cukor), 160
Phillips, D. Z., 2, 22, 95
Plant, Bob, 87, 96
Plato, 67
praxis, primacy of, 8, 31, 65, 94, 95, 99, 155
problem of life, the, 2, 10, 11, 17–19, 24, 27, 31, 35, 45, 46, 54, 55, 70, 103–106, 118, 120, 135–140, 144–148, 150, 152, 153, 158
Process theology, 154
Proust, Marcel, 124
Putnam, Hillary, 57, 156, 160
Python, Monty, 7

Quinn, Phillip, L., 155
Quran, the, 24, 154, 157

Raphael, D. D., 160
Red Balloon, The, (Albert Lamorisse), 52
Rhees, Rush, 7, 21, 45, 77, 86, 156
Rififi, (Jules Dassin), 52
Romanticism, 101, 150
  German, 160
Rosebud, 14
Rosenzweig, Franz, 85, 107, 110–113, 156, 160
Rowe, M. W., 123, 160
Run Lola Run, (Tom Tykwer), 154
Ruse, Michael, 37
Russell, Bertrand, 17, 19, 58, 59, 68, 93, 94, 152, 157

St. Paul, 145
Samouraï, Le, (Jean-Pierre Melville), 52
Sartre, Jean-Paul, 68
Sass, Louis, 42, 149, 162
Saudade, 96
Scanlon, T. M., 155
Schlick, Moritz, 36
Schopenhauer, Arthur, 11, 44, 68, 94, 96, 99, 159
Schroeder, S., 157
Schubert, Franz, 1
Seachris, Joshua, W., 3

seeing
  way of, 5, 9, 11, 19, 29, 39, 46, 47, 53, 54, 57, 62–65, 88, 92–99, 112, 123, 146, 151
Sèraphine, 1
silence, 17, 19, 79, 121, 126, 127, 139, 140, 153
Singer, Peter, 8, 35–41, 47, 152
Sisyphus, 3, 63, 103–106
Sluga, Hans, 21, 153
Smith, Adam, 40
Smith, Michael, 98, 99, 110, 152, 159
Sorrows of Young Werther, The (Goethe), 105
soul-blindness, 113
Sovereignty of Good, The, (Iris Murdoch), 45
Spider-Man, 89
Sraffa, Piero, 156
Stalin, 145
Starry heaven, 51
Stratton-Lake, Phillip, 155
Sub specie humanitatis, 97
suffering, 32, 36–40, 56, 58, 60, 61, 97, 106, 112–114, 135, 138, 144, 149
supernaturalism, 8, 24–29, 61, 93, 95, 152
  God-centred theories, 3
  soul-centred theories, 3

Talmud, 157
Taylor, Richard, 10, 11, 69, 73, 74, 80, 85, 102–106, 152, 157, 160
tendency
  ethics as a, 17–20, 24, 28–30
  philosophy-bashing, 148
Thomas, E. V., 9, 45, 152, 158
Thompson, Galeb, 123, 152, 158, 160
Three Colours: Blue, (Krzysztof Kieslowski), 52
Tolstoy, Leo, 53, 54, 70, 71, 107, 124, 141, 142, 152, 155, 158
Tractatus
  The ethical point of, 22
  the resolute reading of, 153
Trainspotting (Danny Boyle), 35
The transcendent, 3, 32
  longing for, 30, 101, 148
  trace of, 31–34

Trisel, B. A., 152
Tyler, Peter, 5

Ulysses, (James Joyce), 145

Van Gogh, Vincent, 1
Varieties of Religious Experience, The, 16
Verbin, N. K., 50, 60, 152, 156
Von Ficker, Ludwig, 148, 154

Waismann, Friedrich, 30, 36, 44
Waking Life, (Richard Linklater), 154
Wallace, R. J., 159

Where the Green Ants Dream, (Werner Herzog), 158
Wielenberg, Eric, J., 34, 40, 157
Wiggins, David, 42, 75, 157
Williams, Bernard, 38, 78–80, 152
Wittgenstein, Hermine, 126
Wolf, Susan, 4, 125–135, 140–142, 152, 157, 159, 161, 162
Wong, Wai-hung, 13
Woolcock, Peter. G., 155
Woolf, Virginia, 113, 161
world-picture, 2, 85, 87–96, 99, 113, 117, 148, 155, 158

Printed and bound by CPI Group (UK) Ltd, Croydon, CR0 4YY